WITHDRAWN

D0938321

Modern Tragicomedy
and the British
Tradition

Modern Tragicomedy and the British Tradition

Richard Dutton

University of Oklahoma Press : Norman and London

By the same author

Ben Jonson: 'Epigrams' and 'The Forest', Carcanet Press, 1984
An Introduction to Literary Criticism, Longman, York Press, 1984
Ben Jonson: to the First Folio, Cambridge University Press, 1983
Jacobean and Caroline Court Masques and Civic Entertainments, 3 vols., Nottingham Drama Texts, Nottingham University Press, 1981—.

Library of Congress Cataloging-in-Publication Data

Dutton, Richard, 1948-
Modern tragicomedy and the British tradition.

Bibliography: p.
Includes index.
1. English drama — 20th century — History and criticism.
2. Tragicomedy. I. Title.
PR739. T7D87 1986   822'.914'09   86-40072
ISBN 0-8061-2006-1
ISBN 0-8061-2025-8 (pbk.)

Copyright © 1986 Richard Dutton. All rights reserved.
Published in the United States of America by the University of Oklahoma Press, Norman, Publishing Division of the University of Oklahoma. Manufactured in Great Britain. First edition, 1986.

For MAURA, KATE and CLAIRE

Contents

A Note on the Texts

Although the works studied here have achieved the status of modern classics, they have not yet achieved the distinction of definitive hardbound editions, to which academics would for choice refer. Most of them have been published hardbound at one time or another, but such editions are not commonly available even in some of the largest libraries. I have therefore decided to quote in all cases from the most generally available U.K. paperback editions, which are likely to be those with which readers are most familiar:

Beckett: *Waiting for Godot* (2nd edition, 1965) and *Endgame* (1964) are published by Faber and Faber Ltd.

Pinter: Pinter's plays have been collected together in four volumes of The Master Playwrights series by Eyre Methuen Ltd. (A parallel series, *Harold Pinter: Complete Works* is published by Grove Press Inc., New York, with identical pagination). *The Birthday Party* is in *Plays: One* (1976); *The Caretaker* is in *Plays: Two* (1977); *The Homecoming* is in *Plays: Three* (1978); *Old Times* and *No Man's Land* are in *Plays: Four* (1981).

Albee: *Who's Afraid of Virginia Woolf?* is published in Penguin Plays (Harmondsworth, 1965).

Stoppard: *Rosencrantz and Guildenstern Are Dead* (rev. edn. 1968), *Jumpers* (1972) and *Travesties* (1975) are all published by Faber and Faber Ltd.

Storey: *Home* is published (along with *The Changing Room* and

Mother's Day) in Penguin Plays (Harmondsworth, 1978).

Shakespeare: *The Complete Pelican Shakespeare* (general editor Alfred Harbage) (rev. edn. 1969) published by Penguin Books, Baltimore, Maryland. References to *The Two Noble Kinsmen* are to the edition by N. W. Bawcutt (Harmondsworth, 1977).

Modern drama is notorious for the pauses and hesitations in its dialogue, which are denoted in a variety of ways by the different authors. To avoid confusion, I have adopted the slightly unusual form < . . . > to denote my own *editorial* deletions throughout.

Preface

It is generally recognised that the last thirty years have produced a richer and more varied output of drama in Britain than any similar period since the end of the seventeenth century. There have, of course, been any number of individual major talents in the intermean — the Anglo-Irish wits, Sheridan, Wilde and Shaw are obvious examples — but there has been nothing to equal a generation that includes Samuel Beckett, John Osborne, Harold Pinter, Arnold Wesker, John Arden, Edward Bond, Tom Stoppard, Joe Orton, Peter Nichols, David Storey, and a host of others scarcely less eminent; nor does this fund of talent show signs yet of drying up, with younger writers like David Edgar, Howard Brenton, Howard Barker, Christopher Hampton, Michael Hastings, Carol Churchill, David Hare and Stephen Poliakoff joining the ranks.

We should be grateful that we have been blessed with such an embarrassment of riches in our own time, but we should also try to appreciate the conditions that have contributed to their success. With the advent successively of the cinema, radio and television, the live theatre in Britain lost its place as a principal provider of mass entertainment; certain forms of theatre, like the music-hall, died a lingering death in seaside revues and television variety shows, to be remembered nostalgically in plays like Osborne's *The Entertainer* and Trevor Griffiths' *The Comedians*. But as theatre in general contracted, it redefined its role in the community, being seen increasingly as a serious intellectual, artistic and educational resource — something that *ought* to be kept going — not only in the glamorous West End of London but also in the provinces, and if needs be with public subsidies. George Devine's English Stage Company, based at the Royal Court Theatre, was at the heart of an attempt to

1

establish modern drama as a serious force in contemporary culture;[1] and the establishment of the National Theatre on the South Bank in London formally acknowledged the place of drama in the national heritage. Most of the theatres that survived the contraction, and the new ones that emerged as monuments of civic pride or academic endeavour, deliberately broke away from the tyranny of the Victorian proscenium arch. The typical contemporary theatre is a smaller, more intimate place than its predecessors; the division between the actors and the audiences is less clearly marked, and the opportunities for something unexpected or experimental to take place there have correspondingly increased.

Such developments seem to have created, or allowed to emerge, not only new dramatists, but also a new kind of audience. Where once the majority of audiences looked to the theatre for entertainment of a not particularly taxing kind (which they perhaps now find on television), a much higher proportion of those who are prepared to turn out today seems ready to watch something that will offer them a challenge, make them think. Playwrights like Bond and Orton even seem, in their different ways, to have tried to test the limit of tolerance of such supposedly liberal, quasi-intellectual audiences; Beckett's plays, with characters living in ashcans or buried up to their necks in sand, have similarly put severe strains upon the average assumption that plays are, or should be, entertainingly about 'real people' in 'real situations'. Other dramatists may not have been so extreme, but it is a hallmark of the best of recent plays that they have exploited both the physical and intellectual 'freedoms' of the contemporary theatre, taxing the assumptions and expectations of their audiences — for the most part, towards constructive ends.

There is always something rather arbitrary about setting a date to new eras or departures in the arts, but there is a general consensus to the effect that this remarkable phase of British drama was ushered in by two productions, both ground-breaking in their different ways. The first performance in Britain of Beckett's *Waiting for Godot* — his own translation of a play previously written in French and performed in France — was given on 3 August 1955 at the Arts Theatre, London. John Osborne's *Look Back in Anger* was first staged at the Royal

Court Theatre, London, on 8 May 1956. These plays had little in common, except their capacity to disconcert their original audiences — and even in this it was for different reasons. *Waiting for Godot* struck at the audience's most basic expectations of what a play should be: the characters and setting bear only the remotest resemblance to the everyday reality; very little happens; and the dialogue is generally inconsequential and sometimes totally incoherent. *Look Back in Anger*, by contrast, is quite a conventional play, with comprehensible characters in a recognisable setting, lucid dialogue and a plot that is clearly going somewhere. What made it disconcertingly different was its choice of a most unlikely hero: Jimmy Porter was a virtual drop-out, the product of a provincial university, with a lower-middle-class background. He turned his scathing rhetoric on a post-war Britain that seemed to him to have no positive values left, trying to goad his wife and friends out of what he saw as their apathy; but he had little self-respect either and could be downright boorish in his treatment of other people, not an easy man to like or to identify with. It was a far cry from the upper-middle-class, cool and articulate, public-school or Oxbridge characters who peopled the plays of such as Noel Coward and Terence Rattigan.

It would greatly overstate the case to suggest that these plays started two distinct traditions in contemporary British drama, but a significant proportion of the most memorable plays written since seem to line up behind one or other of them. The plays of Wesker or Bond, for example, follow *Look Back in Anger* in being primarily concerned with the social and political state of post-war Britain; the political complexions of the three dramatists are very different, but all focus on the problems of class divisions in society and on a variety of myths and aspirations common to the age which they see as bogus or dangerously blinkered. These are themes which have been picked up again more recently by writers like Edgar and Brenton. There is a persistent strain of outrage or disillusion-ment in these works, centred on an apparent belief that Britain is morally and politically in decline — though the view of that decline varies greatly, depending on the politics of the author. Britain has lost an Empire, but not gained a revolution, or any other redefinition of its role in the world.

There is another kind of play, however, which has more in common with *Waiting for Godot*. The works of Harold Pinter and the early plays of Tom Stoppard are the most striking examples, though the plays of N. F. Simpson and, in the United States, of Edward Albee, also belong here. It is always much more difficult to define what these plays are actually 'about'; they do not confront the world and its issues so directly as the other type, but in an oblique, self-referential sort of way, for which they are often castigated by more politically committed writers. They are very self-conscious of the artificial nature of theatre itself, deeply concerned with the problems of communication in all its forms, inclined to play games with their audiences' expectations, often more concerned with their own style and shape than with having anything practical or principled to say. These plays are the subject of this book. They are often categorised as 'absurdist' but, for reasons I shall explain in Part I, I would prefer to describe them as modern tragicomedies. They are not, I think, as far removed from those plays of social and political commitment as is often supposed. In their own ways, they too express a disillusionment with, and even a sense of outrage at, the post-war world; but they wrap it in a more purely dramatic metaphor, addressing what we might call a spiritual malaise rather than a political one. They use the nature of theatrical experience itself to express these things, in ways akin to ritual, so that it is difficult and probably mistaken to try to abstract social principles or political slogans from them.

I write here in the present tense, but it might be more accurate to use the past, since there have been no significant additions to the body of tragicomedy I discuss in this book for about ten years. All the authors I discuss are still writing, but their works have passed into new phases. Beckett's recent plays have been of a minimalist austerity that makes *Waiting for Godot* and *Endgame* seem luxuriantly wordy and colourful by comparison, and it is difficult to talk about them in the same terms. Pinter has concentrated heavily on cinema since *No Man's Land* (1975), writing a number of major screenplays, notably *The Proust Screen-Play* (published 1977, never filmed), adaptations of Scott Fitzgerald's *The Last Tycoon* (directed by Elia Kazan, 1976) and of John Fowles' *The French Lieutenant's Woman* (directed by Karel Reisz, 1981), and most recently

Turtle Diary (1985). *Betrayal* (1978) and *One for the Road* (1984) are his only new full-length plays in that time. While the former has many stylistic and thematic echoes of his earlier works, it seems to me some way removed from the tragicomic form of his earlier works; it incorporates some interesting devices, apparently adapted from cinematic techniques (it has, in fact, also been filmed) but it would be overstretching definitions to include it here. *One for the Road* represents an even greater break with Pinter's artistic past, with an emphasis on political and human rights issues that would have been out of place in his tragicomedies.[2] Pinter in fact seems belatedly to be following in the steps of Tom Stoppard, the development of whose career is perhaps the most pointed reflection on the history of this kind of tragicomedy. His early plays are verbal and theatrical *tours-de-force*, but they have sometimes been described as all froth and no substance; in particular, they are accused of lacking the compassion and moral concern of great drama, which is apparent in the works of Beckett and Pinter, for all their oblique strangeness. I do not share these reservations myself, but it is noticeable that Stoppard's more recent works have addressed themselves far more directly to social and political issues and to plots where moral and emotional choices loom very large. The turning point, perhaps, was his immaculate TV play, *Professional Foul* (1974), where Stoppard's typical verbal wit and castles-in-the-air confronted the brutal realities of Czechoslovakia after the Russian invasion of 1968. It is arguable that these developments have added a valuable new dimension to his work, but in the process they have certainly drawn him away from the precise mode of tragicomedy. This is particularly significant because tragicomedy has not found favour, either, with any of the newer dramatists, most of whose works start from a direct social or political commitment which is foreign to that form. It may well be, therefore, that we shall need to see modern tragicomedy as one of the facets of a very particular era, approximately 1955-1975.

It has been noted — and not as flippantly as you might suppose — that one thing connecting Beckett, Pinter and Stoppard is the game of cricket. Beckett played the game at Trinity College, Dublin, to a level which warranted a mention in *Wisden*, the cricketers' 'Bible' — a rare distinction for a winner of the Nobel Prize for Literature! Pinter and Stoppard are both known to be avid players and followers of the game, often playing in the same team; it is an interest that surfaces from time to time in their plays. Does this tell us anything useful about their plays, or what they have in common? Well, like a game of cricket, nothing much happens for a good deal of the time, though it may well happen with elegance and style, and there is always the threat or promise that something *will* happen eventually; if something does happen, it is likely to be sudden and perhaps violent, and either exciting or confusing, depending on whether you were paying attention at the time. Also like cricket, their plays are governed by rules that seem baffling, arbitrary, not to say perverse to uninitiated spectators; on the other hand, few games or plays gain such passionate commitment from their devotees as do these. The purpose of *Modern Tragicomedy and the British Tradition* must thus be to explain the 'rules' of these plays to the uninitiated reader/spectator, and also to try to convey something of their special fascination.

This cricketing analogy, with all its English exclusivity, calls attention to the choice of authors examined under the heading of 'Modern Tragicomedy and the British Tradition'. The majority of my examples — Pinter, Stoppard and Storey — belong unequivocally to the great generation of British drama to which I referred at the outset. But it is obvious that Samuel Beckett (for all his cricketing skills), as an Irishman living in France, is only marginally defined by this context; he also has much in common with a good deal of continental drama, and particularly the works of the Romanian French dramatist, Eugene Ionesco. But the English versions of Beckett's plays, and particuarly of *Waiting for Godot* and *Endgame*, have become fixed and influential features of the British dramatic repertoire/tradition, and it is in that light that I approach them here. The American, Edward Albee, is a slightly different case. I have included *Who's Afraid of Virginia Woolf?* here because, although it is written in English and has a lot in common in particular with the works of Pinter, it is very much to one side of the dramatic mode with which I am concerned; it is here for the contrast/comparison it offers with the other texts, helping (I hope) to define and explain their peculiar strangeness and (in some cases) their peculiar Britishness.

6

Preface

I should like to take this opportunity to thank people who have helped me, in various ways, in the writing of this book: Harry Johnson, who introduced me so painlessly to the wonders of word-processing; Moira Linnehan, who kindly sent me a number of U.S. articles on Stoppard; and the staff and students of the English department at St. Martin's College, Lancaster, who listened patiently to a number of early versions of what I have to say here about *Waiting for Godot*.

PART I
Tragicomedy

(i) Tragicomedy

Samuel Beckett labels *Waiting for Godot* on its title page as 'a tragicomedy in two acts'. As so often with Beckett, we may wonder if he is not teasing his readers as much as enlightening them by choosing to use the word 'tragicomedy', which is so tantalisingly indefinite in its connotations. The problems associated with the term are in fact so acute that the author of one of the best books on the subject (J.L. Styan, *The Dark Comedy: the Development of Modern Comic Tragedy*) disavows it altogether, stressing in the preface to his first edition how he has been 'at pains to lose in my title the associations belonging to the spurious term "tragicomedy", which invites us to measure a play by two widely different yardsticks simultaneously, regardless of their possible irrelevance'.[1] Does 'tragicomedy' actually invite us to do this? The problem is that there is no single, agreed definition of 'tragicomedy'. Nor, unlike 'tragedy' and 'comedy', has there been a *consistent* historical tradition of tragicomedy within which we can look for a definition. Writers like Guarini and Fletcher in the Renaissance, and Brecht, Artaud and Pirandello in more recent times, have all claimed to write 'tragicomedies', but it far is from obvious that there is any common thread running through these claims or that their definitions have common points of departure. It is a term that has been expropriated by individuals from time to time for their own purposes, often without reference to historical precedents. As a result, 'tragicomedy' has become one of the most contentious of all critical terms. One can imagine Beckett, always the most scrupulous word-smith, smiling wryly as he used it.

9

Professor Styan is, of course, right to draw attention to the loose and emotive ways in which a term that amalgamates the complex associations of both tragedy and comedy may be misused. Nevertheless, in the preface to the second edition of his book, we find him using 'tragicomedy' without apparent qualifications, and later in the text he describes how Harold Pinter 'practises a new illogicality, yet one pregnant with the logic of feeling that belongs to the subtextual world of tragicomedy'.[2] This suggests that, however 'spurious' tragicomedy may seem at times to be as a critical term, it has a compelling usefulness in some contexts, and most particularly in relation to that style or tradition of recent drama, which centres on the works of Beckett and Pinter, and is the subject of this book. This is borne out not only in Beckett's and Styan's uses of the term, but also in a range of recent discussions of it, including those by Eric Bentley in *The Life of the Drama*, Karl S. Guthke in *Modern Tragicomedy*, Ruby Cohn in *Currents in Contemporary Drama*, Bernard F. Dukore in *Where Laughter Stops: Pinter's Tragicomedy* and David L. Hirst in *Tragicomedy*.[3]

All the participants in the debate concur in finding the term useful, even unavoidable, though they do not concur in an agreed definition. And I here add myself to their ranks. It would be possible, though not I think very helpful, for me to 'place' myself in terms of the debate, comparing my own use of 'tragicomedy' with that of these other critics. My argument in this book does not depend on *definitions* of tragicomedy so much as in trying to elucidate the nature of certain modern plays by comparing them with earlier plays which were indisputably known as tragicomedies; my interest in the term itself extends no further than that. But a comment is called for in the case of Bernard F. Dukore's *Where Laughter Stops: Pinter's Tragicomedy*, the one *sustained* attempt to explain a figure central to my own thesis in terms of tragicomedy. Professor Dukore introduces his own use of the term via a quotation from Pinter himself (taken from *The Sunday Times*, August 14, 1960), in which the playwright described *The Caretaker* as 'funny up to a point. Beyond that point it ceases to be funny, and it was because of that point that I wrote it'. Professor Dukore continues: 'The movement of a funny play to a point where it is no longer funny — where the comic nature of its characteristics ceases to be comic, where the audience stops laughing, where the nonfunny dominates — this movement constitutes the progress, conclusion, and effect of Pinter's distinctive tragicomedies' (p.4). His book then traces this 'movement' in relation to each of Pinter's major works with considerable skill and insight. But I have two major reservations about his method. The first is that it is by no means clear to me that the phrase 'funny up to a point' indicates a specific moment of time within a play, when the forces of tragedy begin to outweigh those of comedy (or however one might want to express it) and the laughter stops. The peculiar quality of Pinter's tragicomedy, like that of the Renaissance to which I will compare, is surely such that, throughout a play, situations can be *simultaneously* comic and tragic, ambivalent in their implications, disconcerting precisely because it is unclear how either we or the characters are really supposed to react to them. Any attempt to pin such ambivalence within the linear 'movement' of the play must inevitably distort it. My second point is connected: it is pleasing to see that Professor Dukore finds Pinter 'funny', albeit only up to a point, because many critics (and particularly many non-British ones) write as if there were nothing comic in his plays at all. Personally, I find Pinter's plays almost painfully funny, with a comedy of incongruousness that has affinities with the best British humour of their period, from *The Goon Show* to *Monty Python's Flying Circus*. But this can only be a matter of taste: it is impossible to legislate on what 'the audience' will find comic or at what point they will stop laughing, and it is surely dangerous to construct a thesis around such unknown quantities. It is perhaps worth adding here that I have never yet seen a film or television version of one of Pinter's stage-plays (as distinct from one of his own purpose-written tele-plays) which does justice to the comic dimension; they invariably seem to play up the doom and menace (partly as a result of excessive use of close-ups rather than the broader picture which is always before us in the theatre) at the expense of the ludicrous. The recent B.B.C. *The Dumb Waiter* was a case in point. If the comedy is so vulnerable that (at least to my mind) it can be lost in translation from one apparently close medium to another, I should prefer an analysis in terms of 'tragicomedy' which is not so dependent upon it. (These comments relate specifically to Pinter, of course, but they seem to me equally valid in relation to any of the other dramatists discussed in this book).

For all these differences of critical opinion, the fact that Beckett himself used the term 'tragicomedy' seems to me important, not least because virtually everyone agrees that *Waiting for Godot* was one of the seminal works of post-war European drama, setting a mode, a tone, a style that was echoed and imitated by younger dramatists like Pinter, Albee and Stoppard from the late fifties to the early seventies. Even where no direct influence may be traced between Beckett and those who followed him — Pinter, for example, is on record as saying that he had not seen or read a play by Beckett when he started writing himself[4] — we may still discern a family likeness between their works, a likeness that is almost axiomatic in current critical thinking. It is my contention that this likeness may best be explored by an examination of the label, 'tragicomedy', starting with Beckett's personal use of the term. As I shall suggest in Part II, I believe Beckett was being neither loose nor casual when he used the term; rather that he was aligning his play — which he knew in many ways to be original and unconventional — with a dramatic tradition that flourished in Renaissance Italy, France and England and which is best known to modern audiences in the late plays of Shakespeare. I do not suggest that any of the plays which may be said to have followed on from *Waiting for Godot* were similarly related to that tradition. But inasmuch as there is this family likeness between Beckett's plays and those, in particular, of Pinter and Stoppard, the latter may be said unconsciously to have extended this revived tradition of tragicomedy. In this specific sense, the term has a critical usefulness.

Most students of contemporary drama will recognise the plays I shall be considering here as having been categorised at one time or another within the so-called 'Theatre of the Absurd' — if not by Martin Esslin in the influential book in which he popularised the term[5] then by others who have sought to extend this sub-genre. In preferring 'modern tragicomedy' to 'theatre of the absurd' as a label for these plays, I do not wish to deny the validity of Esslin's approach, but I do want to point out some of its limitations. Not least amongst these is its tendency to burden some plays with a weight of gloomy European metaphysics they simply will not bear, and to make it more difficult than it should be to account for the genuine strains of comedy which (as I have already suggested) arc in them. Beckett, as an Irishman who has chosen to live in France, and who writes with parallel conviction in both French and English, may fit comfortably in an intellectual tradition that includes Nietzsche, Sartre and Camus — though he may also fit with equal comfort in a number of alternative traditions. But the other dramatists I shall be looking at may only be construed as belonging to such a European tradition with considerable special pleading. Even Stoppard, the writer who most openly advertises his awareness of European movements, seems to show more sympathy in the end for Anglo-Saxon logical positivism and pragmatics than for European existentialism. The fact is that Absurdism, like the existentialism that begot it, underwent a considerable sea-change in crossing the Channel (not to mention, in Albee's case, the Atlantic) and must be regarded with circumspection as a critical term in relation to English-language playwrights. This is not to say that these playwrights are intellectually less challenging than their European counterparts, simply that their traditions and terms of reference are different. I suspect that the term 'Theatre of the Absurd' enjoyed the vogue that it did in the sixties largely because recent British theatre at that time did not enjoy the academic respectability that had been accorded to European theatre broadly since the time of Ibsen, Chekhov and Strindberg. To link some British, and latterly American, dramatists with Absurdism seemed a convenient way of conferring on them all the seriousness implied in European intellectual chic. In now proposing modern tragicomedy as an alternative label, I shall hope to confirm the literary and intellectual standing of these dramatists by relating their work to long-standing dramatic forms and themes rather than by reference to vogue metaphysics.

This is not to deny, of course, that Beckett and Pinter, in particular, have much in common with modern European dramatists, or that they might not usefully be located within a broader theatrical movement which might well involve such figures as Chekhov, Jarry, Pirandello, Artaud and Ionesco. But my own aims here are more modest; I am not really concerned to trace specific traditions, influences and borrowings (except occasionally among my own chosen authors). I start from the observation that, even after thirty years of familiarisation, the average reader and theatre-goer finds *Waiting for Godot* and its progeny difficult — strange, disconcerting, not easily talked about (except perhaps as 'theatre of the absurd', where the critical term has become a comfortable substitute for addressing the texts themselves). My aim here is to dispel some of that 'strangeness' and I find, perhaps paradoxically, that this is more easily done by comparing these plays with works that are super-ficially quite alien — Renaissance tragicomedies — than by considering them in the context of plays that appear to have so much more in common. I believe that Beckett, at least, is demonstrably aware of the parallels between his own work and Renaissance tragicomedy, but I make no greater claim for 'traditions' or 'influences' than that. The analogies I shall draw between Renaissance tragicomedies and modern drama are just that — analogies, whose sole function is elucidation.

In order to draw those analogies I shall have to tackle some topics that will seem remote and strange to readers primarily interested in modern drama: long dead authors and even deader critical controversies, not to mention some very odd plays. It may help readers through this section, therefore, if I briefly outline what I hope to establish by disturbing these sixteenth- and seventeenth-century bones. Firstly, these dramatists consciously and deliberately invented 'tragicomedy' as a new dramatic form, with special qualities. Cutting across the traditional generic boundaries of tragedy and comedy, they aimed for a style of drama which could include everything from the most arcane divine mysteries to the most mundane of characters (such as shepherds, who would normally be the preserve of low-life comedies). This comprehensiveness aimed to take on board the most massive and ineffable topics of human existence — time, fate, providence, virtue, evil, and irrecon-cilable conflicts between reason and emotion. It followed that this could not be achieved within a realistic framework; the issues concerned go beyond common understanding and defy logical analysis. The dramatists therefore cultivated an artificial, quasi-operatic mode ('artificial', something made with human ingenuity, was a critical compliment in the Renaissance), which deliberately distanced the audience, keeping them in a state of bewildered amazement rather than engaged sympathy. The characters too were generally confused and disorientated by what happened to them, never being able to master their own destinies; whatever meaning they had related to their part in some broad pattern of events rather than to their sovereign identity. Dialogue and soliloquy typically reverted to the bewildering perplexity of their situation. Beneath the sophisticated veneer of Renaissance artificiality, this was a form of ritual drama, seeking to appease or come to terms with the unknowable forces which govern our existence; one of its most common motifs was a journey into the unknown (either physical or psychic), which has clear counterparts in modern anthropology and Jungian psychology. Modern drama is very different in form, of course, but in essence this description of Renaissance tragicomedy seems to me to have a lot in common with *Waiting for Godot* and its successors: a form of ritual drama trying to come to terms with the perplexing forces (both within and without) that direct our existence; characters are notoriously unable or unwilling to communicate, often seeming less than full individuals; the language becomes incoherent, inanely repetitive or self-reflective; the plays are defiantly strange and disorientating in terms of the audience's expectations — so that the audience vicariously shares something of the perplexity of the characters; the drama is also often self-consciously theatrical and draws attention to its own artifice (artificial in both old and new senses). For all the differences of style and overt subject-matter, these similarities are worth pursuing.

According to its champions (though not its detractors) tragicomedy is never the random mixture of tragedy and comedy to which J.L Styan objects, but a deliberate blending of traditionally tragic and comic dramatic elements for specific purposes and effects. Unfortunately, there is no single authoritative figure to whom we can turn to verify this claim, so a brief history of the early uses and abuses of the term will be necessary. The concept of tragicomedy was virtually unknown to critics in ancient Greece and Rome. Aristotle and Horace, for example, sanctioned and defined the terms tragedy and comedy in such a way as to imply disapproval of any mingling of the two. In his treatise *On the Best Style of Orators*, Cicero even went so far as to rule that 'In tragedy anything comic is a defect and in comedy anything tragic is unseemly'.[6] This led the critics of the Renaissance, who regularly damned or justified literature by reference to the classical precedents, to frown upon experiments in tragicomedy in their own time.

But the dramatic practice of the classical world was rather less hidebound that its critical theory might suggest, and this left some scope for Italian experimenters in the new form — notably Giraldo Cinthio (1504-73) and Giambattista Guarini (1538-1612) — to justify what they were doing by reference to the ancients. In particular, the Greek dramatists had written satyr plays, about which the critics had had little to say and of which only one example, Euripides' *Cyclops*, had survived into the modern world; since this seemed to mingle comic and tragic elements, it afforded a useful precedent. Similarly, there was the fact that a number of Euripides' tragedies, such as *Electra*, *Helen* and *Ion*, have happy outcomes, in defiance of the supposed rules and certainly against the spirit of Aristotle's *Poetics*, which treats Sophocles as the best model for tragedy. Finally, there was the curious anomaly of Plautus' play, the *Amphitryon*, which the author himself dubbed a tragicomoedia. The god Mercury, who speaks the prologue of the play, first describes it as a tragedy, but then changes his mind: 'Why do you wrinkle your forehead? Because I said that it would be a tragedy? I am a god, and I'll change it if you wish. I'll make a comedy out of the tragedy and yet leave all the lines the same . . . I'll make it a mixture, a tragicomedy ["tragicomoedia"]. I don't think it is proper for me to make it entirely a comedy wherein kings and gods appear. What then? Since the servant also has a part, therefore let it be, as I said, a tragicomedy'.[7] This mixture of 'high' and 'low' characters, which was destined to be a feature of true Renaissance tragicomedy, baffled the Renaissance critics, who tended to treat it as a joke on Plautus' part, and certainly an anomaly.

Whether or not the popular and religious dramatists of the Middle Ages knew much about classical dramatic theory, it is clear that they were little influenced by it. The mystery plays of the York, Chester and Wakefield cycles, for example, break all the supposed rules about the mixing of serious and comic

16

material, and of 'high' and 'low' characters. Even the sixteenth-century school of European religious dramatists known collectively as the Christian Terence, who revered the elegant style of the Roman dramatist whose name they acquired, showed scant regard to the indecorum of mixing aristocratic and peasant characters, or to the conflation of tragic crises with happy endings, any more than they worried about mingling religious and profane (often very profane) subjects. So it is fair to say that a 'mixed' style of drama was the stock-in-trade of popular dramatists throughout Europe in the fifteenth and sixteenth centuries. And, for all the sophistication achieved by the leading dramatists in Italy, France and England, this remained essentially the case in the popular theatres — particularly in England — well into the seventeenth century, apparently because it was what the audiences wanted. Unfortunately, from the point of view of the later reputation of the term, this popular 'mixed' style of drama was dubbed 'tragicomedy' by the scornful educated critics of the time, most notably Sir Philip Sidney: 'But beside these gross absurdities, how all their plays be neither right tragedies nor right comedies, mingling kings and clowns, not because the matter so carrieth it, but thrust in the clown by head and shoulders to play a part in majestical matters, with neither decency nor discretion; so as neither the admiration and commiseration, nor the right sportfulness, is by their mongrel tragi-comedy obtained'.[8] This slur has stuck with tragicomedy for the last four hundred years: any mixture of tragedy and comedy is liable to be dismissed as 'mongrel' populist stuff.

So the situation was far from auspicious for any serious and educated Renaissance dramatist who wanted, for whatever reason, to experiment with the mingling of tragic and comic modes. On the one side, the weight of classical theory was overwhelmingly against him; on the other, he ran the risk that educated audiences whom he probably wanted to impress might damn his experiment along with the egregious 'mixed' popular drama. One of the first authors to try to take an intellectual stand on the matter was Giraldo Cinthio. He was the author of nine plays, which he preferred to describe as tragedies even though six of them had happy endings: apparently he wished to stay safely within the framework of classical critical debate. In his

17

critical treatise, the *Discorso sulle Comedie & sulle Tragedie*,[9] he tried to justify the use of the term tragedy for plays with happy endings: 'Of the two sorts of tragedy there is one that ends in sorrow. The other has a happy end, but in bringing the action towards its conclusion does not therefore desert the terrible and the compassionable, for without these there cannot be a good tragedy. This type of tragedy . . . is shown to us by Plautus in the prologue of the *Amphitryo* when he says that in this play less noble persons are mixed with the great and royal. This he took from the *Poetics* of Aristotle where there is a passage on this sort of tragedy. It is in its nature more pleasing to the spectators because it ends in happiness'.[10] This seems rather a desperate attempt to stay within the confines of critical respectability; Cinthio summons up both Plautus and Aristotle in his defence, but omits to mention that the former had coined the new term, tragicomedy, for his own anomalous play and that, while Aristotle does concede the existence of a 'mixed style' of tragedy, he makes perfectly plain his belief that 'the well-conceived plot will have a single interest, and not, as some say, a double. The change in fortune will be, not from misery to prosperity, but the reverse, from prosperity to misery'.[11] Moreover, Aristotle had *mocked* 'the feeble judgement of the audience' which applauded such tragedies, since 'this is not the pleasure that is proper to tragedy. It belongs rather to comedy' (p.49). Cinthio is on altogether safer ground when, in the prologue to his play *Altile* (1543) he admits that the play might be called a tragicomedy. He firstly discusses it as a tragedy with a happy ending, comparing it with various plays by Euripides: 'But if it displeases you that it should have the name of Tragedy, to satisfy you it could be called Tragicomedy (since our language does use such a name), the outcome of which has conformed to comedy — after troubles it is filled with gladness'.[12] But this is as far as Cinthio was prepared to go; he was clearly uneasy about the term tragicomedy and never attempted either to define or to justify it. His real significance in the history of serious tragicomedy lies in having legitimised a 'mixed style' of tragedy, generally with double plots (in the manner which Terence had exemplified for comedy, but which none of the ancients had really essayed in tragedy), and capable of having a happy outcome for some of its characters. All of these elements were later picked up in the true tragicomedy of, for example, Shakespeare and Beaumont and Fletcher.

The most notable Italian to follow Cinthio's lead, and the most significant single theorist on Renaissance tragicomedy, was Giambattista Guarini, author of the pastoral tragicomedy, *Il Pastor Fido (The Faithful Shepherd)*, begun in c.1580, first published in 1590. This was one of the most influential of all Renaissance plays, being widely admired and imitated throughout Europe in the seventeenth century; it was highly praised by critics as diverse as Voltaire, Rousseau and Schlegel, though today its appeal seems mainly to be to literary historians. The double plot of *Il Pastor Fido* concerns two sets of lovers, Mirtillo (the faithful shepherd) and Amarilli (the chaste nymph), Silvio (the Adonis-like hunter) and Dorinda (a straightforward young lady); their relationships are variously confused and thwarted by the villainous Satyr and Corisca. The scene is Arcadia in the Golden Age, but at a time when Diana, the virgin goddess of the hunt, has placed it under a curse — there must be an annual sacrifice to her of a virgin and, moreover, any nymph found faithless must also die, unless someone volunteers to take her place. Only the marriage of an Arcadian youth and maiden, both descended from the gods, can remove the curse — and an initial complication of the plot is that Silvio and Amarilli, who are known to have suitable pedigrees, have been betrothed to each other by their fathers, but neither loves the other.

In the preface to the 1602 edition of the play, Guarini outlines the plot according to the traditional grammatical pattern applied to the comedies of Terence:

In the protasis is contained the marriage arranged by Montano, father of Silvio, and by Titiro, father of Amarilli, in the hope of liberating by this means their country from the horrible sacrifice; the abhorrence of Silvio and Amarilli toward this match; the plot of Corisca to lead into misfortune the enamoured and incautious girl. In the epitasis is contained the taking of Amarilli as a condemned adultress, the marriage upset, Mirtillo offered in sacrifice, the arrival of Carino, Amarilli unhappy, Titiro tearful, Montano afflicted, and the province grieving.

In the catastrophe is contained the agony between Montano and Carino, the recognition of Mirtillo, the interpretation of the oracle, the death of Mirtillo converted to marriage, all things which had a moment ago been tearful made joyful, the lovers who up to then had been miserable espoused, the province freed from the horrible tribute, and the fable happily changed from very sad to very joyful fortune only through the recognition of the Faithful Shepherd.[13]

This misses out the story of Silvio and Dorinda since, as Guarini explains, that does not belong to 'the principal knot of the fable'. The crucial scene here is one in which Silvio declares his devotion to the chaste Diana, then accidentally wounds Dorinda with an arrow and in his distress learns that he really loves her; the later 'recognition' that Mirtillo is Silvio's long-lost brother, and so a fit match in all respects for Amarilli, leaves Silvio and Dorinda free to marry too — all part of the 'very joyful fortune'.

This resumé of the plot leaves out a good deal, of course, but it will suffice for our purposes. It will be apparent, for instance, that the play is constructed to allow for a wide variety of incident, suspense and emotion, all of which are typical of Renaissance drama. It is all most improbable, to be sure, judged by realistic standards, but it is not gratuitous fantasy and the varied elements that make up this complex plot are far from randomly assembled. For one thing, they all contribute to the central theme of the play which, it has been pointed out, 'is the power of love to transform the human soul'.[14] More immediately to our purpose, however, is the fact that Guarini has carefully constructed the play according to his own definition of what a tragicomedy should be, even closely annotating the 1603 edition, so that we may see how individual elements and scenes are meant to contribute to the whole design. So, for example, we are told that Dorinda 'is a comic personage, and is not a principal, nor of a condition which I have represented in noble character' (by contrast with the three principal lovers who, all being descended from the gods, are characters befitting tragedy). The scene in which Amarilli is condemned for unfaithfulness is, we are told, 'wholly tragic', while that which follows, in which the chorus praises Silvio for his successful hunting of the great boar, is 'wholly joyful'.

The principle by which Guarini combines these potentially conflicting elements of the play is fully spelled out in *Il Compendio della Poesia Tragicomica* (1601), which he wrote to rebut repeated criticisms of the play. Tragicomedy, he insists, is neither tragedy nor comedy, but a third entity, like an alloy composed of two metals but distinct from both:

> He who composes tragicomedy takes from tragedy its great personages but not its action, its verisimilar plot but not one based on truth [i.e. not a historical story, as Renaissance tragedy was usually expected to be], its emotions aroused but their edge abated, its delight but not its sadness, its danger but not its death; from comedy laughter that is not riotous, modest merriment, feigned complication, happy reversal, and above all the comic order . . . Art observes that tragedy and comedy are composed of heterogenous parts, and that therefore if an entire tragedy and an entire comedy should be mixed, they would not be able to function properly together as a natural mixture, because they do not have a single intrinsic natural principle, and it would then follow that in a single subject two forms contrary to each other would be included. But art, a most prudent imitator of nature, plays the part of the intrinsic principle, and while nature alters the parts after they are united, art alters them before they are joined in order that they may be able to exist together and, though mixed, produce a single form.[15]

Tragicomedy, then, aims not just to mix tragedy and comedy but to create a distinct middle mode, the parts of which are artfully subsumed to a unified whole which will give an audience a unique experience.

So far we have concentrated on the plot and the action, but we should not lose sight of the fact that the real emphasis of the play does not fall on these elements. For one thing, some of what might have been the most dramatic events — such as Amarilli's arrest and Mirtillo's subsequent offer to die in her place — are not depicted on stage at all, but are related to us by messengers. Even the shooting of Dorinda by Silvio is not exploited as it might be by a dramatist intent merely on keeping his audience's attention; it comes rather casually at the end of a very mannered (and later much imitated) scene, where the nymph Echo mocks Silvio, who praises the chaste Diana and berates wanton Cupid. When he discoveres what he has done, he is overcome with remorse and simultaneously realises that he really does love Dorinda as much as she loves him. The emphasis is away from the moment of action itself and on the elaborately depicted states of mind of Silvio immediately before and after it. That is not to say that we witness anything resembling psychological realism; the verse offers us a succession of appropriate sentiments vying with each other in baroque style rather than the workings of a man's mind. Nor do we feel that Silvio has developed as a character in this scene; it is simply that he has manifested the appropriate sides of himself at the proper moments.

This is typical of *Il Pastor Fido* as a whole, which is by no means a fast-moving play; each stage of its unfolding calls for appropriate lyric reflection, often from an array of different choruses, or for sententious declamation from one of the principal characters. It is on these poetic embellishments of the action, ornamental reflection and interpretation, that the real emphasis of the play lies; it has more than once been compared with opera and has indeed been given a number of musical settings, including one by Handel. None of the characters ever breaks through this mode by doing anything unexpected or against type. Mirtillo, for example, is always the faithful shepherd, noble and self-sacrificing, even when tortured by jealousy at Amarilli's supposed adultery; she in turn is always pious, invariably seeking divine guidance, even when it seems to have brought her to the brink of an untimely end. The only exception to this is the wicked Corisca who, after a lifetime of selfish villainy, suddenly repents and reforms in time to allow for a totally happy ending. This only underlines the sense that we have throughout the play, that the characters were made for the plot, and not vice-versa; Corisca and the Satyr are necessary plot-instigators, while the others perform their parts dutifully, not so much generating action as reacting appropriately to action generated elsewhere. And if the characters are secondary to the plot, the plot is secondary to the insistent sententious commentary with which its mysterious progress is embellished. The whole baroque structure, finally, is subsumed to the business of tantalising the audience about the outcome — Guarini himself uses the striking image of the enticements of a loose woman, offering 'baits to desire'. We know from the fundamentally comic mode that some sudden reversal must free the characters from impending doom, but we cannot anticipate it or see from where it will come.

(ii) Beaumont and Fletcher

> The irony of Jacobean baroque, however, should be comprehensible to the present age; for the 'sick' humour of comedy, the notion of 'l'absurde' in tragedy provide insights highly relevant to the deeply disturbed, powerful, yet seemingly light-hearted work of those who have been called 'entertainers to the Jacobean gentry'. M.C. Bradbrook.[16]

None of Guarini's English followers in the tragicomic mode went quite so far down this quasi-operatic path, but it remains true that all Renaissance tragicomedy eschews realism on almost every level. Plots are often improbable in the exteme, but artfully shaped so that their development is far from arbitrary — in fact, what we may call the architecture of the whole piece is frequently its most striking feature. The principal characters are very much servants of the action rather than its instigators — to the extent that bewilderment and frustration are among the commonest themes of these plays; we are scarcely interested in the characters as individuals, so much as representative types tested to the utmost by the situations the plot contrives for them. All these characteristics are self-evident in the works of Guarini's true English heirs, the partnership of Beaumont and Fletcher, not least in the *The Faithful Shepherdess*, which echoes the title of *Il Pastor Fido* and many of its basic themes.[17]

In his address 'To the Reader' at the head of that play, Fletcher gets as close as any English dramatist to defining what he means by tragicomedy: 'A tragi-comedy is not so called in respect of mirth and killing, but in respect it wants deaths, which is enough to make it no tragedy, yet brings some near it, which is enough to make it no comedy, which must be a representation of familiar people, with such kind of trouble as no life be questioned; so that a god is as lawful in this as in a tragedy, and mean people as in a comedy. Thus much I hope will serve to justify my poem, and make you understand it; to teach you more for nothing, I do not know that I am in conscience bound'.[18] This is much more rough-and-ready than Guarini, though it says nothing to contradict him; it breaks off with a truculent challenge to the reader just when it promises to be really helpful. It is significant, however, that Fletcher spells out in very clear terms one unique feature of tragicomedy: its allowed mingling of 'a god' and 'mean people', which cuts across all the classical prescriptions distinguishing tragedy from comedy (though, interestingly, it was a prominent feature of Plautus' unique experiment, the *Amphitryo*). Tragicomedy allows not only for intercourse between aristocrats and peasants, but between supernatural beings and the most ordinary mortals. That is something which Shakespeare was to exploit even more thoroughly than Guarini or Fletcher and is, I suggest, an important feature of the appeal of this style of drama to modern dramatists. Modern dramatists do not, on the whole, introduce gods and spirits into their plays as Shakespeare and Fletcher did; but they are just as interested as their predecessors were in the influence of numinous forces — whether they manifest themselves as providence, or the workings of the unconscious mind, or Godot — on the lives of ordinary people.

Few people read or perform the works of Beaumont and Fletcher these days, and I will not try to swim against the critical tide by considering them here in detail. But I think they should be noticed as making a distinctive and — at the time — extremely popular contribution to Renaissance tragicomedy, extending the range of this narrow but intense form. In one of the best books on Beaumont and Fletcher, Professor E.M. Waith has attempted to abstract the characteristic qualities of their drama, listing them under eight heads.[19] It will be sufficient for our purposes here if I repeat something of this process; I will gratefully borrow Professor Waith's heads, though the comments under them are entirely my own. These comments relate in particular to such plays as *Philaster* and *A King and No King*, which I take to be representative of their distinctive contribution to the genre.

(a) *Imitation of the manners of the familiar world*. It is important to the effect of these plays that we are never totally in the realms of fantasy. The action may be stylised, but the principal characters, like the audience for which they were primarily created, are unmistakably gentlemen and courtiers; they speak like them and share their concerns (duty, honour, love, order), however much these may be exaggerated by the exigencies of the plot.

(b) *Remoteness from the familiar world*. Nevertheless, there is an artificiality of conventions that tends towards the operatic; the settings chosen for these plays — generally royal courts and pastoral scenes — are not inherently improbable places but things happen there that defy belief. We are never allowed to forget that, despite the element of familiarity, these are theatrical constructions, inventions of art and not nature.

(c)   *Intricacy of plots*. This artificiality is compounded in the plots which, with all their labyrinthine complexities, are very obviously shaped and balanced: the principal characters and their lovers are so artfully posed in opposition and antithesis to each other; the action is concentrated in 'strong', emotional scenes which are carefully disposed to promote the maximum of comparison and contrast, in a way that is totally consonant with what always seems the self-conscious cleverness of the final revelations/resolutions.

(d)   *The improbable hypothesis*. It is impossible to escape the feeling in a Beaumont and Fletcher tragicomedy that the heart of the play is neither the characters nor the action but an unusual, even perverse *idea*: what if a dispossessed prince were in love with the usurper's daughter? What if the king were in love with his own sister? The whole shape and logic of the plays seems determined to wring these ideas for all they are worth, in ways analogous to Donne's propensity for flogging a conceit to death in his poetry.

(e)   There are no *supernatural beings* in these plays — no ghosts, witches or gods — but the characters (and consequently the audience) often feel themselves to be in the presence of something other-worldly. On the one hand, they may feel what is called 'the secret justice of the gods' (*Philaster*, I.ii.103)[20] running through their lives; on the other, they may feel something inhumanly evil in what happens to them — fits of near-madness or sexual passion that seem to be visited on them rather than to arise from within. They never approach being masters either of themselves or of their destinies.

(f)   *Protean characters*. In one sense, Beaumont and Fletcher's characters are consistent to the point of rigidity: there is no suggestion of psychological flexibility or subtlety. Nevertheless, the extreme situations to which the plots condemn them produce reactions totally at odds with their basic characteristics. It is as if the characters can become whatever is required, apparently in order to heighten the sensational effect of the scene. This is linked, of course, with the recurrent suggestion that the characters have little or no control over their own destinies. We see them as the puppets both of intricate plots and of inscrutable gods.

(g) *'Lively touches of passion'*. Professor Waith is here quoting Dryden's praise of a feature of Fletcher's drama which was one of his great legacies to the Restoration dramatists who wrote in the heroic style. As the characters remain 'fixed' but behave inconsistently, and always 'in extremities', the passions which they endure seem to take on a life of their own: what they express is, as it were, independent of the person expressing it and becomes a thing to admire in and for itself.

(h) *The language of emotion*. When I go on to suggest what parallels I think there are between Renaissance tragicomedies of the type I have been describing and modern drama, I shall concentrate on the patterns of experience on which they focus, on the unstable or ambiguous nature of the characterisation, on the uneasy balance between familiarity and outright artificiality, and to an extent on the rhetorical formality of both dialogue and soliloquies. It would not be realistic to try to compare the actual use of language of dramatists three hundred and fifty years apart — the conventions have shifted so radically — but it is worth noting the essence of Professor Waith's final category.

Fletcher perfected a style of verse totally in keeping with the extremely mannered and artificial nature of his tragicomic drama. Although it may seem perfectly natural in context, and can reach great heights of eloquence, it is much less impressive if we try to abstract and apply it in other contexts. It is easier and more familiar in manner than much Jacobean dramatic verse, being less grammatically convoluted and less crammed with metaphor. But where passages from, say, Shakespeare or Webster often seem resonantly applicable to life as we live it, this is almost never the case with Fletcher. T.S. Eliot rather damningly puts it this way: 'the evocative quality of the verse of Beaumont and Fletcher depends upon a clever appeal to emotions and associations which they have not themselves grasped; it is hollow. It is superficial with a vacuum behind it'.[21] I would prefer to say that it is, for want of a better term, a kind of operatic language, artificial and rhetorical for all its fluent and apparently colloquial surface; it is not to be judged on its local effects but on its contribution to the total effect of the tragicomedy. This seems to me equally true of the language of the modern plays we shall be looking at. Beckett's language is a very stylised mix of the colloquial and the arcane. Pinter has perfected a hyper-realistic version of natural speech, so unnatural in fact as to be immediately recognisable and dubbed as Pinterese or Pinteresque. Stoppard affects a Wildean mix of elegantly modulated patter and philosophical enquiry. Any of them might be accused of being 'hollow' or 'superficial with a vacuum behind it' but that is to measure it by false, quasi-realistic standards. These plays do not offer a literal, photographic picture of the world, any more than do those of Beaumont and Fletcher. They offer something more condensed, oblique and mysterious, an artifice which seeks to convey truths hidden from everyday reality. And they have evolved styles of language perfectly in keeping with those purposes.

Tragicomedy has always been subject to misunderstanding and mistrust, and Beaumont and Fletcher have suffered much from being its most ardent English exponents, attracting much adverse criticism. There is no psychological development in their characters, such as we look for in Shakespeare's mature histories and tragedies, and their plots seem engineered solely to put the principals into positions of extreme mental and moral paradox. The sudden reversals by which these paradoxes are resolved can be construed as cheap, exploitative tricks, or perhaps prurient devices in keeping with the plays' constant resort to perverse emotion and sudden reversals of mood.[22] But the comparison with Shakespeare's history plays and tragedies is unfair and misleading; Beaumont and Fletcher were attempting nothing like their realism. Their plays are, in fact, attempts to find dramatic equivalents for courtly romances, such as Sidney's *Arcadia* and Spenser's *The Faerie Queene*.[23] As such, they *deliberately* eschew the kinds of realism which we regard as hallmarks of Shakespeare's middle period (from say, *Henry IV, Part I*, c.1597, to *Macbeth*, c.1606). It is in the nature of such romances to concentrate on strange and complex situations, as testing grounds of sophisticated moral and intellectual prowess, rather than to deal with the familiar facts of common experience. An apter comparison is with the Shakespeare of *Cymbeline* and the late plays, which I shall now go on to consider. Incidentally, it is common to see both Shakespeare's late plays and the most characteristic works of Beaumont and Fletcher categorised as 'romances'. I prefer the term 'tragicomedy' because it denotes the specifically *theatrical* adaptation of romance materials. That is essentially my definition of the term throughout this book, even in relation to modern drama.

(iii) Shakespeare

Next [Shakespeare] writes a series of what are sometimes called romantic comedies. Really they are the first plays of the theatre of the absurd. Edward Bond.[24]

Unlike Guarini and Fletcher, Shakespeare never described any of his plays as a tragicomedy, nor did the editors of his First Folio impose the term upon him, preferring to squeeze everything into the standard Elizabethan categories of tragedy, comedy and history. Nevertheless, there are compelling reasons for thinking of the plays which Shakespeare wrote in the last phase of his career as tragicomedies — not in the loose, 'mongrel' sense deplored by Sidney, but in ways that relate them specifically to the Guarini-Fletcher tradition. These plays are, specifically, *Pericles, Cymbeline, The Winter's Tale, The Tempest, Henry VIII* and *The Two Noble Kinsmen*. The last two were probably written in collaboration with Fletcher himself; all were written between 1606 and 1613.

Few would quarrel today with the judgement that these plays are significantly different in style and mood from anything Shakespeare had written before, even though we may detect in them frequent echoes of his earlier plays. Many arguments have been put forward to explain their special characteristics, most of them thankfully a good deal more constructive than Lytton Strachey's iconoclastic suggestion that they are the work of an ageing Shakespeare 'bored with people, bored with real life, bored with drama, bored in fact with everything except poetry and poetical dreams'.[25] It has been noted that they were probably written with the special characteristics of the indoor Blackfriars Theatre in mind (though they were also performed at the outdoor Globe) and that they were influenced by the spectacular Court masques then being perfected by Ben Jonson and Inigo Jones. In style and subject-matter they are, like the plays of Beaumont and Fletcher, belated examples of the old 'romance' tradition of literature, to which Sidney's *Arcadia* and Spenser's *The Faerie Queene* belong, a fact that may be related to a strain of nostalgia running through them for the Elizabethan era which fast receded into mythology in the less decorous reign of King James. This tradition, rather than any love-interest in them, explains the label 'romanccs'.

In urging the case for Shakespeare's last plays to be thought of as tragicomedies I wish to deny none of these arguments but rather to supplement them. The starting point of my case is the evident similarity between these plays and those of Beaumont and Fletcher. There are, for example, so many points of similarity between *Cymbeline* and *Philaster* that it is difficult to believe that some sort of cross-fertilisation did not take place, even if we cannot determine in which direction.[26] As Ashley Thorndike put it: 'When we remember that Shakespeare's change from historical tragedy to romance was very abrupt, that it was almost exactly contemporaneous with the success of Beaumont and Fletcher's romances, that Shakespeare and Fletcher wrote two plays together for the King's men, and that three of Beaumont and Fletcher's romances were acted by the same theatrical company as Shakespeare's, then the resemblances between the two sets of plays become very significant'.[27]

Many subsequent critics have conceded 'the resemblances between the two sets of plays' but have been far less well-disposed towards Beaumont and Fletcher. Ever-mindful of Lytton Strachey's strictures against the fairy-tale looseness of Shakespeare's last plays, the younger dramatists have been set up as whipping-boys — their plays set up as examples of unmitigated escapism beside which Shakespeare's forays into a similar mode may be seen to have self-evident depth and purpose. Una Ellis-Fermor puts it this way: 'By one of those paradoxes which this drama continually offers us, Shakespeare used for the culminating expression of his faith in reality the form which its inventors had devised as a means of escape'.[28]

Even the most committed champion of Shakespeare as a writer of tragicomedies seems faintly embarrassed by the Beaumont and Fletcher connection; Joan Hartwig grants them only six pages in her full-length *Shakespeare's Tragicomic Vision*.[29] Her conclusion that 'Beaumont and Fletcher want us to look at the artifice and admire its ingenuity; but Shakespeare wants us to look through the artifice to see why it is worth the effort' (p.32) still smacks of the whipping-boys. She feels the need to be very careful about associating Shakespeare with tragicomedy if it means associating him with Beaumont and Fletcher.

It is true, of course, that there are significant differences between Shakespeare's last plays and the tragicomedies of Guarini and Fletcher. Not just the threat of death but death itself occurs in all of Shakespeare's last plays except *The Tempest*: gods and supernatural beings occur in most of them, fulfilling one part of the definition of tragicomedy that Fletcher prefixed to *The Faithful Shepherdess* but did not adhere to in his work with Beaumont. There is a much greater emphasis on music and theatrical spectacle than we associate with Beaumont and Fletcher — masques, anti-masques, dreams, visions, dances, bears — and a corresponding decrease in unexpected revelations and sensational reverses. Although his characters may spend much of these plays bemused and bewildered, Shakespeare rarely tries to hoodwink the audience. The other characters may not know that Imogen in *Cymbeline* is in disguise, but the audience does; in *The Winter's Tale* Perdita herself does not know that she is a princess, but the audience is in little doubt; Ferdinand in *The Tempest* may believe that his father is dead and that Miranda is a goddess, but the audience knows better. Even in the one significant exception to this rule — the statue scene at the end of *The Winter's Tale* — Shakespeare drops liberal hints to the audience that Hermione is still alive, long before Leontes discovers this for himself.

But these differences between Shakespeare and Fletcher are matters of style and emphasis; they do not preclude the possibility that both were writing tragicomedy in their individual ways. As I shall suggest in respect of Beckett, Pinter and Stoppard, tragicomedy may be a narrower category than either tragedy or comedy, but it is not so delimited as to preclude personal variations of the kind we regard as normal in other genres. Like the works of Beaumont and Fletcher, Shakespeare's last plays concentrate more on action than on character development, and more on trying to make sense of that action, which often seems confusing and arbitrary, than on exploiting its immediate theatrical potential; the focus is primarily on perplexed individuals driven by forces they do not properly understand and incapable of resolving their own destinies. *The Tempest* only deviates from this pattern to the extent of locating the source of the action, the hidden force, within the person of Prospero; if we were to imagine a version of the play in which he did not appear until the final scene, but continued to use Ariel as his intermediary, it would fit the pattern exactly.

We can best demonstrate the essential characteristics of Shakespearean tragicomedy by looking in detail at perhaps the most representative example, *The Winter's Tale*, which M. T. Herrick assures us 'is certainly a tragicomedy, the best one that Shakespeare wrote'.[30] At the outset the play centres on Leontes, King of Sicily, his wife Hermione, and his old friend, Polixenes, who is paying a visit to his Court. Leontes is suddenly smitten with jealous suspicions about Hermione and Polixenes, and engages his trusted counsellor, Camillo, to poison the latter; Camillo, however, warns Polixenes and they both escape to Bohemia. In a fury Leontes consigns Hermione to prison, where she gives birth to a daughter, later called Perdita, whom Leontes baselessly believes to be Polixenes'. Paulina, wife to another trusted counsellor, Antigonus, brings the baby to him but fails to move his compassion; he orders her husband to leave it to die on a desert shore. When word comes from Apollo's oracle at Delphi that Hermione is innocent, Leontes disregards it; he is then told successively of the deaths of his young son, Mamillius, who has grieved at the treatment of his mother, and of Hermione herself. Leontes lapses into inconsolable remorse. Meanwhile Antigonus, struggling with his conscience, abandons Perdita on the shore of Bohemia and is himself immediately killed by a bear, while the ship that brought them is wrecked in a storm with the loss of all hands; Perdita is found and brought up as his own daughter by an old shepherd. Sixteen years pass by in a Chorus related by Time. The grown-up Perdita, still unaware of her true identity, has fallen in love with

Florizel, son of Polixenes. Polixenes has heard of their relationship, which he fears will demean the royal line; at a pastoral shepherds' festival, over which Perdita presides as 'Mistress o'the Feast', he confronts them and peremptorily orders them to part. With the help of Camillo, who has loyally served Polixenes all this time, the lovers escape to Sicily and the Court of Leontes. The intervention of the roguish pedlar, Autolycus, a self-confessed 'snapper-up of unconsidered trifles' (IV.iii.25), makes their escape known to Polixenes, who sets off in pursuit. Perdita's true identity is revealed, to the joy of the still-grieving Leontes and the great satisfaction of Polixenes, who is now happy to bless her match with Florizel, being reconciled with his old friend. All this clears the way for a final scene in which Paulina, who has been Leontes' mainstay in his 'saint-like sorrow', shows them a 'statue' of Hermione; the statue proves to be Hermione herself, who has lived in secret all these years. Her rediscovery is a cue for general rejoicing, which includes the betrothal of the two faithful servants, Camillo and Paulina.

Even such an outline of the story should make apparent the emphasis on action, the sheer concatenation of events, as opposed to character development. Leontes dominates the first half of the play and his jealousy is portrayed with a vividness which some have thought superior even to that of *Othello*.[31] But the jealousy is never projected, as it is with Othello, as a part of his own personality, as a psychologically credible side to his nobility; there is no Iago to stir it and give it substance. It comes suddenly, violently and without warning: 'Too hot, too hot!/To mingle friendship far is mingling bloods' (I.ii.108-9); and it stays with him in spite of the protestations of Camillo, Hermione and Paulina, even in spite of the Delphic oracle. The other characters, in fact, see it less as a personality disorder than as a visitation of alien forces; Camillo consistently describes it as a 'disease' (I.ii.384), while Hermione is convinced 'There's some ill planet reigns' (II.i.105); Antigonus assumes that the King has been misled by some 'putter-on' (II.i.141) and Paulina puts it down to 'dangerous, unsafe lunes' (i.e. fits of lunacy, II.ii.30). All this steers the emphasis away from personality to a suggestion of the character as driven by some extrinsic force; this in turn makes it dramatically more acceptable when, midway through the play, Leontes ceases to be the centre of attention and we concentrate on other characters, who are just as much caught up in the strange pressure of external forces even if they are not personally deranged. The disappearance for so long of Leontes is less disquieting than would be such a disappearance of Hamlet or Othello largely because it is quite apparent that he can do nothing himself to resolve his dilemmas. By the same token, it is possible for the audience to accept that the Polixenes whom we first see in a sympathetic light, as an innocent victim of Leontes' madness, should later appear as an unsympathetic tyrant, threatening Perdita that he will have her 'beauty scratch'd with briers, and made/More homely than thy state' (IV.iv.418-9). In neither case is the audience encouraged to become involved with their personalities; we witness rather what they do and say than what they are.

Although the emphasis falls in this way on the action, the play is notably restrained in its portrayal of some of its potentially most dramatic moments. For example, although Mamillius and Antigonus both die in the course of the play, they do so off-stage, and we only know of it by report. The most striking example, however, is the scene (V.ii) in which Perdita's true identity is established; she is restored to Leontes; he is reconciled to Polixenes; and the two fathers joyfully consent to the marriage of their children. None of this is shown at all; it is all reported in a conversation between Autolycus, who is at best peripheral to the main action, and three anonymous Gentlemen. It is possible to argue, of course, that Shakespeare did it in this muted way to avoid stealing the thunder from the statue scene which was to follow, but that is at best only half an explanation. The dramatist who could present the complex and exciting closing sequences of *Hamlet* and *King Lear* without recourse to lengthy reports of essential off-stage action could surely have deployed things otherwise if he had wished. We must conclude that he employed the muted tones of second-hand report here because it suited his purpose.

That would certainly be consistent with the emphasis on moderation which Guarini insisted was one of the hallmarks of tragicomedy: 'passion, moved but tempered' — we are close to great emotions, but never quite involved in them. It is at the heart of Joan Hartwig's case for seeing Shakespeare's late plays as tragicomedies that they constantly advertise their own artificiality, partly in order to maintain this special Guarinian mood: where the audience is aware of artifice, it is impossible to surrender totally to the pity of quasi-tragic events or to the joy of quasi-comic ones. They are constrained to that special middle-mood response which is the unique effect of tragicomedy (except, perhaps, in its closing moments) and which seem appropriate to this particular reported restoration/reconciliation/betrothal scene. Professor Hartwig would argue further that this self-consciously artificial mode makes special demands on the audience, in that it constantly challenges them to compare the artful picture of life with life as they have experienced it themselves. Shakespeare would thus be using art to force us to examine nature more closely; Professor Hartwig would deny, however, that this is true of the 'artificiality' of Beaumont and Fletcher. It is my contention that this self-conscious art/nature discrepancy, with the special demands it makes of an audience, is a characteristic of all true tragicomedy, though its local operation may differ according to the precise styles and methods of the authors. The sophistication of its conventions, careful modulation of mood and self-evident concern to perplex its audience as much as it perplexes its characters, inevitably make tragicomedy a challenging, even an abrasive mode.

This is one of the surest distinctions between tragicomedy proper and that 'mongrel', mixed style of drama to which most Elizabethan plays — including most of Shakespeare's own — belong and which is often confused with tragicomedy. Dr. Johnson pinpointed the distinction exactly, though he might have been surprised to be told that he had done so. In his *Preface to Shakespeare* (1765), he stoutly defends Shakespeare's plays against pedantic classical objections: 'Shakespere's plays are not in the rigorous and critical sense either tragedies or comedies, but compositions of a distinct kind, exhibiting the real state of sublunary nature, which partakes of good and evil, joy and sorrow, mingled with endless variety of proportion and innumerable modes of combination; and expressing the course of the world, in which the loss of one is the gain of the other; in which, at the same time, the reveller is hasting to his wine, and the mourner burying his friend; in which the malignity of one is

34

sometimes defeated by the frolic of another; and many mischiefs and many benefits are done and hindered without design'.[32] Speaking specifically of *Cymbeline*, however — which in the respects he addresses is a typical tragicomedy — he was magisterially dismissive: 'To remark the folly of the fiction, the absurdity of the conduct, the confusion of the names, and manners of different times, and the impossibility of the events in any system of life, were to waste criticism upon unresisting imbecility, upon faults to evident for detection, and too gross for aggravation'.[33] Dr. Johnson, in short, was quite happy to admit the virtues of mixed or 'mongrel' drama but neither relished nor understood the particular challenge of *Cymbeline's* tragicomic mode, whose artificiality he regards as 'unresisting imbecility'. His reaction to *Cymbeline*, in fact, has a lot in common with unsympathetic responses to the modern tragicomedy of Beckett, Pinter and co.

This middle mood and self-conscious artificiality of tragicomic action is never more apparent than in the sequence of *The Winter's Tale* that leads to the death of Antigonus. As I have already suggested, Shakespeare was going against the prevailing critical wisdom in introducing actual deaths into tragicomedy: 'the danger, not the death' was specifically part of Guarini's formula, and Fletcher always abides by it (except, significantly, in his collaborations with Shakespeare). But, having resolved that Antigonus should die — perhaps as an example of poetic justice, for his part in abandoning Perdita; perhaps as necessary to perplex the audience even further about the possibility of Perdita ever being restored to her proper place in life — Shakespeare goes out of his way to minimise the tragic effect of the death. In the abstract, being torn to death by a bear is quite a horrible way to die; but in the context of the play, Shakespeare does everything he can to channel the horror into something close to comedy. Firstly, the bear itself; there has been much fruitless debate about whether Shakespeare's actors would have used a real bear, taken from one of the bear-pits neighbouring the Globe, or whether it would have been an actor dressed in a bear skin. The balance of probabilities seems to me overwhelmingly weighed towards the latter,[34] but in either case the effect must have been more or less comic: a real bear would not be the savage beast a modern film could offer but a familiar performer in an unfamiliar setting, while an actor in an animal's skin is always apt to be fairly ludicrous, even if he does not make the hash of the part that Snug does of the Lion in *A Midsummer Night's Dream*. Then the death itself is carefully steered off-stage with that most notorious of all stage directions, 'Exit, pursued by a bear', and Shakespeare fixes the tone of events by introducing a comic account of them in the conversation of an old Shepherd and a Clown. Once again, the use of a second-hand account mutes, indeed transmutes, the emotional effect.

The Clown tells both of the wreck of the ship that brought Antigonus and Perdita to Bohemia and of Antigonus' death; it is his sheer exuberant bafflement at having so much to relate which makes the whole experience comic: 'O, the most piteous cry of the poor souls! Sometimes to see'em, and not see'em. Now the ship boring the moon with her main-mast, and anon swallowed with yest and froth, as you'ld thrust a cork into a hogs-head. And then for the land-service — to see how the bear tore out his shoulder-bone, how he cried to me for help and said his name was Antigonus, a nobleman. But to make an end of the ship, to see how the sea flap-dragoned it. But, first, how the poor souls roared, and the sea mocked them, and how the poor gentleman roared and the bear mocked him, both roaring louder than the sea or weather' (III.iii.86-97). The word 'mocked' is self-consciously appropriate, since it reflects what Shakespeare is actually doing, via the Clown, to these tragic events. Nature, in the forms both of the sea and the bear, has destroyed many human beings, but the art of the play — the comic presentation — renders the fact emotionally ambivalent in context, even neutral. It is perhaps worth adding that a speech like this, chaotically yet comically unable to come to terms with the experiences it attempts to relate, has much in common with modern tragicomic practices which audiences often find baffling — I think, for example, of Lucky's soliloquy in *Waiting for Godot* (pp. 42-5) or any of the various attempts that Rosencrantz and Guildenstern make to come to terms with what is happening to them in *Rosencrantz and Guildenstern Are Dead*. Language itself seems to be on the point of collapsing under the pressure of trying to make sense of events which are simultaneously of the utmost importance and laughably insignificant.

In a play by Beaumont and Fletcher the emphasis would fall on the moral and emotional dilemmas in which such strange events place the principal characters. In Shakespeare, however, we are encouraged to look beyond the principal characters to a pattern of perplexing experience which involves everyone in both Sicily and Bohemia; the pressure of moral and emotional confusion is actually voiced most clearly by the secondary characters, those caught up in the events at one remove. The most striking of these are Camillo and Autolycus. The former is strongly characterised as a loyal counsellor, firstly to Leontes and latterly to Polixenes; yet the turn of events is such that he betrays both masters, warning Polixenes about Leontes' jealous suspicions and fleeing with him, and later helping Florizel and Perdita to escape from Polixenes' wrath. On both occasions he is actually aware that he is breaking his trust as counsellor but his conscience forces him to go against his masters' wishes. Just as we see Leontes' jealousy as some kind of visitation from the gods, we begin to see that Camillo is caught up in an unfolding process which he does not understand, and over which he has little control. Had he remained true to type and loyal to his masters, disaster would have ensued, as it is, his double betrayal is crucial to the happy resolution of all difficulties. Indeed, he goes further and even betrays Florizel and Perdita, whom he sincerely wishes to help, by telling Polixenes of their flight and allowing him to follow them:

> *Florizel*: Camillo has betray'd me,
> Whose honour and whose honesty till now
> Endured all weathers.
>
> (V.i.192-4)

But even this does not, in itself, resolve all the play's difficulties; it has to be matched by the equally odd behaviour of Autolycus. He too had overheard the plotting of Camillo, Florizel and Perdita, and contemplated reporting it to Polixenes, but 'I hold it the more knavery to conceal it; and therein am I constant to my profession' (IV.iv.668-70). He then meets the old Shepherd and the Clown, who are anxious to disclaim any real relationship with Perdita because of the King's displeasure at her attachment to Florizel. Worried that this may bring the lovers' flight to the King's notice, Autolycus tries to deflect them, commenting 'Though I am not naturally honest, I am so sometimes by chance' (700-1). When he hears their story, he recognises its potential value to Florizel, and while promising — for a consideration — to help the rustics to an audience with the King, he actually directs them on board the boat that is taking the lovers to Sicily. As he reflects, 'If I had a mind to be honest, I see Fortune would not suffer me' (814-5). Had Autolycus simply acted out of roguish self-interest and betrayed the lovers' flight immediately, Polixenes might have stopped them; had be not intercepted the Shepherd and the Clown, their story might never have reached the Sicilian ears that matter. As it is, the action he takes, prompted by devious self-interest and a perverse form of professional pride, meshes perfectly with Camillo's 'betrayals' to ensure that Perdita's true identity will be revealed at the most opportune moment, reconciling Polixenes with Florizel, Leontes with Polixenes and ultimately Leontes with the supposed-dead Hermione.

With hindsight, therefore, every betrayal and every apparently perverse decision can be seen as a necessary development in a pattern or process which is ultimately benign, ultimately for the greater good of the whole society. Again with hindsight, we can even say that there is a positive dimension to the deaths in the play: the death of Antigonus leaves the way clear at the end for Camillo and Paulina to marry, a kind of reward for being the two loyalest of royal servants despite all appearances to the contrary. And the death of Mamillius makes the survival and rediscovery of Perdita something doubly special: she is now Leontes' heir, and her marriage to Florizel ensures that eventually Sicily and Bohemia will join under a single crown, an Empire where heretofore there have been separate kingdoms. There are similar gestures towards an 'imperial' future in most of Shakespeare's late plays — *Cymbeline, The Tempest, Henry VIII* as well as *The Winter's Tale*. It gives a social and political dimension to the spirit of regeneration and reconciliation with which these plays conclude and can be seen as one tangible benefit to emerge from the suffering and bewilderment which so many of the characters undergo.

By the end of *The Winter's Tale*, in short, we can see that a pattern of experience which threatened pain, death and disaster has actually brought forth reconciliation and the promise of a better future. It is not, in the pejorative sense, a fairy-tale because the suffering and deaths have been real enough, and it is not in any simple sense a case of virtue rewarded because we are given no cause to suppose that the characters as individuals deserve or are responsible for what happens to themselves. There is no sudden and unpredictable revelation akin to those in Beaumont and Fletcher, which resolves and makes sense of everything; even the quasi-magical reappearance of Hermione is only one piece in the play's large jigsaw puzzle. The emphasis is rather on coming to terms bit by bit with the realisation that men's lives are governed by forces too large and inscrutable for them really to understand; Autolycus nods in this direction with his wry decision to accept what Fortune sends him, while the play as a whole reverts constantly to the theme of grace,[35] associating this idea of divine regenerative influence with the persons of Hermione and Perdita. Tragicomedy, in effect, has become a way of embodying a sense of providence, a sense of the real shape and pattern of existence which is not apparent in our everyday lives. All the characteristics we have observed — the characters gripped by extrinsic forces, or acting strangely against their nature; the action oddly distanced or reported; language itself on the point of breakdown — all these combine to present an experience that cannot be conveyed on a literal or realistic level. It must be experienced as we experience myths or dreams, sensing a level of truth in them that is deeper than the reality we normally inhabit. The audience of such a play must surely feel as Alonso, King of Naples, feels in *The Tempest*, when he is baffled by Prospero's magic:

These are not natural events; they strengthen
From strange to stranger.

or again,

This is as strange a maze as e'er men trod;
And there is in this business more than nature
Was ever conduct of: some oracle
Must rectify our knowledge.

(V.i.227-8; 242-5)

It is pointless to try to understand such matters rationally; we can only come to terms with them by surrendering, at least in part, to a state of wonder or, as the Elizabethans would say, of admiration — to the state which Ferdinand achieves in *The Tempest* when he confronts his 'admir'd Miranda' (III.i.37). Like the First Gentlemen in *Cymbeline*, we must accept that, whatever happens, 'Howsoe'er 'tis strange . . . Yet is it true' (I.i.65-7). To surrender in this way is virtually an act of faith in the forces of providence that govern us, an acceptance that however painful and bewildering our life is, it is ultimately for the best. Such faith may not commonly be possible in the twentieth century, but fundamentally the same challenge to our rational understanding and to our consensus realism is made by the 'strangeness' which is a conspicuous feature of modern tragicomedy.

This theme of faith and providence is pushed, perhaps to its limits, in *The Two Noble Kinsmen* (c.1613), a collaborative work by Shakespeare and Fletcher. The main plot is a reworking of the story most familiar to English readers in Chaucer's *The Knight's Tale*, from *The Canterbury Tales*. It tells of the love of two Theban cousins, Palamon and Arcite, for the same woman, Emilia. Shakespeare and Fletcher's play begins, as does *A Midsummer Night's Dream*, with the impending marriage of Theseus, Duke of Athens, to Hippolyta, Queen of the Amazons — a symbolic match, since it shows the great soldier hero, who has already defeated the Queen in battle, being overcome in turn by his love for her. Ceremonial preparations for the marriage are interrupted by the arrival of three Queens whose husbands have been killed at the siege of Thebes; their distress is not so much at their husbands' deaths as at the fact that Creon, King of Thebes, will not allow the bodies a proper funeral — denying them, in effect, the dignity that belongs to a human being. Theseus is loath to postpone the wedding, but agrees to do so when urged on by Hippolyta and her sister, Emilia. The scene moves to Thebes, where Palamon and Arcite are introduced as two noble and idealistic knights, bound to each other by kinship and friendship, deeply distressed by the current government of Thebes, but determined to defend their native city when they hear of Theseus' impending attack. They fight valiantly in the battle, but Theseus wins the day, allows the three Queens to bury their husbands 'With treble ceremony' (I.iv.8) and returns to Athens with the gravely wounded Palamon and Arcite as his prisoners. The two cousins recover in gaol, bemoaning their wretched fate but taking comfort in their friendship, until they catch sight of Emilia; both instantly fall in love with her and quarrel over who has the prior claim on her. They are on the point of coming to blows when Arcite is summoned before Theseus and banished from Athens, on pain of death if he returns; nevertheless, he is so in love with Emilia and so jealous of Palamon that he resolves to go in disguise with some country-people who are to provide rustic entertainment at Theseus' postponed wedding.[36] In this way he impresses Theseus and wins the chaste admiration of Emilia with his skill as a wrestler; he joins their party on its way to the Mayday festivities and meets Palamon, who has escaped from prison. They resolve that, despite their friendship, they will have to fight each other for Emilia's hand. They set to in earnest, only to be interrupted by Theseus, who is furious that knights should be fighting without his permission and doubly so when he discovers that it is his escaped prisoner and the man he banished. His first reaction is to condemn them to death, but once again Hippolyta and Emilia are moved by pity to intercede. Theseus argues that they cannot simply be banished since they would carry on fighting abroad over Emilia, to her dishonour; she suggests that they be bound by oath to leave the kingdom, forget her and never see each other again, but Palamon and Arcite both refuse to take such an oath. Theseus finally decrees that both men should go back to Thebes, to return within the month with three knights apiece to do formal battle for Emilia's hand; she reluctantly agrees, as a way of breaking the impasse and in order to save at least one life, that she will marry the winner of the contest, while the loser will immediately be executed. So their rivalry builds to a solemn climax. Arcite prays to Mars, as god of war, for success in the battle; Palamon prays to Venus, as goddess of love; Emilia prays to Diana, goddess of chastity but also, significantly, of the hunt. Each receives a sign from the gods, but nothing as clear as a promise. In the keenly fought battle Arcite finally wins and Palamon prepares for execution; but at the last minute Arcite's horse (a gift from Emilia) rears and crushes him to death, leaving Palamon to marry Emilia.

The Two Noble Kinsmen lacks the self-evident strangeness of *Cymbeline, The Winter's Tale* and *The Tempest*. It does not have the same quantity of bizarre accident, magical confusion or disorientated characters.[37] Nevertheless the action of the play hinges on one overwhelming dilemma, and the play shares with those earlier works a deep sense of the extent to which human lives are governed by forces essentially beyond their understanding and control. As the play's editor, N.W. Bawcutt, puts it: 'Shakespeare is deeply aware in this play of the extent to which human life is dominated by forces outside human control — we should also take account of terms like "fortune" and "nature" — but although man must reverence and propitiate them, they often work in ways that cause bewilderment or suffering'.[38] It is in the disconcerting way that the authors keep this issue, rather than the individual characters or the action, at the centre of attention, that the play reveals itself as a true tragicomedy. Perhaps the clearest difference between this play and the earlier ones is the fact that all the major characters are intensely conscious of the 'forces beyond human control', particularly the heroic Theseus, who is proud of his kinship with the semi-divine Hercules; the tricks of fortune and the gods do not, therefore, come as real surprises, and the play does not go out of its way to place either the characters themselves or the audience in a state of confusion or wonder. It rather dwells on the problem of how men may live, conscious that they are not in control of their own destinies but essentially ignorant of the forces that actually govern them. This is where the play's emphasis on ceremony, ritual and prayer comes in — the insistence on the proper burial of the dead, the rites of marriage, the fertility rites of Maying, the elaborate prayers before the battle, and even the battle itself, which must be fought with due attention to the ceremonies of chivalry. Such ceremonial activity emphasises the dignity and nobility of human beings, who are not merely brute beasts for all that they lack real understanding — they appreciate the potential significance of their lives; at the same time, however there are nervous attempts to 'reverence' and 'propitiate' the forces which control them and beside which men seem totally insignificant. The compliance of the gods with human wishes can never be predicted or taken for granted, but failure to take them into account as in the case of

Creon's refusal to allow the three Kings a proper burial, will surely (if inscrutably) lead to retribution and disaster. The tragicomedy of *The Two Noble Kinsmen* therefore focuses simultaneously on the nobility and insignificance of human beings; the central dilemma of who should marry Emilia (or indeed whether she should marry at all, since she has shown no personal inclination to do so) invokes a disconcerting double perspective. Seen from one angle, as in tragedy, everything that the characters do is crucially important, a necessity in the wider scheme of man's existence. Seen from the other angle, however, as in comedy, none of it matters at all, since the gods (or whatever) will ultimately dispose everything as they will, and we can only take it on trust that this will be for the best for us too.

Theseus is a crucial element in this double perspective, since as the hero-leader figure of the play he is often called upon to make god-like decisions of life and death, peace and war, and he is frequently petitioned as if he were a god; the widowed Queens and Hippolyta and Emilia repeatedly go down on their knees before him, in scenes which must prefigure the real prayers before the final battle between Palamon and Arcite. On each occasion, we see Theseus determined to be firm and just, but in each case too he is swayed by a sense of compassion, which befits a chivalric hero; the First Queen hits just the right balance when she pitches her appeal, 'For pity's sake and true gentility's' (I.i.25). Although he feels sorry for the Queens, he is convinced that his marriage is 'a service . . ./Greater than any war' (171-2); it is only when Hippolyta and Emilia add their 'prayers' that he puts compassion before his own pleasurable duty and determines to punish Creon. The Queens praise his decision, saying that with it he earns

> (*Second Queen*):   . . . a deity equal with Mars.
> *Third Queen*:   If not above him, for
>   Thou being but mortal makest affections bend
>   To godlike honours; they themselves, some say,
>   Groan under such a mastery
>
>   (I.i.227-31)

That is, in putting compassion before his own inclinations, he has shown a more than god-like magnanimity since the gods ('some say') are often simply driven by their own passions. Theseus does not see it that way himself, claiming that the ability to rise above one's passions is merely what divides man from the beasts: presumably the gods are easily capable of it. He is also quick to allay any suggestion of hubris about his decision to go to Thebes, ordering his friend, Pirethous:

> get you and pray the gods
> For success and return; omit not anything
> In the pretended [i.e. intended] celebration.

(I.i.208-10)

In short, we see Theseus as a firm but compassionate ruler, neither arrogant nor rash, capable of being moved by a fair argument or a pitiful case — as again, when faced with the noble but intractable antagonism of Palamon and Arcite: 'What may be done? For now I feel compassion?' (III.vi.271).

The question which the widowed Queens raise and which the play insistently puts before us is whether the gods themselves are anything like as reasonable and compassionate as this man who so often has to function in their place. It is an important question because it focuses precisely the tragicomic perspective. In his attempt to be a just ruler, a true lover and a champion of chivalry, Theseus stands for everything that is noble and positive about Renaissance man; the possibility that the gods are not like this and that they care nothing for such idealism calls the whole structure of belief into question. That is why the Palamon/Arcite/Emilia dilemma is so significant. In making two equally worthy suitors fall in love with the same chaste young lady, who has no particular desire to marry either of them, the gods have created a situation from which it will be difficult, if not impossible, to demonstrate that they are beings as fair and compassionate as Theseus. Of course, Theseus himself does not harbour any doubts; after he has overcome Creon he sees the moral very clearly and without self-pride:

> Th'impartial gods, who from the mounted heavens
> View us their mortal herd, behold who err,
> And in their time chastise

(I.iv.4-6)

They may take their time about it, but in the end the gods are just, punishing wrong-doers; so there is nothing incongruous in trying to distinguish between right and wrong or, by implication, in trying to live with as much decency and nobility as we can muster. The gods will ultimately endorse such idealism. That is essentially what Theseus himself finally understands to happen in the resolution of the Palamon/Arcite/Emilia dilemma:

> The powerful Venus well hath graced her altar,
> And given you [i.e. Palamon] your love; our master Mars
> Hath vouched his oracle, and to Arcite gave
> The grace of the contention; so the deities
> Have showed due justice
>
> (V.iv.105-9)

That is, it was right that Palamon, as a devotee of Venus, should marry his beloved, and it was right that Arcite, as a devotee of Mars, should win the battle. Mere mortals would expect, under the rules laid down as reasonably as possible by Theseus, that the winner of the one should also be winner of the other, which must have been unjust to whichever was the loser. But the gods have ordained a sequence of events which was just to both parties in the end.

This is a splendidly balanced reading of events, but is it perhaps too Jesuitical? After all, as Palamon complains:

> That we should things desire which do cost us
> The loss of our desire! That nought could buy
> Dear love but loss of dear love!
>
> (V.iv.110-12)

There may be a splendid symmetry about the outcome, but it seems not to take into account the pain, suffering and loss of human life that was necessary to bring it about — or the fact that the winning of Emilia has meant the loss of Arcite, which makes her a more equivocal prize than Palamon had ever anticipated. It may not be the price that a reasonable man would pay, given the choice. Theseus admits that

> Never fortune
> Did play a subtler game: the conquered triumphs,
> The victor has the loss —

But he insists:

> Yet in the passage
> The gods have been most equal

$$(112-5)$$

He concludes with the resolution:

> Let us be thankful
> For that which is, and with you leave dispute
> That are above our question

$$(134-6)$$

That is an answer and no answer. He has made a case for the gods being just, but he has not demonstrated that they are compassionate; now he insists that we have to leave to the gods themselves matters 'That are above our question'. There is, in effect, no final resolution to the tragicomic dual perspective; we have no sanction higher than Theseus himself for this reading of events, unless we take it that the context of these words, at the very end of the play, confers a special resonance upon them. While Theseus lends all his authority to endorsing everything that is positive and idealistic about life, the possibility that it is all finally meaningless is never actually exorcised.

Most of the critics who have concentrated on Shakespeare's late plays have seen in the sequence leading up to *The Tempest* (or even, in Wilson Knight's case, *Henry VIII*[39]) something of a mellow wisdom, a serene but knowledgeable maturity after the storms of the great tragedies. *The Two Noble Kinsmen* does not fit very comfortably into such a pattern, and the problems of joint-authorship have made it relatively easy for them simply to ignore it or to pass over it lightly.[40] Professor Hartwig is typical in this respect; although she admits that the play was, in the custom of the time, registered with the Stationers Company as a 'tragicomedy', she does not regard it as a significant contribution to Shakespeare's achievement in this genre. She relegates it to a few words in an appendix, where she castigates it for its lack of 'joy', a quality she finds central to Shakespeare's solo tragicomedies. This is not the place to argue over the status of *The Two Noble Kinsmen*, but it is worth pointing out that when Ben Jonson — Shakespeare's most formidable contemporary rival as a dramatist — launched his attack on Shakespearean tragicomedy in *Bartholomew Fair*, mocking all its 'tales, tempests and such-like drolleries', he concentrated primarily on this play.[41] It is, I think, more central and a better play than is often appreciated. But my main reason for examining it here is to demonstrate the variety possible within tragicomedy, to underline the fact that even in the Renaissance it was not all light-hearted fairy-tales. This play, more than most of its contemporaries, has something of the bitter-sweet, disillusioned and world-weary flavour of modern tragicomedy.

Summary

We have now seen enough of the works of Guarini, Fletcher and Shakespeare to appreciate that, for all the local differences between particular works, Renaissance tragicomedy is an identifiable genre. It may be useful here to summarise its principal characteristics as a prelude to assessing its relationship to modern tragicomedy. Tragicomedy is primarily concerned with charting the relationship between human beings and the supernatural agencies — call them fate, fortune, providence, God or the gods — which govern their lives. Of course, both tragedy and comedy frequently enquire into such matters, but tragicomedy adopts a particular mode and perspective — signalled in the insistence that both gods and peasants are permissible within the same work — which makes them absolutely central, overshadowing even the characters and the action of the drama; these plays hang on the idea of expressing or embodying (if never quite explaining) the relationship between men and the forces beyond human understanding which shape their lives.

It follows from this that these plays are not, in most respects, realistic in style. The characters may speak a familiar language and their general situation may be broadly recognisable in relation to our own, but they in fact exist within a totally artificial play-world. We see characters in extreme emotional states, but we are not invited to follow the growth of their personalities or to appreciate their psychological complexities. Drama which concentrates on such matters — be it *Hamlet* or *Uncle Vanya* or *Death of a Salesman* — inevitably implies that there is a significant connection between personality and the events with which that personality is involved: not necessarily that 'character is destiny' but certainly that character and destiny are interdependent. Tragicomedy eschews such implications. Neither the dilemmas facing, say, Mirtillo, nor their resolution, arise from his particular personality, and it is significant that there are no essential differences of personality between Palamon and Arcite — one may appeal to Mars and the other to Venus, but they are in other respects indistinguishable to all intents and purposes: there is no way that a *Merchant of Venice*-type casket scene could have revealed which was the more appropriate individual to marry Emilia. Character and destiny thus seem to be independent of each other in these plays; at least, they are not seen to be dependent on each other. By the same token, there is a minimum of realism about the action; gods, spirits and visions may appear, oracles may pronounce, improbable accidents occur. Over and above that, the presentation of the action is generally such as to rob us of any comfortable feeling that cause and effect are linking together according to the known laws: characters may be smitten without warning by violent emotions; others may act perversely against their known natures; key developments may be reported rather than shown, in a way that blurs our sense of their significance; key facts may be withheld either from the characters, from the audience, or from both, in ways that make it difficult to make sense — at least, satisfactory sense — of what is going on.

Given that, broadly speaking, the central concern of these plays is the relationship between gods and men, characteristically they focus on moments of great emotional or moral dilemma, moments which highlight human fallibility: lovers on the point of being obliged, for reasons of state, not to marry, or to marry the wrong person; two men desperately in love with the same woman; good Kings becoming dangerous tyrants; loyal subjects tempted to treason; honourable men tempted to incest. Instinct and morality are crucially at odds with each other in ways that the characters themselves cannot resolve, so that the characteristic moods of tragicomedy are frustration and bewilderment, only offset for the audience by a greater or lesser conviction that the forces which created these dilemmas must ultimately also resolve them. It is this balance between all the doubts encountered in the course of the action and the certainty of the outcome which is, so to speak, generically guaranteed (though the means of it may be obscured till the last moment and may be as ambivalent as that in *The Two Noble Kinsmen*) that creates the peculiar 'middle mood' of tragicomedy.

What I have described as the generic guarantee of a propitious outcome to a tragicomedy carries with it problems that are partly philosophic and partly artistic. Any play which promises a happy ending, whatever the odds, runs the risk of seeming unrealistically complacent about man's lot — Panglossian in its conviction that all is for the best in the best of all possible worlds. This is essentially J.F. Danby's complaint about Beaumont and Fletcher, that they were fundamentally underwriting the absolutist assumptions and incipient Cavalier attitudes of the Jacobean Court with a promise of divine approval.[42] In a slightly different context, it is also essentially the complaint of those who regret that Shakespeare abandoned the complex realism of the great tragedies for what they see as the altogether less challenging mysticism of the late plays: where magic or the gods can resolve all problems, why should ordinary mortals worry? The charge in both cases boils down to culpable escapism, to the suggestion that these plays are only sophisticated fantasies which have nothing useful to tell us about man as a social and moral being; they do not relate meaningfully to the real world, or make us question its values. This may be one definition of self-indulgent, decadent art.

The charge is laid most forcefully at the door of Beaumont and Fletcher by E.M. Waith, who concludes his analysis of *A King and No King* with the judgment that the play, 'has no meaning. It says nothing about incest, pride, jealousy or wrath, but it presents an arrangement of dramatic moments in which these passions are displayed. Each moment has its meaning, but the whole has none that can be readily defined . . . . The emphasis is upon the formal pattern, to which everything else is sacrificed . . . .. The appeal is made directly to an emotional and aesthetic response'. He reinforces this conclusion when he considers the relationship of their tragicomedy to satire, romance and the art of declamation: 'The new effect of the combination of satire and romance upon the pattern of tragicomedy can be described as a major increase in formalisation and a corresponding decrease in meaning'; similarly, the 'remoteness from actuality and emphasis upon rhetorical elaboration [of declamation] strengthened the forces that were pushing tragicomedy away from meaning and toward greater formalisation'.[43]

While this remains, in essence, the modern view of Beaumont and Fletcher, any amount of critical ink has been spilled to defend Shakespeare's last plays from similar imputations. Perhaps the most convincing piece of evidence in his defence is that Shakespeare stops short of the all-or-nothing absolutism of his younger contempories. Although the climax of *The Winter's Tale*, for example, is full of joy and wonder, it is tempered by the reflection that Mamillius and Antigonus are indeed dead, and that Leontes and Hermione have wasted sixteen good years of their lives — her face is wrinkled, as a mere statue would not be. Similarly, at the end of *The Tempest*, Gonzalo's ecstatic assessment of the wonders of providence —

> Was Milan thrust from Milan that his issue
> Should become kings of Naples? O, rejoice
> Beyond a common joy, and set it down
> With gold on lasting pillars: in one voyage
> Did Claribel her husband find at Tunis,
> And Ferdinand, her brother, found a wife
> Where he himself was lost; Prospero his dukedom
> In a poor isle; and all of us ourselves
> When no man was his own.

(V.i.205-13)

— has to be set against both his own character as an inveterate optimist (see, for example, his daydream of setting up a utopian republic on the island, II.i.139-65), and the fact that neither Sebastian nor Antonio shows any real sign of falling in with the prevailing mood of goodwill. The famous interchange between Prospero and Miranda captures the ambivalent mood perfectly; she is full of wonder and enthusiasm — 'O brave new world/That has such people in't!' — while he is far more sceptical and world-weary: "Tis new to thee' (V.i.183-4). Like the art of the play as a whole, Prospero's magic cannot resolve all of life's difficulties. Professor Hartwig makes it the centre of her case that Shakespeare constantly brings the limitations of his art in these tragicomedies to the attention of his audience, in such a way that their unreality ceases to be escapism and becomes a critical yardstick for assessing life itself — art and artifice becoming useful servants of nature, rather than substitutes for it.

I am not convinced that Shakespeare is unique in giving tragicomedy this critical edge, though I agree that it is easier to locate in his plays than in those of many other practitioners of the genre. As we have seen, Renaissance tragicomedy had close links with pastoral literature, which in turn had close links with satire. At the heart of all these forms lay the abiding question of Renaissance literature: what is the proper relationship between art and nature, between man's creative and imaginative capacities and the imperfect world into which he is born? The question surfaces openly in *The Winter's Tale* in a debate between Perdita and Polixenes about the practice of 'improving' plants by artificial means (IV.iv.79-103), but it is implicit in all the plays we have considered here. More commonly it is man himself who is under consideration, rather than plants: what are the possibilities of human improvement, of attaining the ideals of chivalry, of being truly civilised, of creating a true and holy Empire on earth? Tragicomedy dreams the dream, but it does so in a way that underlines all the difficulties and limitations. Human beings alone are not capable of achieving these ideals; their art is far too compromised by the nature to which they belong. That is what, I suggest, prevents even Beaumont and Fletcher from being pure escapists: their plays may resolve all the problems of the world, but they do so with a panache that reflects its own impossibility. Like Donne 'proving' a little room an 'everywhere', or two parted lovers not parted at all, or riding westward the best way of looking east,[44] Beaumont and Fletcher's happy endings are baroque exercises in paradox, teasing the limits of the audience's reason and common sense. Art can never supplant nature, and only a fool would think that it can improve on it very much: the sudden, overwhelmingly

51

artful reversals that these plays engineer are thus intellectual and emotional challenges to any audience worth its salt, just as the golden world they conjure out of catastrophe is a challenge to the brazen, imperfect reality we actually inhabit.

This section will to some degree have failed if it has not, in sketching out a definition of Renaissance tragicomedy, also suggested how much that genre has in common with a certain style or mode of modern drama. The kind of tragicomedy I have been describing did not die out with Shakespeare and Fletcher. It lived on, suitably transposed, in the heroic drama of seventeenth-century France and Restoration England, perhaps echoing on into the melodrama of succeeding centuries.[45] But it would be unrealistic to suggest that it survived, as a living tradition, into modern times, however much the term 'tragicomedy' has been appropriated to other causes. If Beckett did look to Renaissance tragicomedy in writing *Waiting for Godot* — as, in the next chapter, I shall suggest he did — he must have done so as a conscious act of antiquarianism; he has been described as 'in many ways the last heir to the Renaissance, an heir who has religiously devoted himself to selling off every last stick and stone of his inheritance'.[46] Tragicomedy might very well be described as one of those sticks or stones. The only way in which this kind of drama might be described as having a living tradition is in Shakespeare's late plays, which his reputation has kept almost continually in the repertoire, even when they were neither fashionable nor particularly popular. Their influence would be difficult to assess, but perhaps it ought not to be ignored, particularly in the case of Pinter, who was an actor before he began writing plays and was certainly conversant with even the least-performed of Shakespeare's texts; one of his earliest professional roles, for example, was that of Abergavenny in *Henry VIII* for a Third Programme radio production (January 1951). As an actor, he would certainly have to confront the peculiar demands imposed by this style of drama.

But the thesis of this book does not hang on demonstrating a living tradition of tragicomedy so much as pointing out that a number of modern dramatists, for whatever reasons, have seen fit to write in a style or mode that has a significant amount in common with Renaissance tragicomedy — enough in common, in fact, to make it useful to approach these plays via a comparison with their predecessors. The usefulness is all the greater for the fact that the works of both eras are notoriously 'strange' and difficult for audiences to understand. It is my contention that the strangeness is deliberate in both sets of works and deployed towards broadly similar ends — so that an understanding of the one may help an understanding of the other. Of course, this modern drama has nothing to do with kings and princes and their bizarre dilemmas — Stoppard was quite in tune with the age in shifting the focus from Prince Hamlet to two of the dimmer luminaries of the Danish Court. Nor do its characters come into contact with gods or super-natural agencies — though a provocatively-named Godot may or may not hover in the wings. But the new tragicomedy shares with the old a concentration on characters caught up by numinous forces which they do not understand, about which they are barely articulate and over which they have no control. These forces may today be located as much within the psyche as beyond the natural world, but the dramatists remain studiously non-committal about such rational distinctions, which are irrelevant or invalid in the realms of experience they explore. It is precisely because these plays avoid 'rational distinctions' in this way that they have been assailed with charges of being 'meaningless' or 'form without substance' or 'complacently self-obsessed' — in ways strikingly reminiscent of the critical response to Beaumont and Fletcher.

In this context I feel constrained to describe tragicomedy, both old and new, as a form of ritual drama. I am mindful in this of Raymond Williams' strictures in *Modern Tragedy* against a term that seems capable 'of infinite extension . . . ritual, in the sense of a form of worship of a particular god, cannot be glibly identified with the many forms of dramatic action, in which . . . there is no proper ritual action at all'.[47] But ritual is not necessarily a form of worship of a particular god; it may be any form of communal activity undertaken to appease or come to terms with forces beyond our understanding (and in this context it makes no difference if such 'spirits' are psychological or super-natural). Such activity is at the nub of tragicomedy, a term for which Professor Williams has no apparent use — completely overlooking Beckett's label, for example, when assimilating *Waiting for Godot* within his 'modern tragedy'. It is in this sense, therefore, that I shall talk of ritual drama throughout this book.

PART II
Waiting for Godot,
by Samuel Beckett*

Beckett makes one overt allusion to Renaissance tragicomedy in the text of *Waiting for Godot*, beyond using the term on his title page. In the play's longest speech, the hapless Lucky mentions 'the divine Miranda' (p. 43) — a clear reference to *The Tempest* — though, as with everything else in that speech, the precise significance of the reference is far from clear. It may help us to uncover the tragicomic roots of the play as a whole if we can make some sense of this allusion. Like Perdita in *The Winter's Tale*, Miranda is one of the heroines in Shakespeare's late plays, mysteriously imbued with a special grace or aura which is linked — though never very precisely — with what I have described as the generic guarantee of a happy outcome in these plays. Her name reflects this special role, meaning 'wondrous' or 'admired one' and points to the awe-struck state of suspended disbelief which all such romances seek to inspire in their audiences as much as in some of their characters, rational apprehension giving way to something like faith. A perfect example of such 'admiration' is in fact given by her lover in the play, Ferdinand; when he first sees her, he assumes she must be divine:

> Most sure the goddess
> On whom these airs attend . . .
> . . . O you wonder! (I.ii.424-5; 429)

His devotion to 'admir'd Miranda' is immediate, unquestioning and complete, as Prospero's trials prove; this makes him fit both to win her hand in marriage and to be a spectator of that

---

*First performed in English in London, 1955

'majestic vision', the masque of Iris, Juno and Ceres which Prospero conjures up to celebrate their betrothal.

The experience of Ferdinand, which in a sense parallels that of the real audience confronted with the 'strangeness' of *The Tempest* itself, has to be seen as part of a broader process. Although it may seem odd to say so of a character who rarely attracts much attention, he is the real 'hero' of the play. Our interest is largely focused on Prospero and the various more or less wicked characters whose destinies he helps to shape, but it is Ferdinand who has to face the strange world of the island alone, believing his father and friends to be dead. He falls in love with the quasi-divine heroine, undergoes several trials and privations to prove his worth, and is finally accepted as a fit bridegroom for a marriage that will unite Naples and Milan in a new and prosperous Empire. This pattern of experience is traditionally one undergone by a hero, and we would readily identify Ferdinand as such, were it not for Prospero's unusually dominant position as the arbiter of affairs. The heroic pattern is, moreover, central to the tragicomic experience, as Joseph Campbell demonstrates in his book, *The Hero with a Thousand Faces*.[1]

Campbell comments on the modern assumption that tragedy is superior to comedy (or, in my terms, tragicomedy) because it is inherently truer to life as we know it: 'The happy ending is justly scorned as a misrepresentation; for the world, as we know it, as we have seen it, yields but one ending: death, disintegration, dismemberment, and the crucifixion of our heart with the passing of the forms that we have loved . . .. In comparison with all this, our little stories of achievement seem pitiful' (pp. 25-7). But he argues that the assumption is misconceived:

> The happy ending of the fairy tale, the myth, and the divine comedy of the soul, is to be read, not as a contradiction, but as a transcendence of the universal tragedy of man. The objective world remains what it was, but, because of a shift of emphasis within the subject, is beheld as though transformed . . .. It is the business of mythology proper, and of the fairy tale, to reveal the specific dangers and techniques of the dark interior way from tragedy to comedy.
>
> (pp. 28-9)

Campbell uses the terms 'tragedy' and 'comedy' in a broad anthropological sense, at which literary critics might wince, and he does not use tragicomedy at all. But it is in his focus on the passage from seeming tragedy to actual comedy that he declares his true relevance to this study since, as we saw in the last chapter, that passage is the specific experience in narrative literature of romance and in drama of tragicomedy (and not necessarily of the dramatic genre we call comedy).

In Campbell's analysis, this passage from tragedy to comedy is traditionally figured forth in the adventures of a hero; we should, however, think of this rather as an allegorical depiction of a development from one frame of mind, or psychological state, to another: 'hence the incidents are fantastic and "unreal": they represent psychological, not physical, triumphs' (p. 29). And he attempts to reduce these allegorical heroic adventures to a single formula:

> The standard path of the mythological adventure of the hero is a magnification of the formula represented in the rites of passage: SEPARATION—INITIATION—RETURN: which might be named the nuclear unit of the monomyth.
>
> A HERO VENTURES FORTH FROM THE WORLD OF COMMON DAY INTO A REGION OF SUPERNATURAL WONDER: FABULOUS FORCES ARE THERE ENCOUNTERED AND A DECISIVE VICTORY IS WON: THE HERO COMES BACK FROM THIS MYSTERIOUS ADVENTURE WITH THE POWER TO BESTOW BOONS ON HIS FELLOW MAN.
>
> Prometheus ascended to the heavens, stole fire from the gods, and descended. Jason sailed through the Clashing Rocks into a sea of marvels, circumvented the dragon that guarded the Golden Fleece, and returned with the fleece and the power to wrest his rightful throne from a usurper. Aeneas went down into the underworld, crossed the dreadful river of the dead, threw a sop to the three-headed watch-dog Cerberus, and conversed, at last, with the shade of his dead father. All things were unfolded to him: the destiny of souls, the destiny of Rome, which he was about to found, 'and in what wise he might avoid or endure every burden' (Virgil, *Aeneid* VI, 892). He returned through the ivory gate to his work in the world.
>
> (pp. 30-1).

It is a striking feature of this venturing forth 'from the world of common day into a region of supernatural wonder' that it is commonly perceived by the hero's fellow men as a death: 'the really creative acts are represented as those deriving from some sort of dying to the world', from which the hero 'comes back as one reborn, made great and filled with creative power' (pp. 35-6). It should be apparent that most of this fits Ferdinand in *The Tempest* perfectly (and that the pattern of apparent deaths and potent rebirths is a common one in Shakespearean tragicomedy, if not always invested in a single character). Ferdinand is separated from his father and shipmates, who all assume that he is dead; he is haunted by Ariel's music which seems to tell him ('Full fathom five thy father lies', I.ii.397-405) that his father is dead and introduces him to 'a region of supernatural wonder', inhabited by the 'god o' the island', Prospero, and his 'goddess' daughter, Miranda; he encounters 'fabulous forces', when Prospero's magic renders him unable to draw his sword and later summons up the spirits for the masque; the 'decisive victory' proves to be the winning of the heart of Miranda, and his acceptance by Prospero, so that when he is restored to his father and friends — as if from death — he brings not just his own person but a great boon in the shape of the future merger of Naples and Milan, healing former dissensions by his marriage to Miranda. The one significant deviation from Campbell's pattern is that Ferdinand is really rather a passive character; as a prince of Naples he has the nobility required of a hero, and he shows himself steadfast enough in carrying out the tasks that Prospero sets for him, but he never shows any of the courage or resourcefulness that comparisons with Prometheus, Jason and Aeneas would warrant. He is always something of a pawn in Prospero's plans, most significant in being who he happens by birth to be, which is why he is always likely to seem a rather insipid character on stage. But this in turn relates to the peculiar characteristics of tragicomedy, where the emphasis is on the idea or pattern of experience rather than the personality of the characters involved: it would be improper for a heroic character to dominate the action, or to bring about the resolution by the force of his own endeavour, since this would cut across the basic pattern of perplexing mystery which tragicomedy always embodies. It is in tragedy proper that we see true heroes in the

Campbell mode — Oedipus, Faustus, Hamlet etc. — confronting mysterious forces stage centre, but in their case we do not see the return, the end of the cycle, though in some cases we may infer that their death or suffering has not been entirely in vain. In most of the Renaissance tragicomedies we have considered it would be more appropriate to think of Campbell's heroic pattern being dispersed into various facets of the play rather than focused on individuals, which is perhaps a logical extension of minimising the emphasis on individual endeavour: repeatedly we find the themes of characters who are lost or separated from their families or homelands, often not knowing their own identities; of deaths real, apparent or symbolic; of confrontations with strange or miraculous forces; and of a resolution which not only puts right what was wrong but goes beyond that to promise even greater happiness in the future. Characteristically in tragicomedy, the pattern is the collective work of providence, fate or what you will, acting on and through a whole society rather than favoured individuals.

May we infer, then, that Lucky's reference to 'the divine Miranda' in *Waiting for Godot* is a muted echo of these tragicomic themes, a pathetic likening of himself to the Ferdinands of the world — a further extension of the obvious irony in his name? It would be disproportionate to conclude as much on the basis of so little evidence, were it not for the fact that this is totally consonant with so much else in the play. It will not, perhaps, have passed notice that one career which paralleled most closely Campbell's heroic pattern ('a separation from the world, a penetration to some source of power, and a life-enhancing return', p. 35) was that of Jesus Christ. And from the outset, Beckett makes the tragicomic progress of Christ one of the central concerns of his play. The issue obsesses Vladimir for a time:

Vladimir: Two thieves, crucified at the same time as our Saviour. One —
Estragon: Our what?
Vladimir: Our Saviour. Two thieves. One is supposed to have been saved and the other . . . (*he searches for the contrary of saved*) . . . damned. < . . . > And yet . . . (*pause*) . . . how is it — this is not boring you I hope —

how is it that of the four Evangelists only one speaks of a thief being saved. The four of them were there — or thereabouts — and only one speaks of a thief being saved. < . . . > One out of four. Of the other three two don't mention any thieves at all and the third says that both of them abused him. < . . . >

Estragon: Well? They don't agree, and that's all there is to it.
Vladimir: But all four were there. And only one speaks of a thief being saved. Why believe him rather than the others?
Estragon: Who believes him?
Vladimir: Everybody. It's the only version they know.
Estragon: People are bloody ignorant apes.

(pp. 12-13)

In the face of Estragon's bored indifference, Vladimir puzzles out one of the perplexing inconsistencies of the Gospels: the life-enhancing boon which Christ was supposed to secure with his death was salvation, the possibility of redemption from all sins, including original sin. The story of the thief who was crucified with him, repented and was promised salvation is often quoted as a particular earnest of Christ's power and grace: the first person he saved was no more than a common criminal, which leaves room to hope even for the likes of Vladimir and Estragon. Yet only St. Luke records the story and it vexes Vladimir that a matter of such importance should lack more convincing verification. It is typical of the play as a whole, and of the characters' tenuous grasp of the realities of their existence, that Vladimir should actually have got his facts wrong: all four Gospels mention that Christ was crucified with two other people; only St. John fails to specify that they were thieves (or robber, bandits, criminals or malefactors, as various translations have it) and both St. Matthew and St. Mark record that both these thieves reviled or taunted Christ. So the mathematical odds are even worse than Vladimir imagines; he thinks that one evangelist supports the story of the penitential thief, one denies it, while the other two are unhelpfully neutral. In fact two deny it, only one supports it and the fourth is neutral. To believe the one, as he acknowledges that 'everybody' does, requires an even greater act of faith than he allows for.

It is difficult to resist the conclusion that the story of the penitent thief is significant to Vladimir, as that of Miranda is to

60

Lucky, because it relates directly to the situation in which he and Estragon find themselves. The mysterious and very possibly mythical Mr. Godot for whom they are endlessly waiting (or on whom they attend, if we allow for the ambiguity in the original French title)[2] is imbued by them with all the attributes of a hero/Christ figure on the point of return. He will give their life purpose and direction; he will make sense of everything, even their wait, and give them something to do. His coming, in short, would be like the miraculous denouements of Renaissance tragicomedy — but only if he really exists and has the powers they believe him to have. Vladimir and Estragon are both like the thieves on the cross, hoping — with varying degrees of faith — for redemption. In that sense, they have roles in a predestined tragicomic process, representing both the highest and the lowest of human potential. As Vladimir rather grandly puts it: 'at this place, at this moment in time, all mankind is us, whether we like it or not < . . . > Let us represent worthily for once the foul brood to which a cruel fate consigned us' (p. 79). The 'foul brood' of mankind, whom Estragon had earlier dismissed as 'bloody ignorant apes', inevitably includes themselves, however much they try to resist the implication.

While this is the principal tragicomic situation outlined in the play, it is not the only one. Perhaps because the status of 'Godin . . . Godet . . . Godot' (Pozzo superciliously confuses the issue) as a hero-redeemer is constantly in doubt, there are indirect suggestions that either Estragon or Lucky should take his place: they are not yet invested with any supernatural powers, but are repeatedly likened to figures at the 'separation' stage of the hero's progress, when he is singled out for his special mission in life. At this point in the cycle the hero is generally mocked by those who do not understand his specialness and made to perform demeaning tasks: the mockery of Christ and being made to carry his own Cross are cases in point, as is Prospero's insistence that Prince Ferdinand carry logs, demeaning himself to prove himself worthy of the highest honours. Such figures, who carry the scorn and even the physical burden of a society, are called scapegoats, an idea alluded to when Lucky's pathetic, shambling dance is called 'The Scapegoat's Agony' (p. 40). Pozzo also mockingly calls

Lucky 'Atlas, son of Jupiter' (p. 31). Like Vladimir with the Gospels, Pozzo has got his mythology wrong. Atlas was not the son of Jupiter — or even of Zeus, since this is Greek and not Roman mythology. He was actually the son of Iapetus, one of the Titans whom Zeus/Jupiter's Olympians overthrew. Once again, however, it is a pointed mistake: Atlas was condemned to bear the weight of the earth and the heavens on his shoulders because of his disrespect for Perseus (and so for the gods who favoured Perseus) — a classic example of the scapegoat. To make him 'son of Jupiter' inevitably draws an analogy with the scapegoat Christ who, in being crucified, carried the sins of the world on his shoulders.

Ironically, when the analogy is openly drawn in the play, it is Pozzo rather than Lucky who is likened to Christ. In the first act, Pozzo is confident and self-assured for the most part, but when he has a sudden spasm of agitation he blames Lucky for his distress (pp. 33-4); Vladimir had seemingly sympathised previously with Lucky, but now he suddenly turns on him: 'How dare you! It's abominable! Such a good master! Crucify him!' (p. 34). This may, of course, be tongue-in-cheek, since it is perfectly obvious on stage that Pozzo is still the well-fed master and Lucky the 'crucified' slave. There is a similar confusion in the second act, when Estragon tries to call Pozzo Abel and Lucky Cain; Pozzo seems to respond to both names, calling out 'Help!' (p. 83). Cain, the first murderer, slew his blameless brother Abel, for which God punished him, making him 'a fugitive and a vagabond in the earth'.[3] Oddly, both brothers have come to be seen, in different traditions, as scapegoats. Abel, as the innocent shepherd victim, is traditionally seen as a prefiguring of Christ. Cain, in his banishment 'east of Eden' and marked by God so that all men should know him, became for many Romantics (who similarly glamorised Satan) an image of the heroic rebel — a sinner no doubt, but nobly human and long-suffering in the face of a tyrant God. It is difficult to see how Pozzo, who swings from self-importance in the first act to self-pity in the second, could fit either role, but the pathetic and long-suffering Lucky might fit both. Perhaps we should be content to note that Lucky is at the centre of successive allusions to the scapegoat syndrome, the whole tragicomic concept of one man bearing the sins and burdens of others on himself.

Of course, it may well be that Lucky does not relish this role as much as did Christ or Ferdinand. When Estragon offers to wipe away his tears, *'Lucky kicks him violently in the shins'* (p. 32), which links up significantly with another sequence of allusions relating to Estragon himself. Throughout the play, references are made to the problems he has with his legs and feet; the first thing we see on stage is Estragon *'trying to take off his boot'*, a process which takes two sides of dialogue, punctuated with his moans. When Vladimir finally asks, 'How's your foot?' Estragon replies, 'Swelling visibly' (p. 12). When Pozzo asks, 'Which of you smells so bad?' Estragon bluntly admits, 'He has stinking breath and I have stinking feet' (p. 46). In the second act, he acquires what may or may not be new boots, which he says do not hurt because they are too big (pp. 67-9); by the end of the play, however, he is again in trouble: 'My feet! (*He sits down, tries to take off his boots.*) Help me!' (p. 90). The effort now seems too much for him.

Lucky's kick on the shin thus adds insult to injury, mixing pain and offensiveness. 'There's the wound!' announces Vladimir triumphantly. 'Beginning to fester!' (p. 67). All this, of course, ties in with the play's unremitting emphasis on the animal facts of human existence, with numerous references to eating, smelling, urinating, farting, pain and clumsiness. But there are surely mythical allusions even here. Wounded feet and legs are traditionally associated with certain Greek heroes, notably Achilles, whose heel was the only vulnerable part of his body; Oedipus, whose very name means 'swollen foot' because his feet were pinned at birth in the father's attempt to kill the child destined to kill him; and Philoctetes, the man who killed Paris when Troy finally fell but who missed most of the siege because of a snake-bite to his leg, which caused him to groan so much and smell so badly that his friends abandoned him.[4] Wounded feet are thus ambivalently both signs of human vulnerability and earnests of true heroic stature. Estragon, the martyr to his feet and to the festering wound on his shin, is thus akin to the boy with the swollen feet who grew up to read the riddle of the Sphinx (as well as kill his father and marry his mother) and to the social outcast who finally avenged the dishonour to Greece over which the Trojan war was fought.

Vladimir seems to underline Estragon's potential hero/scape-goat status when the latter announces, 'They're coming', which causes both of them great consternation but no one actually comes; Vladimir explains it by saying, 'You must have had a vision' — a line he is forced to repeat. He puts the confusion down not to a mistake or to an illusion, but to a 'vision', something vouchsafed only to special people.

Like Lucky, moreover, Estragon is linked with the pattern of Christian redemption as well as with classical mythology. When Pozzo asks his name, he gives it as Adam (p. 37) and when Vladimir objects to the idea of his going barefoot (the feet motif again), he replies:

> Christ did.
> *Vladimir*: Christ! What's Christ got to do with it? You're not going to compare yourself to Christ!
> *Estragon*: All my life I've compared myself to him.
> *Vladimir*: But where he lived it was warm, it was dry.
> *Estragon*: Yes. And they crucified him quick.
>
> (p. 52)

Thus Estragon links himself both with the first sinner and with the redeemer of sins, the whole tragicomic pattern of The Fall. But at this point we must pause to recognise that these themes and connections are by no means as neat and obvious in a viewing of the play, or a first reading, as they can be with hindsight. Nor do they call attention to their own significance: when Estragon calls himself Adam, we are as likely to be concerned with whether or why he is lying to Pozzo as thinking of Biblical connotations; the whole incident passes without comment, moreover, as Pozzo ('*who hasn't listened*') launches into a soliloquy. The analogy with Christ looks like taking on significant proportions but soon fizzles out in a grim joke when it becomes apparent that Estragon's thoughts are focused very much on the practicalities of suffering rather than its spiritual dimension. There is a similar randomness or inconsequentiality about all the other classical and Christian allusions we have been tracing. They do not readily add up to the coherent themes I have been suggesting, nor are they easy to follow. The allusions to Oedipus and Philoctetes, for example, will only be apparent to someone with a knowledge of Greek literature and are never made overt, while it takes time and a fairly sophisticated knowledge of mythology to make anything of the 'Atlas, son of Jupiter' confusion, which passes in a moment in performance.

This is typical of the mode of the play as a whole, where ideas are raised and either not pursued at all, or pursued with a perversity which leads nowhere, to nonsense or to music-hall routines. We constantly hear echoes of a civilisation in which words meant something and conversations led somewhere, and these echoes are just audible enough to mock the failure of the present in such matters — but not audible enough to suggest that such meaning and purpose can now be recovered. Lucky's anarchic soliloquy is the great example of this. It is also true of the play's repeated allusions to tragicomic themes and their scapegoat—hero—redeemers: they are certainly in the text, but so randomly and inconsequentially that it would be foolhardy to make too much of them. They are just sufficiently present to remind us flickeringly of the great tragicomic patterns of classical mythology, Christian doctrine and Renaissance drama, but not to assure us that these patterns are any longer viable.

This is central to the bitter-sweet quality of *Waiting for Godot*. Throughout the play, the *possibility* is kept before us that Godot may come, or that Lucky or Estragon may prove an adequate substitute for a Godot who does not exist, but none of these possibilities ever turns into achieved reality. It is as if the sudden reversal at the end of a Fletcher play had never occurred, as if Hermione had not been reunited with Leontes, or the newly betrothed Ferdinand with his father and friends. In Beckett's tragicomedy, the pattern is not completed, the generic promise is not fulfilled, the tantalising never ends, the miracle does not come. And that is the essence of modern tragicomedy, whatever different forms it takes. Beckett and his successors do not abandon the concerns and mannerisms of earlier tragicomedy but they redeploy them, adding new perplexities to the old 'strangeness' by *failing* to produce the wonderful conclusion or the last-minute 'impossible' explanation.

With this in mind, we may be better placed to confront those aspects of *Waiting for Godot* which audiences still find difficult to come to terms with, for all that they have been part of our common consciousness for the past thirty years. For example, while Vladimir and Estragon have many intensely human characteristics, including fear, inquisitiveness, a tendency to boredom, poor memory, bad breath and stinking feet, they lack many of the qualities which make a dramatic character 'real': we know nothing about their past, families, education or employment. They are often referred to as tramps, but there is nothing in the text to warrant this apart from their generally bedraggled appearance and arguable resemblance (mainly in the hats) to the Charlie Chaplin tramp. We do not know how or when they first met, why they stayed together (but apparently not at night) or who beat Estragon, if indeed he was beaten. We do not know in which country or in which era they live. We cannot even be sure that the names they use are their real ones; not only does Estragon call himself Adam, but Vladimir answers to 'Mr. Albert' (p. 49). We can trust nothing that they say — it is all uncorroborated and rarely consistent throughout. Above all, we cannot be sure what to make of their supposed relationship with Godot. Pozzo and Lucky only compound these problems. In theory, a second pair of characters ought to make more sense of the first pair, giving us a new and possibly objective perspective from which to assess them. But Pozzo and Lucky beg more questions than they answer — about a relationship which is even less ordinary than that of Vladimir and Estragon, and about a radical deterioration in their condition (Pozzo becomes blind and Lucky dumb) overnight. At least, Vladimir perceives it to be an overnight phenomenon: Pozzo refuses to commit himself, and becomes quite irate when he is asked to relate experiences to time. The Boy or Boys epitomise the whole problem. He seems to be the same character on both appearances, and Vladimir certainly thinks that he is; but the Boy denies it, just as he denies knowing Vladimir and Estragon on both occasions — so he may be lying deliberately, or telling the truth, or he may just have a bad memory. On both apperances he admits to having a brother, but that hardly proves in itself that he is the same person. The evidence, as ever, is tantalising, but inconclusive.

If we think of these problems in relation to the tragicomedies that we considered in Part I, we will find them less puzzling, indeed less unusual than they at first appear. It was characteristic of such tragicomedy that character was subordinate to action, and that action in turn was subordinate to a governing idea, or to a middle-mode perspective, shaping everything in such a way that the whole pattern of the play should seem more important then particular characters or particular incidents. In such a play it is quite usual to find perplexed characters in perplexing situations, but also to find that the personality of those characters is relatively insignificant. In the very nature of such drama, they will not be forceful enough to resolve their own difficulties, a task which must be left to God, providence or (to put it another way) the author. Similarly, it is quite usual for the laws of time, and of cause and effect, to be bent or broken in tragicomedy, for characters to act quite inconsistently or to change out of recognition: we are in the presence of forces and effects beyond rational understanding and common sense.

Vladimir and Estragon are more character-types than fully-rounded characters. Beckett invests them with certain limited, familiar characteristics, but he makes no pretence of giving them the kind of social or psychological individuality that we might look for in characters created by, say Arnold Wesker or Arthur Miller. Vladimir is the thinker of the two, the one who worries about philosophical and moral questions, like that of the thieves crucified with Christ; he takes the lead in questioning the Boy both times he appears and sings the sardonically cyclical song with which the second act begins: he at least has the inclination to make sense of what is happening to him. Estragon, by contrast, is more closely identified with the physical exigencies of life, like the problems of his feet and legs. He is the one who breaks up a silence '*violently*' with 'I'm hungry' (p. 20) and later asks Pozzo for his chicken bones (shocking Vladimir, who is typically caught between a concern for social niceties and outrage at the treatment of Lucky). Similarly, when Vladimir starts his ruminations about the Gospels, Estragon replies, 'I remember the maps of the Holy Land. Coloured they were. Very pretty. The Dead Sea was pale blue. The very look of it made me thirsty' (p. 12). His senses and his appetite predominate, to the exclusion of worries about salvation. His main concern about Godot — 'your man', as he insists to Vladimir (p. 21) — is whether they are 'tied' to him, as if his coming might constitute a physical impediment to their freedom of manoeuvre — perhaps like the rope that actually binds Lucky to Pozzo. Beyond such broad considerations it would be difficult to define the personalities of Vladimir and Estragon; more significant than their individual traits is the fact that they complement each other almost perfectly.

Late in the play Pozzo asks, 'but are you friends?' and Estragon, *laughing noisily*, exclaims rhetorically, 'He wants to know if we are friends!' before Vladimir puts him right: 'No, he means friends of his' (p. 85). So the question of whether Vladimir and Estragon are actually friends, like so many others in this play, is raised but never answered. Estragon's noisy laughter and arch comment is as ambiguous as any other pointer in the play: either their friendship is so self-evident as to require no confirmation or it is so unthinkable as to provoke laughter. All we can really say is that they have an affinity with each other which need have nothing to do with personal inclinations. We might say that the shape or idea of the play *demands* that they remain together, and any consideration which might challenge that demand is circumvented. It is hardly surprising that they have frequently been likened to clowns, or music-hall double-acts, or comedy teams like Laurel and Hardy — groupings where the team is more important than the individuals involved, one physical presence setting off the other. By the same token, people often talk of them as complementary facets of the same personality, the friction between them reflecting the dualities of ego and id, or nature and nurture, or the left and right sides of the brain, or the male and female mix in all of us. We shall meet this kind of symbiotic pairing frequently in this book: it is almost a hallmark of modern tragicomedy. In their different ways, Mick and Aston in *The Caretaker*, George and Martha in *Who's Afraid of Virginia Woolf?*, the title characters in *Rosencrantz and Guildenstern Are Dead* and both main pairs of characters in *Home* are variations of this original: mutual dependencies that go far deeper than personality. One thing they all have in common, for all the banter and energy they may generate, is a fundamental sterility: usually, as with Vladimir and Estragon, the relationships are asexual; sometimes — especially in Pinter — we detect undertones of impotence, homosexuality or other forms of infertile sexuality. None of these relationships shows any prospect of creating the miracle of new life, which is particularly striking, given that these are as much the primary units of modern tragicomedy as the lost princes and unrecognised, nubile princesses were of its Renaissance predecessor.

At first glance, the relationship between Pozzo and Lucky seems quite different. Vladimir and Estragon are essentially equals, while the links between this master and slave appear to be imposed by force, as symbolised by the rope with which Pozzo leads Lucky around. This, at least, is what we might call the liberal democratic assumption about such a relationship — perhaps shared by the majority of a modern theatre audience — and Vladimir gives voice to it when he explodes, 'It's a scandal!' (p. 27). But the reality proves to be rather different — if, that is, we can accept as true the only version of affairs (Pozzo's) we are offered. He claims that Lucky is really clinging to him, rather than vice versa; Lucky has outlived his usefulness, and Pozzo is on his way to the fair to sell him, which he considers a humane gesture to an old slave: 'The truth is you can't drive such creatures away. The best thing would be to kill them' (p. 32). He adduces Lucky's failure to sit down and rest as evidence that he is eager to please him; the argument is difficult to refute because we never hear an alternative one, though we might be inclined to explain this behaviour as fear of punishment or even the sheer inability of ageing knees to bend so far with little prospect of ever getting up again. The nature of the relationship takes on a further unexpected dimension when Pozzo waxes first generous and then bitter: 'Guess who taught me all these beautiful things < . . . > My Lucky! < . . . > But for him all my thoughts, all my feelings, would have been of common things < . . . > I can't bear it . . . any longer . . . the way he goes on . . . you've no idea . . . it's terrible . . . he must go < . . . > I'm going mad' (pp. 33-4). We are offered the picture of a humane and sensitive being, now deeply distressed by the appalling condition into which his old and valued servant has fallen; he is desperate to part with him because he finds his presence so painful. We might reflect that this is still a very one-sided relationship — everything is seen from Pozzo's angle, but it is noticeable that this emotional outburst (which sceptics might dismiss as a sentimental display for public consumption) puts an end to Vladimir and Estragon's 'liberal' concern for Lucky. Estragon even seems to start angling to replace him, if the vacancy is going to exist. And Lucky demonstrates that he is not entirely helpless by kicking him on the shin. The second act gives us even more cause to revise our opinion of this relationship. When they reappear both have fared badly since we last saw them, but Pozzo much worse than Lucky: Lucky has become dumb, but since he was largely mute before and incoherent when he did speak, it does not seem so great a loss; Pozzo, however, is blind and physically decrepit, a pathetic shadow of the vigour and assurance of which he previously boasted. Relatively speaking, Pozzo is surely now worse off than Vladimir and Estragon, worse off even than Lucky, particularly since he is additionally cursed with the memory of better times. As Vladimir puts it, *'Memoria praeteritorum bonorum* — that must be unpleasant' (p. 86), having no notion of it himself; the irony of the Latin quotation is that it is itself a memory of better times, of the classical past. Yet Lucky is still with Pozzo, still being led by him, when it would seem pathetically easy to abandon Pozzo if he really wished to. Perhaps Pozzo was right that Lucky really does prefer to stay with him — or perhaps the fact that Lucky remains in an inert heap for most of his time on the stage in this act means that he no longer has the will or energy to act independently.

Throughout the play, therefore, Beckett seems to be testing any easy assumption that the relationship of Pozzo and Lucky is simply a matter of the powerful callously exploiting the downtrodden, from which the latter would naturally extricate himself if he could. Pozzo is never a pleasant character, being arrogant and generally complacent in the first act, and pathetic without being sympathetic in the second; it is always possible to feel sorry for Lucky, since he is clearly one of life's victims. But sentiment should not obscure the fact that their relationship, for want of a better term, *works*. They remain together, linked by a longer or a shorter rope and, for all that Pozzo gets all the obvious advantages out of this arrangement, Lucky never rebels; if Pozzo may be believed, he may even be trying to perpetuate matters.

There have been well-intentioned attempts to construe this relationship as a parable about society in the real world: tyrants and people, capitalists and workers, or whatever. Such attempts seem to find it necessary to explain *why* Lucky never rebels, and the answer invariably depends on the political persuasion of the proponent. The right-wing argument is essentially that men are by nature unequal, that some form of aristocracy is inevitable however it dresses itself up, and that Lucky is commendably resigned to his natural lot in life. Left-wingers would explain his apathy and inarticulateness as a direct product of exploitation, an erosion of his humanity by the constant suppression of its true potential (which would, however, be restored if the revolution ever came). Beckett's text seems to invite such speculations, but steadfastly refuses to endorse any one over another, reflecting rather the audience's preconceptions back upon themselves. The play refuses, in effect, to focus on the personalities (as distinct from character-types) of its characters. In the last resort, all we can really say is that Pozzo is a species of selfishness and Lucky a species of selflessness, and that they belong together. In other words, they are typical characters from tragicomedy, stripped of any 'accidental' personality and subsumed to their roles in the perplexing pattern of the play. The rope is a symbol of symbiosis, perhaps, as much as of submission, and they are as interdependent as Vladimir and Estragon, abeit in a different style. As 'friends', or at least equals, Vladimir and Estragon represent a horizontal axis; as master and servant/slave, Pozzo and Lucky represent a vertical one.

This dual symbiosis is important to the total effect of the play in several respects. On the one hand, two such *fundamental* relationships, echoing, paralleling and cutting across one another in so many ways, contribute to the impression that we are dealing with a much broader society than we ever actually see. There are several references to people who never appear — those who beat Estragon at night, for example, the other slaves Pozzo claims to have, the Boy's brother, and the Gozzo family Vladimir claims to have known ('The mother had the clap', p. 23), but their existence is always rather hypothetical. Nevertheless, the interaction of these four characters, with their mixture of contrasting and complementary characteristics, suggests a much broader range of possible relationships: they are the microcosm of a society — albeit, as my list suggests, not one with much of a regenerative future. This is crucial in terms of the traditional working out of the tragicomedy, since whatever resolution of perplexities may be achieved, it must have ramifications of more than merely local or personal significance. If Godot were to come, and be all that Vladimir suggests, it would put an end not only to the boredom, frustration and lack of purpose experienced by Vladimir and Estragon, but also to whatever is unreasonable in the relationship of Pozzo and Lucky: the fact that Pozzo has little time for 'Godin . . . Godet . . . Godot' and that Lucky seems to know nothing about him is irrelevant. It is in the nature of tragicomedy that its resolutions are as far-reaching and comprehensive as they are surprising — if not exactly unlooked-for. But the symbiotic nature of these relationships also helps to explain why, if Godot should not prove to be the redeemer they need, neither Estragon nor Lucky could take his place, for all the tantalising hints that either of them might be a suitable scapegoat/hero/redeemer figure. The fact is that they are integral parts of society as it is: for all that they may be mocked or exploited, they do not have the special status of outsiders or outcasts which is critical to the first phase of the redemption process. Perhaps, in this dislocated, topsyturvy world, it would be correct to say that all the characters are equally outcasts and outsiders (not excluding the Boy) so that there is no longer anything special about that condition.

What I have been describing in both the thematic imagery and the character relationships of *Waiting for Godot* is a kind of still-born tragicomedy, one to which no magical providence brings a happy ending, for all the hopes and hints that it might be possible. This diagnosis is confirmed by an analysis of the ways in which language is used in the play. In Fletcher's plays,[5] we noticed how, characteristically, the action was shaped into a succession of 'strong' scenes, in which what happened was rather less central than the principal characters' *reaction* to what happened; typically, this was delivered in a rhetorical soliloquy or sometimes an operatically-stylised dialogue, in which the characters grappled verbally with the moral and emotional dilemmas that had materialised. The presentation was disconcertingly ice-and-fire, since passions were usually running at fever pitch, but the action was so formalised and the characters so predictable that the audience could never empathise with what was going on. In keeping with the tragicomic 'middle mood', their attention was split between the apparent insolubility of the immediate dilemma and the promise inherent in the genre that a resolution to all perplexities would be found, somehow.

In *Waiting for Godot*, the language veers between two characteristic extremes: soliloquy, and the form of dialogue normally used by Vladimir and Estragon, which is constantly in danger of drying up for the lack of any real communication between them, but is kept going by in-built repetitive patterns which substitute for logic and even, at times, for sense. This is the more or less neutral mode of waiting itself, dispassionate, avoiding extremes of pessimism and optimism, mainly concerned with passing the time. We see this at its most elemental in the second act, when Vladimir and Estragon forget themselves to the extent of speaking simultaneously, which is obviously an extravangance if the point of the exercise is only 'to see the evening out' (p. 77):

> *Vladmir/Estragon*: *(turning simultaneously.)* Do you —
> *Vladimir*: Oh, pardon!
> *Estragon*: Carry on.
> *Vladimir*: No no, after you.
> *Estragon*: No no, you first.
> *Vladimir*: I interrupted you.
> *Estragon*: On the contrary.
> > *They glare at each other angrily*
> *Vladimir*: Ceremonious ape!
> *Estragon*: Punctilious pig!
> *Vladimir*: Finish your phrase, I tell you.
> *Estragon*: Finish your own.
> > *Silence. They draw closer, halt*
> *Vladimir*: Moron!
> *Estragon*: That's the idea, let's abuse each other.

> (p. 75)

This 'abuse' consists of an interchange of eight terms chosen as much for their assonance and verbal symmetry as their sense — mormon, vermin, abortion, morpion, sewer-rat, curate, cretin and critic. It is not explained why the last term ends the sequence, though it is spoken '*with finality*'; it does, however, seem metrically appropriate, as the run of hard c, r, t sounds cancels out the soft on, in, ions. They then switch to 'make it up', with a run of tritely romantic phrases which echoes the over-politeness of the first passage quoted. This in turn gives way to a sequence of 'exercises', which once more have as much to do with sound as with sense — movements, elevations, relaxations, elongations. Both of these phases round off with a rhetorical and ambiguous 'Off we go!', the first from Estragon, the second from Vladimir, and the whole sequence seems to revolve around the only line which is foregrounded from the surrounding symmetry: between two silences, Vladimir remarks, 'How time flies when one has fun!' This is language close to the state of music, where pattern, shape and repetition, assonance, dissonance and rhythm dominate to the exclusion of rational sense. The characters do not *mean* anything in what they say; it is a mutually concocted routine to make time fly

Vladimir: While waiting.
Estragon: While waiting.

This is an extreme example, coming as it does when the energy of the play is pointedly flagging, and immediately before the final appearance of Pozzo and Lucky, which provides a new lease of life. Nevertheless, it is not untypical. There is always a sense in which the dialogue is driven more by its own form and pattern, more by the need to preserve itself, than by any real attempt to communicate, or by any conviction that such communication might be possible. As an audience, we are entertained by the characters' rhetorical responses to the tragicomic dilemma of waiting: we are not involved in it as a personal experience. We appreciate the witty and elegant artificiality of the language, while half our attention is elsewhere — wondering what external resolution can be found to their perplexities, since it is increasingly self-evident that they cannot find one for themselves. Thus we too are vicariously waiting for Godot.

The soliloquies, or at least sustained solo passages, that occasionally erupt out of this dialogue cut across the self-sustaining but also self-cancelling neutrality with marked injections of energy; the clearest examples are Pozzo's lyrical disquisition on the twilight (pp. 37-8), Lucky's 'tirade' (pp. 42-

5), Vladimir's attempt to break out of 'idle discourse' (pp. 79-81) and his reflection on the passing of Pozzo and Lucky (pp. 90-1). Leaving aside for a moment Lucky's speech, each of these is different in mood and context, but each follows a similar pattern: an attempt to explain something or express enthusiasm fails to evoke any response in the listeners, runs out of steam and ends in despair. Note how each one ends: 'pop! like that! (*his inspiration leaves him*) just when we least expect it. (*Silence. Gloomily.*) That's how it is on this bitch of an earth' (p. 38); 'Come, let's get to work! (*He advances towards the heap, stops in his stride.*) In an instant all will vanish and we'll be alone once more, in the midst of nothingness! *He broods*' (p. 81); 'of me too someone is saying, he is sleeping, he knows nothing, let him sleep on. (*Pause.*) I can't go on! (*Pause.*) What have I said?' (p. 91). It is as if some inexorable law of gravity applies to their thinking and speaking; however seriously or enthusiastically it takes off, it cannot help but come to ground, with a negative emphasis that cancels out anything affirmative in the original effort. We are forced back to the neutral mode of the dialogue, aware that a rhetorical gesture has been made to find a way out of the total perplexity of the waiting situation, but more than ever convinced that only a miracle can succeed in providing it.

Lucky's soliloquy is a significant exception to this pattern, and so an interesting challenge to this conviction. It seems to defy both the 'laws' of neutrality and of gravity. It rattles along without any need of support or reciprocation and shows no sign of flagging when the other three characters contrive to break it off ('unfinished', as he says) by removing his hat. But is would be perverse to read into this linguistic fluency any real hope of salvation, since it proves to lack both the minimal purpose of the other soliloquies and the consoling involvement of the dialogue: it is a jumble of words and half-words, ideas and half-ideas, with no coherence or conviction, a perfect metaphor for the absence of meaning or purpose throughout the play, but elsewhere kept at bay by the tragicomic shaping and middle mood of the whole. What makes the speech particularly painful, and perhaps explains the determination of the other characters to silence him, is the fact that even incoherence is not the final answer; if it were possible to be *certain* that nothing had any meaning, that there was no purpose in life, it might also be possible to cultivate a peaceful resignation to the fact. But Lucky's jumble contains just enough echoes of a comprehensible world ('divine Miranda', 'Bishop Berkeley') and just enough *potential* themes to make such resignation impossible: indeed, if you stare hard enough at the speech, it almost begins to make sense.

Take, for example, the obsession with stones that emerges in the second half of the speech. The name 'Steinweg', which is mentioned twice, is German for 'stone-way', while 'Peterman' means 'stone-man' and may allude to St. Peter, the rock or stone on which Christ said that he built his Church. Such a Christian reference would tie in with the parallel obsession with the skull, since the place of crucifixion was called The Skull, and from there Christ was buried in a tomb cut from the rock and sealed with a stone — his resurrection thus being literally a spiritual triumph over the confines of the material world. This in turn would tie in with the reference to Bishop Berkeley, the eighteenth-century philosopher, famous for his proof that the material world does not exist, which in turn is famous for Dr. Johnson's graphic refutation: 'I shall never forget the alacrity with which Johnson answered, striking his foot with mighty force against a large stone, till he rebounded from it — "I refute it thus"'.[6] It is probably also relevant that 'stones' was a vulgar old expression for testicles, which ties in with the likely sexual innuendo of 'Testew and Cunard' — and so on and so forth. But that way madness lies. All these connections are plausible, not to say tempting, but they are not provable and they can be manipulated in too many ways for their own good. 'Peterman', for example, looks invitingly like the heart of a run of allusions relating to Christ, the resurrection and the founding of the Church. But a good dictionary tells us that it also means a fisherman, or a kind of beer, or a particular style of thief; it may even simply be a reference to Pozzo's lost 'Kapp and Peterson' (p. 35) — an expensive brand of pipe. There is, in short, no inherent sense in what Lucky says, but there is a kind of parody of sense, something that tempts us to make more of it than is actually there. It is a perfect trap for that part of the human mind which is determined to impose shape, sense, purpose and meaning on the world, whether it is there or not. It reopens, in effect, the argument about the relationship between art and nature which, as we noticed,[7] was central to the theory of

Renaissance tragicomedy: it is an artful mirror of artlessness, an unrandom evocation of randomness. As such, we must appreciate that its final effect is as neutral as other aspects of the play's language; it is no more adequate, or inadequate, than any other attempted solution to the perplexities in which the characters find themselves.

In every aspect, then — theme, style, characterisation, language — *Waiting for Godot* is the tragicomedy that Beckett declares it to be. The only thing missing is the providential reversal or revelation — the arrival of Godot, in effect — which will resolve all perplexities and promise a better future. But what are the implications of Godot's failure to arrive and so of the tragicomic pattern's failure to fulfil itself in the traditional manner? Does this make the play grimly pessimistic in emphasis, or does it leave some room for hope? Audiences, and indeed directors, have been fairly evenly divided on this question. Some point to the unmistakable downward slide in the second act as evidence of the grimmest implications; Pozzo is reduced to a blind and helpless figure, Lucky is dumb, and Vladimir and Estragon are increasingly desperate at the lack of progress: even the Boy's brother is reported to be sick. Others, and particularly those who attach significance to the Christian allusions running through the play, argue that there is a paradoxical ray of hope in this, reflected in the '*four or five leaves*' that appear on the tree (p. 57); the way that Vladimir and Estragon stick to their vigil in the face of repeated disappointment and disillusionment is a victory for human dignity, perhaps proof that they really are, as Pozzo mockingly puts it, 'Made in God's image!' (p. 23). Their tenacity may fall short of being an act of faith, but the refusal to surrender has an integrity about it which should not quickly be discounted.

Beckett himself is chary of commenting on the meaning or implications of his works but, when pressed on *Waiting for Godot*, he has more than once quoted a passage from St. Augustine: 'There is a wonderful sentence in Augustine < . . . > "Do not despair: one of the thieves was saved. Do not presume: one of the thieves was damned" < . . . > I am interested in the shape of ideas even if I do not believe in them . . .. That sentence has a wonderful shape. It is the shape that matters'.[8] The quotation from Augustine is interesting because it picks up the theme that Vladimir himself raises in the play; the reference to 'the shape of ideas' is similarly interesting, in that it describes perfectly one of the qualities of tragicomedy that I have referred to repeatedly in this book — its subsuming of every feature — action, character, style — to a single, shaping idea, a determinant inescapably present in the artificial patterning of scenes and sentences.

In Renaissance tragicomedies that patterning carries a generic promise of a positive resolution, a prediction of joy. Here, if we are to accept Beckett's own account, the promise is no more than ambivalent; providence not only works in mysterious ways, but cannot be relied upon in the last analysis at all: one of the thieves was saved, but one of them was damned. The ambivalence is picked up in the play's direct references to fate or fortune. Vladimir, for example, complains of 'a cruel fate' (p. 79), but this is a piece of sententious posing and has to be set, say, against the implications of Lucky's name — which may or may not themselves be ironic. The play's signals are resolutely neutral, or self-cancelling, to the last; the play calls for both pessimism and optimism, or neither.

There is, however, a final consideration provoked by the 'tragicomedy' label. The sudden, night-into-day reversals of Fletcher's plays, and even the complex, symbolic resolutions of Shakespeare's tragicomedies, have often been castigated as escapist and (particularly the former) as blandly endorsing the world as we have it. But, as I argued in Part I,[9] there is another way of looking at such endings; their patent artificiality is not smug conservatism, so much as a challenge to the audience to weigh the difference between the theatre and life, art and nature. The *failure* of *Waiting for Godot* to provide such an ending paradoxically has exactly the same effect, because it poses exactly the same challenge: is the absence of Godot true to life or is it only true to the theatrical requirement to keep the audience interested and involved? Does it say more about the relationship between man and God or about the tastes and expectations of the contemporary audience? *Waiting for Godot* finally lives up to its generic promise in the sense that it leaves the *real* resolution not to the actors but to the audience. The ending of the second act with the same words as the first (though the lines are mirror-image reversed between Vladimir and

Estragon) is a final reminder of the dividing line between art and nature, a line of critical importance in investigating the mysteries of life, and in the process of becoming simultaneously aware both of our potential and of our limitations. It is for this reason that terms like 'optimism' and 'pessimism' ultimately carry no force in relation to this play, or indeed to any of the others I shall look at in Part III. The middle-mode, neutral balance of tragicomedy challenges us to think; it does not endorse one mood or philosophy over any other.

Part III

1

Endgame,
by Samuel Beckett*

Endgame, too, has its echo of *The Tempest*. But where Lucky remembered divine Miranda, Hamm derisively recalls the world-weary Prospero: 'Our revels now are ended. (*He gropes for the dog.*)' (p. 39). The difference is of a piece with the difference between *Waiting for Godot* and *Endgame*. The latter is at once a bleaker and a more perplexing play. Vladimir and Estragon have their basic health, for all their disappointments and discomforts, whereas Hamm is confined to a wheelchair, blood intermittently flowing from his head, and Clov is stiff-limbed, unable to sit down. Pozzo and Lucky degenerate physically in the course of the earlier play, but their situation is never so extreme, so dehumanised as that of Nagg and Nell, immobile in their ash-cans. The bare stage of *Godot*, with its focal tree, is an open metaphor for anywhere, at any time, but those ash-cans and the rest of the colourless set in which they stand pose a more disturbing challenge to our understanding, to our sense of the reality of the situation. *Endgame* is chillingly fixed within a room, but one that is as difficult to account for, in conventional terms, as are the events that take place within it.

The play in effect challenges us to find a metaphor that will explain or accommodate its abnormalities. The two favourite 'solutions' have been to see it as depicting either one of the last pockets of life after a (nuclear?) holocaust or the dying moments inside the skull of someone who has suffered a cerebral haemorrhage. But neither of these is totally satisfactory: the emphasis of the play seems more on progressive degeneration than on sudden cataclysm, and anyway it refuses to succumb to a single, rational interpretation. Perhaps it is more fruitful to

---

*First British performance in French, in London, 1957

81

start from the observation that, for all the difficulties it poses, *Endgame* is an intensely self-reflexive play, endlessly commenting on its own genesis and progress. Clov's opening words, for example — 'Finished, it's finished, nearly finished, it must be nearly finished' (p. 12) — refer as much to the play/performance as they do to anything else, while Hamm is always conscious of the theatrical context in which he exists. When Clov asks, 'What is there to keep me here?' Hamm replies, 'The dialogue' (p. 39). Towards the end he becomes irate when Clov misunderstands the force of something he says, '(*angrily*). An aside, ape! Did you never hear an aside before? (*Pause.*) I'm warming up for my last soliloquy' (p. 49). These moments of self-consciousness provide a running commentary on the play and its meaning, though it is one we should always treat warily:

> Hamm: We're not beginning to . . . to . . . mean something?
> Clov: Mean something! You and I, mean something! (*Brief laugh*). Ah that's a good one!

(p. 27)

Bearing this in mind, we may approach the bleak and perplexing nature of *Endgame* through two of its most sustained passages of self-commentary, the stories told by Nagg and Hamm. These are not overtly 'about' the play itself — though the latter, as we shall see, is intriguingly adjacent in its subject-matter — but both are verbal entertainments, interrupted by their authors with observations on style and performance, and as such mirror the wider verbal entertainment of which they form a part. They are very similar, in effect, to plays-within-plays in Renaissance drama, which always mirror in some sense the plays in which they occur. Nagg's story (pp. 21-2) is a well-polished produce of the raconteur's art, as carefully tailored as the trousers of which it tells, gathering in fluency and profanity until its disdainful climax. As such, it stands out markedly from the dialogue around it, with Hamm's peremptory observations and Nell's wistful reminiscences, and even more markedly from the broader context of meandering repetition, aimless conversation and staccato demands for 'pap' and painkiller. The very fact that the story has a discernible climax sets it in antithesis to the play. It tells of a time when men had pride and a purpose in what they did, setting themselves a Renaissance goal — however difficult it might prove to achieve — of improving in their art on the nature of the world as they found it. ('"But my dear Sir, my dear Sir, look — (*disdainful gesture, disgustedly*) — at the world — (*pause*) — and look — (*loving gesture, proudly*) — at my TROUSERS!"'). It is set ('the bluebells are blowing') against the season of spring, with all its traditional associations of vigour and aspiration. The irony, of course, is that it is the tale of a pair of trousers told by a legless man, a mocking survival of the past in every respect. It has no real validity in the present, as the indifference of the immediate audience, and Nagg's own depressed conviction that 'I never told it worse' underline. This is typical of the play's constant evocations of the past. Echoes of a time when life had a purpose, language had grace and meaning, and the arts communicated vigorously with their audiences only underline the loss of such qualities in the *Endgame* world — epitomised by the picture with its face to the wall.

This, surely, is the force of the Shakespearean echoes in the play. The revels to which Hamm alludes — the mysteries of the masque of Juno, Ceres and Iris which Prospero stages for Ferdinand and Miranda — are a long time gone in this world. It seems absurdly melodramatic, moreover, that Hamm should evoke the climax of *Richard III* — 'My kingdom for a nightman!' (p. 22) — in his fit of exasperation with Nagg and Nell: melodramatic and in poor taste, given that a nightman is someone employed to remove night-soil — so that Shakespeare's moment of high drama has been reduced to a moment of pique and disgust. The two quotations, ironically transposed as they are, have similar effects in the broader context of the play. Both evoke masters of enterprise, politicians in their different styles — Prospero, the Renaissance mage, and Richard, the Machiavel — but focus on their moments of world-weariness and defeat. These are important moments in the Shakespearean originals, no doubt, but only moments; yet the moods they represent threaten totally to engulf the less ambitious and less articulate world of *Endgame*.

What caused the decline from Renaissance energy to *Endgame* apathy is never explained, though possibilities are obliquely suggested in other memories, particularly Nagg and Nell's recollections of a free and mobile past. Nagg's story is actually associated with their happiness, rowing on Lake Como, though also with a capsizing that almost drowned them (p. 21). They also remember cycling on a tandem in the Ardennes, on the road to Sedan — a memory coloured by its association with a crash that lost them their 'shanks'. For the audience, the further association of these two places with the First World War may obliquely hint at what brought such a carefree, sugar-plum existence to an end. An even obliquer hint in the same direction may occur in the preamble to Hamm's story, where he refers to 'Something dripping in my head, ever since the fontanelles' (p. 35). The latter phrase is an extremely odd one. The fontanelle is the soft, uncovered spot on a new-born baby's head, before the plates of the skull have joined together. So Hamm seems to be saying 'ever since birth'. But why be so circuitous about it, and why use the plural? It may be that Beckett is playing on the sound and shape of a relatively unfamiliar word, and so conjuring with the more familiar sound and shape of 'Dardanelles' — the scene of the disastrous Gallipoli campaign in the First World War. The phrase 'ever since the Dardanelles', in the context of a head-wound, would be much more conventional English than 'ever since the fontanelles', and perhaps the net effect of this aural pun is a running together of birth and battle which would be quite appropriate in this play.

If this punning seems a little far-fetched, it is worth noting that two lines later Hamm/Beckett again plays with the aural ambiguity of words: 'Perhaps it's a little vein. (*Pause.*) A little artery. (*Pause.*)'. Does the listener hear 'vein' or 'vain'? — particularly given that Nagg has previously (pp. 19-20) mocked Hamm's self-dramatisations about the dropping in his head (including the phrase, 'Perhaps it's a little vein') as a piece of vanity. The addition of 'A little artery' seems at first to confirm that we are dealing with blood vessels, but the pause after *that* phrase allows the word 'artery' to reverberate and perhaps break down into art-ery — a product of art or affectation, chiming with vanity. No precision is possible here because the text is straining at — playing with — the limits of language itself, in typically tragicomic manner. This is the nature of language in the post-Renaissance, post-First World War of *Endgame* — an unpredictable medium, an untrustworthy tool, a gamble. And the stories that language embodies have the same qualities.

Hamm's story is not as finished as Nagg's; it has an open-endedness which is far more in tune with the play as a whole. Indeed, it co-exists with the play, and may even overlap it, in very pointed ways. When the main telling of the story dries up (p. 37), it does so with observations — 'I'll soon have finished with this story. (*Pause.*) Unless I bring in other characters. (*Pause.*) But where would I find them?' — that might be those of Beckett on his play at this juncture, as much as of Hamm on his story. And in fact the story does not end here. Hamm intermittently adds details and tried new wordings for it until the dying moments of the play.

The contiguity of Hamm's story and Beckett's play is announced in the preamble, when Hamm's gloomy reflection — 'It's finished, we're finished. (*Pause.*) Nearly finished.' — so closely echoes Clov's opening words to the play. Thereafter, a range of possible overlaps emerges, hinging principally on the fact that the story is a first-person narrative. Hamm never asserts that the 'I' of the story is in fact himself, and the *narrative tone* he adopts for the story-telling always preserves some distance between the two of them, but there are sufficient similarities in their manner and circumstances to suggest that it is likely. His puzzled reaction to the idea of introducing new characters into the story — 'But where would I find them?' — further confirms the possibility; his powers of pure invention seem to be as diminished as any other commodity in the play, so the likelihood that his story is based on 'fact', however embroidered in the telling, is all the stronger. The most marked similarities between the character in the story and the character in the play are the histrionic, dictatorial manner and the implication that he alone can dispense food and patronage; on the other hand, the 'I' in the story seems to be fit and mobile, busily putting up his festive decorations and only troubled by a touch of lumbago — a far cry from the haemorrhaging figure confined to his wheelchair. This is easily explained, however, if the events of the story are some time in the past, when Hamm was a younger man; this would further allow the possibility that the 'little boy' was Clov and the man his father, who (if this is 'true') must have disappeared from the scene very shortly after these events:

Hamm:	Do you remember when you came here?
Clov:	No. Too small, you told me.
Hamm:	Do you remember your father?
Clov:	(*wearily.*) Same answer.

(p. 29)

Of course, this version of how Clov came to be with Hamm may be just as much, or as little, fiction ('you told me') as the story itself.

The timing of the story in the past, perhaps the late Victorian era, is suggested by a few incidental details. The character speaks of lighting a meerschaum pipe with 'let us say a vesta', while distance is measured by 'a good half-day, on horse'. While the timing of the 'present' in the play is never fixed, these details seem pointedly anachronistic, like the memories of Nagg and Nell. They chime, moreover, with one of the marked characteristics of the character telling the story, his obsession with a certain kind of scientific or technological factuality, constantly measuring the weather: 'zero by the thermometer'; 'fifty by the heliometer'; 'a hundred by the anemometer'; 'zero by the hygrometer'. The mixture of meerschaum and scientific data perhaps evokes the popular image of Sherlock Holmes:[1] it certainly evokes the dispassionate, rather autocratic assumption of an absolute and verifiable physical truth which is often associated with late-Victorian science and finds its archetype in Sherlock Holmes. At its most extreme, it can be a heartless doctrine of the survival of the fittest, as in the character's contemptuous conviction of his own superiority over the man on his belly and his little boy ('as if the sex mattered') — a conviction not even shaken by the fact that this is Christmas Eve, with its message of peace on earth, good-will to all men. The outward show of decorations takes precedence over any question of human feelings or spiritual needs.

The position of the arrogant man of science is not as secure, however, as he would like to believe. For one thing, a heliometer would not give him the reading he so confidently ascribes to it; a heliometer measures the angles between the stars, or possibly the diameter of the sun, but not its brightness, for which some form of photometer would be necessary. Moreover, if all his measurements *were* correct, he would be in the midst of extreme, not to say apocalyptic weather conditions — hardly the time to be lording it over some unfortunate suppliant. This may help to explain the anticlimactic ending: just as the character relishes his triumph over the defiant suitor, Hamm's powers of invention flag and the performance ends lamely and ironically, like a sermon: 'Let us pray to God'. At least for the time being, religious faith of a sort wins out over scientific truth.

In what ways does this story mirror or comment on *Endgame* as a whole? Whether or not it literally describes Hamm's past and how Clov came into his service, it emblematically describes (as does Nagg's story) a stage in the intellectual and emotional journey to the *Endgame* world. Where Nagg's tailor had a zeal to improve on nature as he found it, the 'I' in the story is determined to dominate both it and his fellow men by force of character and by the powers of scientific reason. Both approaches fail. The myth of progress (and the art of story-telling which it in some respects resembles) evaporates in the light of human inadequacy and of the overwhelming forces both of time and of nature that oppose them. The world that is left in *Endgame* has neither zeal nor conviction, neither faith nor reason, though habits of arrogance and servitude linger on in Hamm and Clov respectively, like the memories of Nagg and Nell. The movement towards extinction seems assured. And yet it never comes: 'Finished, it's finished, nearly finished, it must be nearly finished'; 'It's finished, we're finished. (*Pause.*) Nearly finished'. Both Clov and Hamm start from the proposition that they have finished but retreat, reluctantly, to 'nearly finished'. Unlike Christ, whose final words on the Cross they are doubtless both of them echoing, they cannot achieve the satisfaction of completion. Like Hamm's story, like the play itself, they 'remain' (the play's final word) rather than end.

The speaker in Hamm's story doubted whether the little boy existed, much less could still be alive. Clov's survival into the present may just be testimony that he was wrong. By the same token, Clov's claim (p. 49) to see with his telescope 'a small boy' may be true, despite all the suggestions throughout the play that such development is impossible. The existence of such a 'potential procreator', as Clov calls him, might imply that life of a sort would go on, perhaps even if Clov were to leave Hamm. This is a measure of the irreducible level not so much of optimism as of pertinacity in the play. Hamm and Clov seem to form one of the sterile symbiotic relationships which are a hallmark of modern tragicomedy; each apparently needs the other to survive — Hamm chairbound, unable to reach the larder on his own, Clov mobile but not knowing the combination of the larder. They seem indispensable to each other, even though little love is lost between them: 'It's we are obliged to each other' is how Hamm Irishly puts it at the end (p. 51), though Clov's version is equally valid: 'If I could kill him I'd die happy' (p. 24) — a sardonic summing-up of their interdependence. Yet the existence of the boy would allow the possibility of their independent survival: the boy could replace Clov with Hamm, and Clov might survive outside, since Hamm's claim that 'Outside of here it's death' would demonstrably not be true. This would be a new character for Hamm's story, just as he despaired of finding one. Life, the story and the play would go into another chapter, another act, bleaker no doubt than the present, further fallen from the glories of the past, but unquenched.

This is the real location of the play: not a particular time and space, but a place in the life-cycle, whether it be of an individual, or of a society and its civilisation, or of the human species. It represents a syndrome of moments before extinction, dragged out interminably by habit and will: finished, nearly finished is the emotional climate of the whole play, however we interpret its perplexing particularities. It is an emotional climate that virtually precludes the tragicomic hope of redemption which is so central to *Waiting for Godot*. Indeed, *Endgame* could be seen as a remorseless closing down of the possibilities both of meaning and salvation which the earlier play had grudgingly kept alive. 'We're not beginning to . . . to . . . mean something?' asks Hamm (p. 27), with an incredulity that underlines just how unthinkable that is in this play. The emphasis here is not on waiting and the future, but on remembering a past to which the present seems a pointless addendum. Yet the past, as it is recalled and transmuted into 'art' by Nagg and Hamm, really has less to pride itself on than might be assumed: the trousers never achieved the desired perfection, and scientific rationalism was not the answer to everything it claimed to be. The presumption that the past was better — that life and civilisation had meaning, and so could make sense of the immense mysteries of time, age and death — is shown to be fallacious, and as that happens priorities change. The mere fact of survival into the present takes on an unlooked-for dignity, which is compounded by at least the possibility that it will go on into yet another generation. In such ironic topsyturveydom, the mere fact of 'remaining' becomes itself the miracle solution for which tragicomedy is always looking, and the play's 'strangeness' becomes a way of celebrating the mysterious fact that life goes on despite the odds. The mere performance or reading of so artfully self-absorbed a play becomes a proof of that fact. Every new performance or reading of *Endgame* is thus a little miracle in itself, a continuation and celebration — however weary — of the mystery of life, a tragicomedy despite itself.

2

The Birthday Party,
by Harold Pinter*

Harold Pinter is the master of modern tragicomedy. Beckett led the way, of course, but after *Waiting for Godot* and *Endgame* his plays have developed along experimental, post-modernist and minimalist lines, often related to tragicomedy but not precisely of the form that I have tried to define, though some — notably *Krapp's Last Tape* (1958) — come close. By contrast, Pinter's main achievement — all the full-length plays from *The Birthday Party* to *No Man's Land* (1974) — has been in the tragicomic form. It is worth repeating here that Pinter did not know Beckett's dramatic works when he began to forge his own idiom;[2] they came independently to tragicomedy as the proper dramatic response to their times. The characteristic elements of Pinter's drama are well known, and have been appraised according to a wide variety of lights: the acutely naturalistic ('Pinteresque') dialogue, which carefully registers the repetitions, hesitations and equivocations of colloquial speech without ever quite sounding natural; ordinary settings in which abnormal events occur; characters with dubious pasts and inadequate or ambiguous explanations of themselves; violence or the threat of violence; characters with apparent psychological or sexual inadequacies; games played with an intensity that threatens one or more of the players. My contention is that these are essentially the ingredients of tragicomedy and that the precise nature of the mixture — the unmistakable Pinter mixture — is best understood in those terms.

The Birthday Party was the first of Pinter's full-length plays to be performed, and it baffled critics and audiences alike in a disastrous London production that lasted only a week.[3] With hindsight, it now seems one of his most accessible works —

---

*First performed, London, 1958

almost over-explicit by comparison with the spare, elliptical style of his later plays. But it may be helpful for someone coming newly to Pinter or to *The Birthday Party* itself to try imaginatively to recreate the problems that it may have posed for its earliest audiences. It opens with an immediately comprehensible scene on a set which has none of the aggressive strangeness we associate with Beckett: a hen-pecked old man is being nagged by his small-minded wife about a number of mundane issues, such as his cornflakes and fried bread, the weather and the contents of the paper he is reading. The most challenging feature of this in 1958 is likely to have been that, while such scenes were familiar enough in real life, they were not the stuff of which drama was conventionally made. Audiences used to the sophisticated and articulate dialogue of such as Noel Coward, Emlyn Williams and Terence Rattigan may have been bemused by inane exchanges about cornflakes, the more so because they are so insistently repetitive, in Pinter's teasingly naturalistic manner:

Meg:	Here's your cornflakes. $<$ . . . $>$ Are they nice?
Petey:	Very nice.
Meg:	I thought they'd be nice.

$$< \ldots >$$

Meg:	Is it nice out?
Petey:	Very nice.

$$< \ldots >$$

Petey:	I've finished my cornflakes.
Meg:	Were they nice?
Petey:	Very nice.

(pp. 19-21)

The irritatingly all-purpose 'nice' in fact recurs ten times in three very spare pages of dialogue, in a way that audiences now — appropriately, I think — take as comic, but which may then have seemed an all too faithful transcript of a bit of life that no one was interested in. If it appealed at all, perhaps it did to those who saw something exciting in the then new, so-called 'kitchen sink' style of drama, associated with writers like Arnold Wesker and Alun Owen (the latter, incidentally, a friend of Pinter's). These writers concentrated on the unglamorous aspects of working-class and lower middle-class life. Indeed, the set which Pinter prescribes for the play — a not very special seaside house, with its kitchen-hatch — seems to promise something of this style, a promise which looks all the more like being fulfilled when Stanley, the only boarder, appears, unshaven and wearing his pyjama top.

Anyone reconciled to a piece of slice-of-life, 'kitchen sink' realism must, however, be disconcerted by the way the play develops. But it is not easy to put a finger on where exactly the realism breaks down. Meg's attempts to mother Stanley may seem excessive but are far from unbelievable. Stanley's pretensions to be a professional pianist do not ring true but are credible enough little vanities in response to Meg's mothering: he resists her fussiness but plays up to the fact that she shows a pride in him. Stanley's brief interchange with Lulu merely confirms our amateur-Freudian suspicions about him ('You're a bit of a washout, aren't you?' p. 36). Goldberg and McCann are certainly an unusual pairing, an East End Jew and an Irish Catholic, and the former asks a lot of questions, but there is nothing inherently improbable about their behaviour in the first act. On the other hand, by the time they are established as significant characters, the emphasis of the play has swung firmly away from 'kitchen sink' realism at least. Plays of that type characteristically focus on a family or community and its life-style almost as their principal concern. Goldberg and McCann are very pointedly outsiders here as, for all Meg's 'mothering' is Stanley Webber. The play is not about the typical life-style of Meg and Petey's house, but about some unusual intrusions into it.

That fact has scarcely registered when the first piece of real oddity occurs:

> *Meg*:   It's [Stanley's] birthday today.
> *Goldberg*:   His birthday?
> *Meg*:   Yes. Today. But I'm not going to tell him until tonight.
> *Goldberg*:   Doesn't he know it's his birthday?
> *Meg*:   He hasn't mentioned it.
>
>   (p. 42)

Of course, we know Meg to be a bit simple-minded and over-motherly, but to decide arbitrarily that today is Stanley's birthday is downright strange, outside the established realistic parameters of the play. Perhaps Meg is actually deranged?

Stanley tells her categorically, 'This isn't my birthday, Meg' (p. 46), but he accepts her present, a child's drum, puts it about his neck and starts beating it, perhaps humouring her. But '*the beat becomes erratic, uncontrolled, Meg expresses dismay. He arrives at her chair, banging the drum, his face and the drumbeat now savage and possessed*' — on which note the act ends.

Is Stanley also deranged, or on the point of a nervous breakdown? The fact is that realistic explanations will no longer serve in this play; the evidence we have for why things happen, for why characters act and speak as they do, is just too sparse or ambiguous to provide realistic answers. The second act opens that same evening (at least, that is the natural inference, and there is no authorial indication to the contrary; this is typical of the grey areas of non-information in any Pinter text). Stanley seems to be over whatever possessed him with the drum; he concurs moreover with McCann's pointed insistence that today is his birthday. To which of them was he lying, and why? We have far more possibilities than we can constructively use: he may have been resisting Meg's mothering; he might be humouring the strangers, whose arrival made him nervous from the start; he may simply be mad, and so on. The play has elements of a mystery thriller about it: there are strong inferences to the effect that Stanley once belonged to and betrayed some 'organisation' (p. 48) that Goldberg and McCann belong to, and that is why they have come to do whatever it is they do to him. But mystery thrillers are *generically* realistic: that is, although a variety of explanations of events may for a time seem equally feasible, in fact only one explanation squares exactly with all the known facts and is indisputably 'real'; hence the highly parodiable stock scene in the library or the drawing room, where the detective eliminates all the false possibilities in favour of the only true one. Tom Stoppard gets a good deal of comic mileage out of such 'generic realism' in *Jumpers* (see Chapter 9) and *The Real Inspector Hound*. But Pinter eschews it altogether, just as, in *The Birthday Party*, he subverts and finally abandons 'kitchen sink' realism. We never do know why Goldberg and McCann have come for Stanley, or even exactly what they do to him, any more than we know why Stanley lies about his birthday. It is, in effect, a play of mysteries. Perhaps this is what defeated the original audiences? Or perhaps it was the *mixture* we have been tracing

— an apparent realism that gradually devolves into something altogether more perplexing.

What is the nature of the play's mysteries? Most of the difficulty attaches to the *identity* of the three characters, Goldberg, McCann and Stanley — their past, their relationship, their motives, and at the heart of all these Stanley's unspecified guilt. In Goldberg's case, the mystery of his identity correlates in an obvious way with a considerable degree of confusion about his name. When he first appears with McCann, the latter addresses him as 'Nat' — almost obsessively so, since he reiterates the name ten times in less than three pages of dialogue (pp. 37-9). Does this suggest a degree of unease about their relationship, even though it seems to go back a long way? Goldberg even asks at one point, 'What is it McCann? You don't trust me like you did in the old days?' (p. 38), but we never find out what those old days consisted of, or why things have changed. It is not entirely surprising, therefore, when, in a fit of sentimental reminiscence, Goldberg slips into another name:

> 'Simey!' my old mum used to shout < . . . >
> *McCann*: I thought your name was Nat.
> *Goldberg*: She called me Simey.
>
> (p. 53)

Could this shift be related in any way to the fact that Goldberg has only just met Stanley for the first time in the play? If so, we still have to explain why Goldberg repeats the whole conundrum with Lulu, to whom he introduces himself unequivocally: 'I'm Nat Goldberg' (p. 65), only later to reminisce again about being called Simey, though this time it was what 'my wife' used to shout:

> *Lulu*: I thought your name was Nat.
> *Goldberg*: She called me Simey.
>
> (p. 69)

Nevertheless, Goldberg reacts 'murderously' when McCann ventures to call him Simey (p. 86) and lapses thereafter into another reminiscence about his childhood, where this time he is known as 'Benny' (p. 88).

It is all quite perplexing. There is no consistency about the changing of Goldberg's tune; it cannot, for example, be explained away as an attempt to hoodwink particular individuals. The one common thread to all the names he acknowledges is their Jewishness — an aspect of his identity constantly underlined by traces of Jewish idiom in his speech (e.g. 'When I was an apprentice yet . . .' p. 37; 'Simchahs' p. 66; 'schnorrers' p. 88) and by references to traditional Jewish food, like 'gefilte fish' and 'rollmop and pickled cucumber'. But even this aspect of his personality is less secure than at first it seems. For one thing, he seems able to drop the idiom and accent at will. When McCann asks him about the 'job' they are on, Goldberg *speaks in a quiet, fluent, official tone* (p. 40). Just prior to that, McCann has praised him with the singularly infelicitous observation, 'You've always been a true Christian', to which Goldberg replies with studied ambiguity, 'In a way'. Later, his reminiscences include a Sunday School teacher girlfriend, who was presumably not Jewish. None of this means that he is *not* Jewish but it is sufficient to raise significant doubts. The possibility that *every* facet of Goldberg that we see in the play may be part of a very complex piece of play-acting is one we can never discount. It is a possibility we shall have to confront about one or more characters in most of Pinter's plays, so this is something of a test case.

McCann is not so ambiguous a figure, though even his identity is less secure than it may at first seem. He is known by his surname for most of the play, until Goldberg mentions him to Petey as 'Dermot' (p. 81). Petey queries the name and Goldberg confirms it. Barely a side of dialogue later, however, Petey refers to McCann as Dermot:

> Goldberg   (*sharply*): Who?
> *Petey*:   Your friend — Dermot.
> Goldberg   (*heavily*): Dermot. Yes.

Later again, however, Goldberg seems to change the name: 'Because McCann — (*Gently.*) Seamus — who came before your father?' (p. 88). Perhaps Goldberg is just using Irish names indiscriminately in a generic way, as some people call all Irishmen Paddy, but the discrepancies are odd. McCann's Irishness would seem to be indisputable, but in fact it is never categorically affirmed; it is entirely a matter of nuance and supposition. He drops Irish place-names very conspicuously in his conversation — Carrickmacross, Roscrea, Tullamore, — makes a point of only drinking Irish whiskey and asks pointedly Irish questions in their examination of Stanley: 'What about Ireland?' 'What about the blessed Oliver Plunkett?' 'What about Drogheda?' (pp. 61-2). The possibility that he is a member of the I.R.A. seems very strong when he starts singing 'Glorio, Glorio, to the bold Fenian men!' and reciting 'The night that poor Paddy was stretched' (pp. 70-1). But it is noticeable that he avoids Stanley's straight question: 'Where do you come from?' with 'Where do you think?' and it is Stanley himself who continues with 'I know Ireland very well' (p. 52). Similarly, Meg takes it for granted that McCann is Irish in her observation to him, 'My father was going to take me to Ireland once' (p. 69), and it is this which stirs McCann to the patriotic fervour noted above. The fact is that McCann's Irishness is as suspect at root as Goldberg's Jewishness — a mask of mannerisms and implications with no substance. The very oddity of an alliance between — what? — a Jewish gangster and an I.R.A. man is surely enough to start us asking questions.

The mystery is compounded, however, by Stanley's apparent association with both halves of this odd alliance. He is on edge from the moment it is mentioned that two men are coming to stay, but it is never clear whether he actually knows Goldberg and McCann. He *glimpses their backs through the hatch* (p. 37) when they first arrive but is not wearing his glasses. Later he presses Meg about their names and she just about remembers Goldberg, but when she asks on the strength of this, 'Do you know them? *Stanley does not answer*' (p. 45). At the beginning of the second act, McCann raises the issue formally:

	I don't think we've met.
Stanley:	No, we haven't.

Nevertheless, when McCann starts whistling an Irish tune, 'The Mountains of Morne', Stanley joins in, as if associating himself with the stranger: '*During the next five lines the whistling is continuous, one whistling while the other speaks, and both whistling together*' (p. 48). And, as we have seen, it is Stanley who volunteers the information that he knows Ireland very well, going on to list platitudinously the virtues of the place and its people. His links with Goldberg emerge more circuitously. In conversation with McCann, Stanley paints an innocuous picture of his own past in Maidenhead, with its Fuller's tea-shop and Boots library; he tries to get McCann to admit that he has been there, but the latter insists, 'I don't know it' (p. 49). It is Goldberg later who lists as part of his own modest life-style 'tea in Fullers, a library book from Boots' (p. 66); he does not locate this in any particular place — but by then Stanley seems to have shifted his story from Maidenhead to Basingstoke (p. 52). We are simply left with the implication, as with McCann, that *something* links Stanley and Goldberg.

On the precise identities of Goldberg, McCann and Stanley, therefore, and consequently the relationships between them, the play remains inscrutable. All we are really in a position to assess is the *dramatic* relationship between them — the ways in which they relate to each other as actors on stage: dominant, equivocal, submissive; questioning, sidestepping, answering; positive, neutral, negative. This is seen at its clearest in the two scenes (pp. 55-63, 91-5) where these characters are left alone on stage, and the action takes on the distinct form of ritual both times.[4] The threats, questions and accusations with which they assault him in the first scene and the promises with which they assail him in the second are not credible by any realistic terms of reference. But we recognise in the repetitions, parallel phrasings and near-chantings to which Goldberg and McCann subject Stanley the presence of forces which are barely human; Goldberg and McCann cease as it were to be individuals and become channels via which Stanley is subjected to, in the first instance, an intense psychological dismemberment and latterly a mocking attempt to repair the damage. We recognise in the questions and accusations echoes of the themes running through the complex issues of identity we have been tracing:

McCann: You betrayed our land.
Goldberg: You betrayed our breed.

Presumably this is Ireland and Jewishness respectively, but the net casts far wider than that, dragging in Stanley's relationships with Meg ('Why are you driving that old lady off her conk?') and Lulu ('Why do you treat that young lady like a leper?'). The questions range from the absurdly trivial ('Enos or Andrews?')

to the most arcanely philosophical ('What makes you think you exist?'). At the outset, Stanley tries to answer the questions and rebut the accusations more or less rationally, but by the end he no longer has the resources; he screams and tries to attack them with a chair. Effectively, Goldberg is right when he says, 'You're dead. You can't live, you can't think, you can't love. You're dead < . . . > You're nothing but an odour' (p. 62).

Stanley never says another coherent word in the play. It is as if the ritual interrogation has stripped him of whatever life or personality he had, leaving him incapable of speech and latterly of any kind of response at all. The second of these scenes is a kind of mocking attempt to put the pieces of his identity together again, but on terms that Goldberg and McCann dictate:

McCann:	We'll renew your season ticket.
Goldberg:	We'll take tuppence off your morning tea.
McCann:	We'll give you a discount on all inflammable goods.
Goldberg:	We'll watch over you.

(p. 92)

As in all tragicomic ritual, strange and mysterious forces have intervened in the life of a community that conspicuously lacks spiritual and cultural energy: these forces take control of one member of the community, who is often an 'outsider' (Stanley is not actually a member of the family) and who has, or appears to have, special potential (note Stanley's pretensions to be a concert pianist). They make him a victim or scapegoat, who is called upon to carry the whole burden of guilt for the community — McCann pointedly calls Stanley 'Judas' (p. 62), the member of the human race singled out to betray the Son of God, as it were on our behalf: paradoxically, without that betrayal the crucifixion and resurrection would have been impossible. It is signficant in this respect that, when Lulu is ordered to 'confess' (p. 91), McCann is described as a recently unfrocked priest; his association with the strikingly named Carrickmacross — carry my cross? — is similarly suggestive. It all reinforces the impression that this side of the play is a kind of perverted Christian ritual.

The very nature of ritual, with its intrusion of supernatural or metaphysical forces into everyday lives, helps to put into context one of the oddest features of the play, Goldberg's obsession with the Necessary and the Possible: 'Is the number 846 possible or necessary?' he demands of Stanley twice, finally insisting on his own solution to this old philosophical conundrum (p. 60). He later tells Lulu of a lecture he delivered at the Ethical Hall, Bayswater, about the Necessary and the Possible ('It went like a bomb', p. 67). It is a theme which inevitably goes to the heart of the apparent contradictions inherent in concepts like fate and free will, providence and accident: in what sense is man a free agent, and in what sense is he governed by inscrutable forces which he may not understand, but to which he may ultimately be answerable? These forces may, of course, operate as much through the unconscious parts of one's own personality — in the forms like fear, lust or guilt — as through external means (Goldberg/ McCann?) that we might more readily label as fate or historical necessity.

These questions, and the pattern of experience in which they are wrapped for Stanley, are immediately reminiscent of what we found in Renaissance tragicomedy: the parallels, for example, between Stanley and Ferdinand in *The Tempest* are marked.[5] The obvious difference, however, is that where Ferdinand's symbolic 'death', trial and induction into the higher mysteries lead to a splendid 'rebirth', with the promise of marriage and a new Empire, in Stanley's case we see only a parody of such things. At his 'rebirth' (this is, after all, *The Birthday Party*), he is completely catatonic:

McCann: You're a dead duck.
Goldberg: But we can save you.
McCann: From a worse fate.

(p. 92)

This 'salvation' will consist of supplying him with the equipment for a barely adequate existence — ointment, hot poultice, baby powder, back scratcher, stomach pump, oxygen tent, crutches etc. — conjuring up suggestions of a life of continuous illness and discomfort.

Goldberg: We'll make a man of you.
McCann: And a woman.

The promise of something quasi-heroic is immediately undercut by a reminder of what have been implied as Stanley's sexual inadequacies or ambivalences, particularly in respect of Lulu. It is signficant that the whole liturgy concludes with Goldberg and McCann saying the same word, 'Animals'. Far from achieving the elevated power and status of the traditional tragicomic 'victim', the effect of Goldberg and McCann's intervention has been to reduce Stanley to the speechless dependence of an animal. It is a complete inversion of the traditional tragicomic conclusion, which invariably enhances the status of humanity; it is a mockery of a providential outcome.

This is underlined by the brief reappearance of Petey and Meg at the very end of the play, a return to the dispiriting 'normality' from which these strange occurrences sprang. Petey remains a champion of 'realism', albeit a feeble one, throughout the play — there is nothing mysterious about him. It is Petey who puts the shilling into the meter to restore the lights after the blackout. (I wonder how many of the audience even pause to consider a practical reason for the blackout when it happens? — the play seems so firmly in a symbolic, ritual mode by then that the blackout seems merely appropriate, the work of numinous forces.) It is also Petey who proposes the commonsense solution of getting Stanley to a doctor. So it is fitting that he should be the one to try to recall Stanley to his old self, to break him from the hold that Goldberg and McCann obviously have over him: 'Stan, don't let them tell you what to do!' (p. 96). But Pinter's stage direction to this line ('*broken*') indicates the effect of what has happened to Stanley on the household that had adopted him. Thus Meg's last few lines, her fantasies of the 'lovely party' the night before, at which she was 'the belle of the ball $<$ . . . $>$ I know I was', are poignantly ironic. This image of triumph, charm and sexual potential is exactly what we should expect at the end of a traditional tragicomedy, where 'gods' and 'mean people' mingle.[6] Here it is a sham, a mockery of any such possibilities.

3
The Caretaker,
by Harold Pinter*

Like all of Pinter's plays, *The Caretaker* has a veneer of social realism and an apparent concern with contemporary mores. Indeed, it would not be difficult to imagine a version of this play (written, perhaps, by Arnold Wesker) in which a concern for social problems was its most significant dimension: immigration and shortages both of work and housing (Davies' fear of 'aliens', loss of work and homelessness); urban decay (the state of the room, and Mick's ambitions as a landlord); irresponsible medicine (Aston's electrotherapy), and so on. All of this seems firmly located in the naturalism of the set, with its solid pile of more or less rubbish and the leak in the roof. But it is clear from the outset that social and political concerns are not the primary emphasis of the play that Pinter wrote; the apparent realism of the set and of the issues raised in the dialogue dissolve at every point into the hopes and fears, and so ultimately into the identities, of its three characters. It is at this level that we can see that the play is not a social documentary, but a modern tragicomic ritual, a search by each of the characters for meaning and redemption, which ultimately leads nowhere.

The play is scrupulously modelled around a sequence of parallels and contrasts which underscore the futility of the search. Davies, the outsider, is introduced into a room occupied by Aston but (apparently) owned by Mick; the former is gentle and unassuming, the latter aggressive and self-assertive. Davies tries to ingratiate himself with each in turn, and succeeds to the extent of being offered rather ill-defined posts as caretaker by each of them separately; but he is finally rejected by both of them, for reasons that are no clearer than they were for his

*First performed, London, 1960

101

earlier acceptance. At the end of the play he has all but been pushed out again into the violent every-man-for-himself world from which Aston had originally saved him and offered him refuge. The play thus passes through a perfect cycle, ending effectively where it began, with no discernible progress made. All we can really say from the 'neutral' structure of *The Caretaker* is that each of its three characters indulges in some kind of hope — looks, in fact, for a kind of miracle — from the new presence in the room. But none of them finds it, and we are left to wonder whether any of these hopes was ever realistic in itself, or whether their mutual incompatibility rendered them still-born. As with all tragicomedies, it is a process — for the audience even more than for the characters — not so much of acquiring practical wisdom as of coming to terms with perplexing and frustrating realities that are not always apparent in our daily lives.

This process focuses on the room, the play's only set, and on the hopes and illusions with which each of the characters invests it. Davies, for example, looks upon the room as a potential refuge from the real or imagined threats of the world outside, which he locates insistently in foreigners of all denominations: 'All them Greeks had it, Poles, Greeks, Blacks, the lot of them, all them aliens had it < . . . > All them Blacks had it, Blacks, Greeks, Poles' (p. 17). The man who attacked him in the cafe is repeatedly characterised as 'a Scotch', 'a Scotchman' and 'that Scotch git', while he was chased away from the monastery by 'an Irish hooligan'. At the outset, his main worry about the room seems to be its proximity to another flat occupied by what Aston twice calmly refers to as a family of Indians, but which Davies obsessively identifies as 'Blacks'.[7] Davies is wrong, however, to think of the room as a refuge from such threats, because here he is himself the alien, and liable to attack for that very reason:

Aston:	Welsh, are you?
Davies:	Eh?
Aston:	You Welsh?
	(*Pause*).
Davies:	Well, I been around, you know . . . what I mean . . . I been about . . .

(p. 34)

His unwillingness to admit his country of origin — he lamely claims not to be able to remember when Aston asks directly where he was born — suggests that he is anxious not to be labelled as any kind of outsider. The two names he admits to, Bernard Jenkins and Mac Davies are ingratiating mixtures of Scots, Irish and Welsh, a rather feeble attempt perhaps to be all things to all men, but sadly out of place in the London of Mick and Aston; he tries to make up for it with his familiar talk of his 'mate at Shepherd's Bush' (p. 22) and getting 'onto the North Circular, just past Hendon' (p. 24), but he is clearly out of his depth alongside Mick, the gregarious Londoner:

> You know, believe it or not, you've got a funny kind of resemblance to a bloke I once knew in Shoreditch. Actually he lived in Aldgate. I was staying with a cousin in Camden Town. This chap, he used to have a pitch in Finsbury Park just by the bus depot.
>
> (p. 41)

These inconsequential observations carry on, bringing in Putney, Fulham, the Caledonian Road, the Nag's Head, the Angel, the Essex Road, Dalston Junction, Upper Street, Highbury Corner, St. Paul's Church and a detailed account of the bus service in that part of London: 'Dead spit of you he was. Bit bigger round the nose but there was nothing in it'. Of course, in fact, there was everything in it: Davies is very pointedly not a son of these London streets, for all his resemblance to this probably mythical 'bloke'.

The whole speech is part of a sustained attack on Davies/Jenkins as an outsider. Mick's repeated breaking of his name into 'Jen . . . kins' is a way of emphasising its strangeness, its not belonging, and the whole process culminates in the direct question:

> *Mick*: You a foreigner?
> *Davies*: No.
> *Mick*: Born and bred in the British Isles?
> *Davies*: I was!
>
> (p. 42)

It is one of the least equivocal exchanges in the entire play, with Davies desperate to establish his Britishness as a way of glossing over his alien status in this particular room. He seems to succeed for a time, but never totally. The fact is that his view of the room as a refuge is always a mistake. The same forces that threaten him outside — be they real or imagined — also threaten him there. The ways in which Aston quietly and Mick more brutally insist upon his being a foreigner in this world are only verbal equivalents of the physical and psychological pressures which the room brings to bear upon him, as if trying to exclude him. Mick's silent, ominous, leather-jacketed presence before Davies even appears makes a mockery of all the latter's attempts to settle comfortably there. Mick's direct assault at the end of the first act, the nightmarish 'attack' of the electrolux in the dark, the danger of the gas stove (even though it is not connected), the discomfort of the open window — all these point to Davies' status as the vulnerable outsider, who can never properly be assimilated there. The room as a refuge is always an illusion.

But it is an illusion that is fostered, at least part of the time, by the attitudes of the other two characters. When they are not at work making Davies feel like an outsider, they seem bent on making him feel at home. Again, this centres on *their* respective views of the room which, as in the case of Davies, seems intimately bound up with their personalities. Mick is aggressively extrovert, constantly determined to be seen as a pillar of the social and business communities — a pose always rather at odds with his leather-jacketed appearance. His announcement that the room belongs to him comes between the two soliloquies in which he tells Davies, 'You remind me of my uncle's brother . . .' and 'you've got a funny kind of resemblance to a bloke I once knew in Shoreditch' (pp. 40, 41). As we have already noted, these speeches seem calculated to make Davies aware of how much a foreigner he is; they depict Mick as a man with extensive family and social connections, gregarious, with an intimate knowledge of London and its colourful characters. We may wonder, of course, just how genuine any of this is. 'My uncle's brother' strikes a wrong note from the start, since the phrase logically denotes either another uncle of Mick's, or his father. Why use this odd periphrasis unless he is just making things up as he goes along or striving too hard for effect, spuriously implying a wider web of family than actually exists? Much of what Mick says has this hollow ring to it, would-be respectable/impressive, rather than sincere. Note, for example, the way his badgering of Davies occasionally lapses into ultra-politeness: 'I hope you slept well last night?' (p. 40).

All of this is carried over into his view of the room, which he insists upon seeing as a legal and financial asset far beyond its all too apparent worth; hence his constant talk of solicitors, contracts, rateable value, references, furnished or unfurnished status and so on. The use of legal jargon seems simultaneously to be a way of disconcerting Davies and of imposing respectability on a squalid reality. The same principle holds when he switches to the jargon of salesmen and advertising magazines:

> I could turn this place into a penthouse < ... > I'd have teal-blue, copper and parchment linoleum squares. I'd have those colours re-echoed in the walls < ... > You could have an off-white pile linen rug, a table in ... in afromosia teak veneer, sideboard with matt black drawers, curved chairs with cushioned seats, armchairs in oatmeal tweed, a beech frame settee with a woven sea-grass seat, white-topped heat-resistant coffee-table, white tile surrounds < ... > it wouldn't be a flat it'd be a palace.
>
> (p. 69)

Much of the comedy of this disconcertingly funny play derives from the sheer incongruity of such language in relation to such property and such people, reaching ludicrous heights when Mick asks Davies: 'Who do you bank with? *Pause.* Who do you bank with?' The question is far less funny the second time. The pause allows us time to reflect that we are on the borders of some very uncomfortable areas — insanity, menace, insecurity, homelessness. Karl Marx thought that history repeated itself, coming first as tragedy and then as farce; repetitions in Pinter commonly work the other way round: a line that may be comically incongruous once takes on a dangerous edge when it recurs. So it is when Mick finally turns against Davies, repeating earlier words almost verbatim:

> You mean you wouldn't know how to fit teal-blue, copper and parchment linoleum squares and have those colours re-echoed in the walls? [etc.]   (p. 81)

Nevertheless, for at least a time, Davies seems to represent for

Mick the key to fulfilling those illusions of respectability which are so much part of him and which he vests so heavily in the room and its potential. This lies at the heart of his proposition that Davies should stay on as caretaker.

Of course we can never rule out the possibility that *anything* Mick says may be a devious way of badgering Davies. But his overheated discussion of the room may be judged too persistent and detailed to be dismissed simply as malicious make-believe; perhaps, as he claims himself, it comes painfully close to revealing something deeply part of his own personality: 'You're the only man I've told, about my dreams, about my deepest wishes, you're the only one I've told' (p. 81). This 'admission' is itself histrionic and might be dismissed as pure play-acting, particularly when he goes on, 'and I only told you because I understood you were an experienced first-class professional interior and exterior decorator'. This is pure make-believe; he earlier claimed to be taking Davies on as a caretaker only because he looked like 'a capable sort of man' — with a knife (p. 59). Nevertheless, the possibility that Mick had briefly opened himself up to Davies more than he had intended is one we cannot entirely discount. It fits, for example, with his shifting position on the smell Davies gives off. Early on, he is quite forthright: 'You're stinking the place out' (p. 44). Just before he turns against Davies for the last time, however, he comes close to contradicting this: 'You don't stink < . . . > If you stank I'd be the first one to tell you' (p. 79). At this point Davies may still represent for Mick some weird possible key to respectability, so he may be willing to twist the truth. The line is far from unequivocal, however, since Mick *had* in fact been the first one to tell him that he stank; the line bristles with irony, conscious or unconscious. This hardens into something like gleeful spite when he finally rejects Davies: 'And to put the old tin lid on it, you stink from arse-hole to breakfast time' (p. 83). For most of the play Davies is an unacceptable presence in the room for Mick, but there are — perhaps — moments when he is willing to overlook this, for reasons we can only speculate about. It is as if he is playing cat-and-mouse with him for most of the time, but every now and again the aggression gives way to a kind of fascinated interest.

Aston seems to be antithetically different from his brother, a quiet introvert who is genuinely well-disposed towards Davies, until the latter rejects his friendship. It is Aston who has acquired all the junk with which the room is littered, just as — significantly — it is he who introduces Davies. The junk all has some theoretical potential but, like the unconnected gas stove, seems doomed to remain a pile of useless clutter which is slowly making the room uninhabitable. Aston himself apparently lacks either the skill or the initiative to make anything of the things he has collected. The toaster with which he tinkers for much of the early part of the play, and to which he pointedly returns in the closing moments ('That ain't the same plug, is it, you been . . .?' asks the rejected Davies, p. 84), is a constant reminder of the problem. It is no closer to being fixed at the end than it was at the beginning, and even if it were (assuming that Mick is telling the truth about having to use the light socket for the electrolux), there would be no electricity for it in the room. This is symptomatic of what we know about his life in general. 'I'm supposed to be doing up the upper part of the house for [Mick] (p. 49). He is convinced that, 'I can work with my hands, you see', but claims to be frustrated by the lack of a workshop in which to do it; that is why he is anxious to 'get that shed up outside' — a surrogate for fixing up the room itself. Mysteriously, he comes to think of Davies' presence as a help out of his impasse. This passage, in which he describes his woodworking aspirations, is followed by the discovery that the bag he has brought in is not Davies' own, but one that Aston had actually paid for (incongruously elegant smoking-jacket and all), with the apparent intention of keeping Davies happy. This in turn leads immediately into *his* offer that Davies could be a caretaker. It is as if Davies' staying and taking on this elevated title — with its own uniform, implements and bell to polish, but only the haziest of duties — will somehow confer dignity on Aston's own efforts, perhaps facilitating the building of the shed or even making it unnecessary: a flat with its own caretaker might no longer need 'doing up'. In that sense, a caretaker might be the answer to Aston's inadequacies. But Davies resists the offer, apparently because he fears that the new title and status would make him more vulnerable to the threatening forces outside the room. He feels relatively safe shuffling between Bernard Jenkins and Mac Davies but worries that his own bell announcing 'caretaker' might invite trouble from 'that Scotch git', or the social security people, or 'any Harry'. This, at least, is what he claims. So one personality problem crosses the path of another, frustrating its ambitions.

But this account of Aston's character or personality is incomplete; it is, so to speak, what Davies sees or wants to see in him — a sincere but vulnerable victim of life, who might eventually be excluded from the room to make way for Davies. Yet, just as in the case of Mick, where it is possible to detect a certain vulnerability within his general aggressive assurance, so with Aston there seems to be an element of deviousness in his pathetic simplicity. This is particularly apparent in relation to what Davies takes to be his most vulnerable feature, his mental condition. The longest, and in many ways most resonant, speech in the play is that in which Aston describes the experience of having been forcibly subjected to cerebral electrotherapy or shock treatment (pp. 63-6). In it, he depicts himself as a classic hero-victim or scapegoat, someone not quite of this world: 'I used to get the feeling I could see things . . . very clearly . . . everything . . . was so clear . . . everything used . . . everything used to get very quiet . . . everything got very quiet . . . all this . . . quiet . . . and . . . this clear sight'. Because of this special gift, or oddity, he was an outsider, spurned by people in the cafe or the factory, and finally attacked by the doctors in the mental hospital (which, significantly, was 'right outside London'). What they did to him amounted to a metaphorical death, a change of being: 'The trouble was . . . my thoughts . . . had become very slow . . . I couldn't think at all . . . I couldn't . . . get . . . my thoughts . . . together <. . .> but I didn't die. The things is, I should have been dead. I should have died'. The speech is graphically convincing, particularly underscored by the slow fade of lighting which leaves only Aston clearly visible by the end; it is apparently an island of truth in a sea of equivocations and patent falsehoods.

But Pinter himself, in a rare direct comment on his own work, has pointed out that we *need* not construe the speech in this way.[8] Of course, we should not need the author to point out such things, and in fact we do not. But the unreliability of this particular narrative is less easy to pin down than is that of Mick's early soliloquies, where the verbal oddities ('my uncle's brother') call attention to the far-fetched nature of what he is saying. In fact it is just as likely that Aston is making up everything he says as that Mick is; he merely disguises it better by using the nature of the story itself to cover up his hesitations and inconsistencies: 'The trouble was, I used to have kind of hallucinations. They weren't hallucinations they . . . <. . .> Then one day . . . this man . . . doctor, I suppose . . . the head one . . . he was quite a man of . . . distinction . . . although I wasn't so sure about that. He called me in. He said . . . he told me I had something.' Given that Aston is describing himself in a mental hospital, having shock treatment, it is quite natural to interpret the pauses, meanderings and changes of tack as the consequences of that treatment. But in a play where 'every word [they] speak is open to any number of different interpretations'[9] these falterings could be explained just as adequately by the hypothesis that he is making it all up as he goes along, 'feeding' his audience, Davies, as by the assumption that he is telling the naked truth. The possibility invests Aston with a deviousness far more subtle than Mick's bluster. All his vulnerable 'sincerity' becomes a way of teasing Davies into thinking that his chances of staying in the room are better than they are; the self-promotion as a scapegoat figure becomes a cruel parody of the role that Davies actually plays.

Mick and Aston, in this view, are just as much a symbiotic pairing as Vladimir and Estragon or Rosencrantz and Guildenstern, though (unlike those pairings) their links are most apparent in their silent actions rather than in their dialogue. Their entrances and exits, for example, add up to a smooth and sophisticated game of blind-man's-buff or pass-the-parcel — with Davies as the blind man or the parcel, never knowing which way he will be pushed next. The whole process is shown in miniature in the rough game Mick plays with the bag that Aston brings for Davies (pp. 47-8). On the surface, this is another example of Mick's aggression, while Aston seems to try to protect Davies ('Scrub it', 'Give it to him'). But if we follow the action carefully, we see that it is not so simple; on at least one clear occasion, '*Aston gives it to Mick*', which seems to act as a signal that it is time for the game to stop, because then '*Mick looks at Aston*' — one of the earliest confirmations of what is increasingly apparent as the play progresses: an element of collusion, telepathy or shared instinct between the brothers in their dealings with Davies. We could not expect to spot this in the opening moments of the play, where Aston's solicitous attention to Davies follows Mick's sinister exit, but the ending should come as no surprise —

Aston comes in. He closes the door, moves into the room and faces Mick. They look at each other. Both are smiling, faintly.

(p. 84)

The faint smile signals the end of the game, and the exclusion of Davies.

The tension of the play, then, grows out of a number of irreducible ambiguities in the motives and actions of the brothers. To see the whole action as a complex game or joke played at Davies' expense would be to ignore the fact that, in inventing the role of caretaker for him, both Mick and Aston seem to dig deeper into their personalities than such a game or joke would require; but to take either of them at his word or surface appearance would be to ignore an element of collusion which rules out total sincerity. Davies is not allowed to be simply redeemer or merely victim, but is tantalisingly strung between both possibilities for most of the play. As a consequence, his attempts to find a niche for himself in the room, usually by playing one brother off against the other, are doomed to failure: he cannot keep up with the ambiguities of the role in which he is being cast by them.

Davies' untenable position is best reflected in the piece of Aston's 'junk' with which he is repeatedly associated: '*Davies* <. . .> *comes face to face with a statue of Buddha standing on the gas stove, looks at it and turns*', (p. 18); '*[Davies] picks up the Buddha and looks at it*', (p. 37). Unlike the rest of the junk, the Buddha has no practical potential; it is an alien artefact which Aston has picked up for no very persuasive reason: 'Looked quite nice to me. Don't know why <. . .> Yes, I was pleased when I got hold of this one. It's very well made' (pp. 26-7). Although Aston is unable or unwilling to explain what appeals to him about the statue, it is something he wishes to keep central in the room: '*Aston stands, goes to the sideboard drawer, picks up the statue of Buddha, and puts it on the gas stove*', (p. 49). This is immediately prior to telling Davies of his woodworking ambitions, which leads to the first caretaker offer. So the Buddha is something to which our attention is repeatedly drawn, always in relation to Davies' being — and perhaps staying — in the room. We might be tempted to see it as a symbol — but of what? In a play by Beckett we would never have to ask that question; the play itself would invest every artefact with an open-ended range of symbolic associations, just as the tree in *Waiting for Godot* is a gallows, the Cross, The Tree of Life and heaven knows what else besides (it is, of course, also a tree). In Pinter's indeterminate ambiguities, the Buddha remains inscrutably itself. Had it been, say, a crucifix, a symbol with which most of the audience would be familiar, we would instinctively have identified it with the victim/redeemer role at which Aston plays, but which really belongs to Davies. But — at least before the popular interest in Eastern religions in the late Sixties — we can safely assume that Buddha would have no such resonances for a British audience. Like Davies, when asked 'What do you think of these Buddhas?' we would probably reply, 'Oh, they're . . . they're all right, en't they?' (p. 27). And that is surely the point; it is something and nothing. It is whatever anyone wants to see in it, and so reflects Davies' uncertain role in the room. This is particularly ironic to anyone who *does* know about Buddhism since, where Christianity stresses the significance of the interceder/redeemer figure, Buddhism emphasises the potential within each individual to reach enlightenment by himself. Which is a wry reflection on the Mick—Aston—Davies triangle, where the individuals are never themselves but are constantly playing at roles imposed by the very existence of the triangle. It is totally appropriate, therefore, that the complex game of charades comes to an end when Mick '*hurls the Buddha against the gas stove. It breaks*' (p. 83). All the ambiguous tensions break with it. The brothers are formally united with their faint smiles, and Davies is back to being what he has always really been, unequivocally one of life's victims.

The Caretaker is a typical modern tragicomedy in the way it teases the audience about the likelihood of social and psychological redemption for its characters. Davies' search for a refuge from the forces that threaten him, matched by the possibility that he himself supplies a solution to the inadequacies in the lives of Aston and Mick, offers all the ingredients for a ritual of renewal and redemption: but the irreducible ambiguities in that triangle of relationships prevent anything more than the most tentative assembling of the ingredients. As in Renaissance tragicomedy, we find soliloquies at strategic moments in the play, in which the characters appear to voice their deepest cares and perplexities — Davies' tale of his search for shoes at the monastery, Aston's tale of his shock treatment, Mick's vision of a penthouse. But on examination, each of these dissolves into half-truth, implausibility or public performance for effect. As modern characters, they either do not comprehend the perplexities in which they find themselves, or they refuse to face them squarely, or they are chary of admitting too much to other people; and for whatever reason, in failing to express their perplexities adequately, they seem to deny themselves the possibility of a redemption, an answer to all their problems, that might be there for the taking. They are brought to this by irrational forces, acting through fear, guilt and ambition, and as ever we look to such forces ultimately for a benign conclusion. It is in coming so close to something like a miracle, but all too humanly failing to achieve it, that *The Caretaker* stands as an object lesson to modern times.

4
Who's Afraid of Virginia Woolf?
by Edward Albee*

In many respects, *Who's Afraid of Virginia Woolf?* must seem
out of place in this book, not so much because it was written by
an American, Edward Albee, but because it lacks the
strangeness, the pervasive challenge to the audience's sense of
normality, which is the hallmark of the other tragicomedies
studied here. It is the play furthest removed from the tone and
style of *Waiting for Godot*. The characters, for example, are all
realistically drawn, with credible histories and psychological
profiles. They may tell lies from time to time, or indulge in
make-believe, but never to the extent of mystifying the
audience; we recognise that they are playing games of a sort, and
the most important of these — the fantasy creation and
elimination of George and Martha's son — is clearly explained
as such by the end of the play. It may seem odd that Nick and
Honey should stay to take the verbal and mental abuse to which
George and Martha subject them, but that can be put down to
the fact that they are newcomers to a college run by Martha's
father and so anxious not to offend. Much of the excessive
behaviour on all sides — from Honey's throwing-up to
Martha's seduction of Nick, and the latter's impotence which
frustrates the seduction — can be explained by the copious
quantities of alcohol which are consumed throughout the play.
In these respects, *Who's Afraid of Virginia Woolf?* seems less a
modern tragicomedy than a traditional drama of marital
conflict, reminiscent perhaps of Eugene O'Neill or Tennessee
Williams.

Nevertheless, the play deserves a place here, because in all
other respects — in its structure and thematic patterns, its

---

*First performed, New York, 1962

mixture of game-play and quasi-religious ritual, its exploration of sterile symbiotic relationships — it is a copy-book modern tragicomedy. As we noticed in Part I, Renaissance tragicomedy was a broad enough genre to accommodate a considerable range of forms and styles; there is no reason why modern tragicomedy should be different. This is, we might say, tragicomedy stripped of much (but not all) of its strangeness, bringing its mysteries to the surface rather than leaving them submerged. The roles of Nick and Honey are crucial here. They are outsiders in the 'strange' world of George and Martha. The processes by which they come to understand that world and to discover an affinity with it put them in a special relationship with the audience — one rarely found in tragicomedies, though it has affinities with the way that Shakespeare allows us to see the magic machinery behind *The Tempest*. It is as if *they* experience the strangeness on our behalf, being bewildered and affronted while we are able to remain rather more detached, to see the dramatic process essentially from the outside. In these unusual respects, *Who's Afraid of Virginia Woolf?* offers an interesting parallel to, and commentary on, the plays of Albee's more oblique contemporaries, and it is in that light that I shall approach it.

The clearest acknowledgement of the play's affinity to the works of Beckett and Pinter comes in the titles which Albee gives to each of the three acts, 'Fun and Games', 'Walpurgisnacht' and 'The Exorcism'. These make explicit motifs and processes which, as we have already seen, are certainly present in European tragicomedies, but which audiences are normally left to intuit and interpret for themselves. The playing of games, for example, is a recurrent feature of this kind of drama — games of language, games of identity, games of aggression where, as often as not, the audience and at least one of the characters are bemused about the rules of play and indeed about the point of it all. Think of Vladimir and Estragon playing at being Pozzo and Lucky, or Mick and Aston playing pass-the-parcel with Davies' bag, or Rosencrantz and Guildenstern tossing coins and playing questions; it is commonly a metaphor for the wider situation in which the characters find themselves — itself a game with dubious rules and an uncertain point. With George and Martha there is little mystery; playing games has become a whole way of life, the thing that keeps them together for all their mutual antagonism. We see this in Martha's impersonation of Bette Davis and George's threatening to shoot her with a shotgun that emits nothing more lethal than a parasol; each is constantly trying to upstage the other, whether or not there is a third-party audience. However we interpret the progress of particular games, we are left in no doubt that the game-playing ultimately relates to the self-respect of the characters concerned, to the hopes and illusions that they foster about themselves — and this can be extended to include visitors as well as the home team. In attack, the aim is always to minimise the opponent's self-respect by subjecting him or her to sarcasm or humiliation; in defence, the aim is to construct a personal history that the opposition will be too shamefaced or confused to challenge. So, for example, we have Martha's depiction of herself as admired by her father (Daddy) and loving and adoring him in return, which is then capped by George's coyly fictional account of being responsible for the deaths of both of his parents. Both of these stories are questioned to breaking-point in the course of the play, but their truthfulness is never crucially important; we recognise them as well-worn counters in a marriage-long game of mutual antagonism.

The attempts by George and Martha to outdo each other in self-esteem or self-pity elicit a series of more naive self-revelations from Nick and Honey, who have clearly not achieved the same degree of sophistication in the game, though there is some evidence that they are not entirely strangers to it. These revelations enable George to call a truce in the game he and Martha are playing (and which, until Act 3, he is patently losing) by transposing the action to a new but similar game of Get the Guests. Martha in turn attempts to regain the initiative in the original game with a round of Hump the Hostess. It is Nick's unsatisfactory performance in this party-piece that leads to one of the revelations that the play gives us very little room to doubt (since she gains no advantage by making it); Martha confesses: 'There is only one man in my life who has ever . . . made me happy <. . .> George who is good to me, and whom I revile' (pp. 112-13). She lists, among the perverse virtues that contribute to this fact, George's ability to keep 'learning the games we play as quickly as I can change the rules' — a perfect metaphor for their antagonistic symbiosis.

To all appearances, 'Fun and Games' might run indefinitely, but there are forces at work which conspire to bring them to crisis point. Principal among these must be the specific chemistry between George and Martha, Honey and Nick; it is implied that George and Martha have 'performed' for their guests before, but never with the intensity they manage for Nick and Honey. George represents the backward-looking art of history, Nick the forward-looking science of biology; George seems to be spiritually broken while Nick is in his prime, a recent 'intercollegiate state middleweight champion' (p. 37). Martha is, or can be, blowsily attractive, while Honey is mousy and slim-hipped. But as *couples* they complement each other perfectly and, allowing for the discrepancies between their ages, the similarities may seem to outweigh the differences: an ambitious arrival in the faculty; a marriage entered into without the idealism one might have looked for; and the rankling absence of real children. It is as if these similarities reopen old wounds for George and Martha. Their game-playing has become formulaic and predictable, even cultivated for public consumption. But this confrontation with a version of their old selves, when their hopes and illusions were at their height, spurs the game-play into an unprecedented ferocity ('Total War', p. 95), pushing it beyond restraints which George and Martha have hitherto respected with each other.

This helps to explain the title of the second act, 'Walpurgisnacht' — the German witches' sabbath, that lingering acknowledgement of Celtic and Teutonic deities in an otherwise Christian world. It is a night when supernatural forces are at work, when spirits of the dead walk abroad and divinations of the future are made — a time when usual notions of what is normal or acceptable are broken. The confrontation between George and Martha, Nick and Honey raises the ghosts of the formers' past and looks into the latters' future. Looked at in this light, the play is by no means as securely realistic as it may at first seem; as this title suggests, we are not just watching a series of sophisticated domestic quarrels but a struggle for power between spiritual forces. The private lives of these characters are presented to us as a metaphor for a much profounder drama, which is why the realistic dialogue repeatedly — and increasingly — devolves into ritual and incantation, the proper modes for addressing experience outside the normal range of human comprehension. This quality of the play is reflected in the chant which gives it its name. Martha's transposition of 'Virginia Woolf' for the Big Bad Wolf of the old nursery rhyme is, on one level, a not particularly funny joke. We may suspect that its mock intellectualism was another attempt to embarrass George before the other members of the faculty. We are told that George laughed at it, but not why. Did he think it was funny? Or that Martha was making a fool of herself rather than him? Or simply because he recognised another round in their unending games? Any of these is psychologically credible and would explain his irritation when, during the play, Martha repeatedly reminds him that he had laughed — as if this were a point in her favour. But on another level, and perhaps the one that really gets under George's skin, 'Virginia Woolf' points to the real stakes in the games they are playing. The name of the novelist conjures up images of talent and intelligence translated into madness, despair and suicide.

Who's Afraid of Virginia Woolf? moves constantly in this way between a relatively conventional realism, in which the actions of the characters square readily with what we know of their personalities and their intake of drink, and a symbolic level in which the characters are driven by dark forces deep within themselves, agents in a ritual drama which they do not fully understand and over which they have little control. These dark forces — the spirits released on 'Walpurgisnacht' — are not merely psychological. The language of the play insists that we see the characters symbolically in a number of other contexts too, primarily historical and religious ones. The names George and Martha, for example, inevitably evoke for an American audience George and Martha Washington, the founding father and mother of their country: we are invited to see them as an archetypal American couple, in the same way that George can refer to their mythical son as 'our own little all-American something-or-other' (p. 116). Their drama is, at least in part, a sour and disillusioned version of The American Dream — the title, as it happens, of another Albee play, and a shorthand phrase for all those hopes of life, liberty and the pursuit of happiness/wealth seemingly guaranteed by the idealistic New World. But the play is not simply an allegory about America and its failings; it evokes a much broader sweep of history, notably in its choice of New Carthage as the name for its campus setting. This is plausible enough, given the actual example of campus towns with classical names like Ithaca and Syracuse, but it is a strikingly gloomy precedent — a city conquered and totally eradicated by Rome in those 'Punic Wars' where George sarcastically locates his own childhood (p. 61), though he later glosses this cryptic comment as 'the Great Experiment, or Prohibition'. This chimes exactly with the passage from the modern history book which George reads when briefly left on stage alone: '"And the west, encumbered by crippling alliances, and burdened with a morality too rigid to accommodate itself to the swing of events, must . . . eventually . . . fall."' (p. 104). The reading of history throughout the play is extremely pessimistic — civilisations fallen, dreams and ideals tarnished or forgotten — and this even extends to the study of history itself. As represented by George, history is a thing of the past as much as it is about the past, a discipline in decline, its humanist assumptions undermined by the new science, represented by Nick. The genetic engineering of the biologist threatens to determine the fate of mankind (at least in George's imagination, see p. 29) in a way previously reserved for the forces of history.

Between them, George and Nick represent the study of what makes human beings the creatures they are — the social, political, economic, evolutionary, physical and biochemical determinants that carry man through time. As Nick puts it: '*You've* got history on *your* side . . . I've got biology on mine. History, biology' (p. 71). In context, this is the younger, fitter man putting his older adversary in his place, and it might well seem fitting (a less jaundiced view of history) if the generation of Nick and Honey were seen rightly to be taking the place of those cynical failures, their hosts. But that is surely not the real emphasis of the play. If there is something pathetic about an old historian who feels cheated by the history of his own marriage, there is something more than ironic about a biologist railroaded into marriage by a *hysterical* pregnancy. George's bitterness about the biologist seems to focus on the fact that, where a historian can never really be more than an analyst of destinies, the biologist might determine them himself — a potent image of virility. But in fact, the two couples prove crucially alike in having produced no children and, to all appearances, in being unlikely ever to do so. George and Marcha's joint infertility is spelled out in the closing moments of the play; Nick's impotence with Martha may be the temporary effect of drink, but Honey's slim hips — to which George repeatedly calls attention — suggest her inability to bear children. George's sarcasm about the biologist's dream of genetic engineering thus proves to be an unnecessary gambit in the game at large; biology in this play offers no more hope for the future than does history. This is one of the dark lessons taught by the spirits of Walpurgisnacht.

Similarly, religion seems to offer little in the way of consolation, much less of redemption. Martha and Honey offer parallel examples of conventional religious backgrounds, respectively Catholic and Protestant, which have produced something less than spiritual idealism. Martha now describes herself *'uncertainly'* as an atheist, but George insists on 'pagan': Martha is the only true pagan on the eastern seaboard' (p. 50). George's use of the term 'pagan' alludes to Martha's sexual appetite, or perhaps more generally to her unprincipled self-indulgence, though it also fits later with his furious denunciation of her as a 'SATANIC BITCH' (p. 84) — her insistence on having everything her own way has a kind of demonic enthusiasm about it. Her personality is the antithesis of the pious self-renunciation that a convent education is supposed to bring about. Honey's father, we learn from Nick, was 'a man of God' — not exactly a priest, but a man with a vocation who went about baptising, preaching, building churches and, in the process, 'ended up pretty rich', which George sardonically describes as 'very nice' (p. 69). His sarcastic insinuations make the point well enough. Mammon seems to have done rather better out of Nick's father-in-law than God, and there is every reason to supose that Nick's decision to marry Honey was influenced by this wealth ('not God's money'), which she has inherited. The reduction of religious faith to the level of materialistic sexual politics, at which most of this play operates, is further reflected in George's mock deference to Martha's father: 'He's a God, we all know that' and his reference to the latter's rooms as 'Parnassus' (pp. 23, 25). Both George and Nick have, for the most dubious motives, married the daughters of men ironically aligned with God.

It is in their normal use of language, however, that we may appreciate most readily just how little religious values mean to these characters. Throughout the play they swear about as much as they drink, and it is noticeable that they resort to oaths much more readily than to obscenities (though 'bitch' is fairly standard in the vocabulary of George and Martha) — Jesus, God, Dear Lord, God in Heaven, Good God, My God, Jesus God, for God's sake, for Christ's sake. The words are used almost exclusively for effect, with no thought of their real connotation. Swearing is just a way of registering emotions, modulated to suit individual personalities — Martha's brassy self-assertiveness, George's weary resignation, Nick's clean-cut exasperation, Honey's mousy astonishment, or whatever. But it is ultimately a reflection of a language as sterile as the characters who use it; they swear so often that it passes virtually unnoticed, as part of the verbal scenery. This is surely significant in a play which is so largely about the lack of meaning and purpose in people's lives: those dimensions which have traditionally afforded meaning and purpose in life have been relegated to the role of making language more colourful. Albee points up this fundamental irony in the opening and closing moments of 'Fun and Games', where formulaic invocations of God and Christ mirror each other (pp. 11, 57).

While the repetition and parallelism of those lines calls attention to the irony from the outset, it is not until the final act that its full force becomes apparent. Albee's title for the last act is 'The Exorcism' — the driving forth of an evil spirit by the speaking of a holy oath or name. The exorcism aims to lay the ghosts of 'Walpurgisnacht'. Hence the particular poignancy of the last two outbursts of such swearing: George justifies his 'killing' of the apocryphal son with the insistence: 'YOU KNOW THE RULES, MARTHA! FOR CHRIST'S SAKE, YOU KNOW THE RULES!' and Nick finally makes sense of it all: 'JESUS CHRIST I THINK I UNDERSTAND THIS!' — a line so loaded, that Albee has him say it twice (p. 137). The effect here is not dissimilar to those blatant anachronisms in medieval mystery plays, where uncouth carpenters nail Christ to the Cross swearing 'by Christ' and 'by him that saved us', since it should by now be clear to the audience that the characters are undergoing a trauma analogous to the crucifixion of Christ. That is a large, even blasphemous claim to make about a play that on one level simply depicts a drunken, overblown marital quarrel, but the detailed context insists that we see it this way. The realism of the surface contains beneath it a far more complex 'spiritual' struggle, reflected in all these allegorical allusions to history, biology and religion. So the 'death' of George and Martha's 'son' is imbued with all the force of a scapegoat rite — the innocent victim created by the two of them, a perfection to offset all their own inadequacies and failings, is driven out by their incessant warring and finally sacrificed as the necessary price for any possibility of reconciliation.

The fact that their son is fictitious, a piece of make-believe, does not matter in this context. This is the point where the realistic 'surface' and the mysterious depths of the play intersect. What matters is that George and Martha have vested all their most precious hopes and illusions in this joint creation. He is the sum of their historical, biological and ultimately religious dreams, the only thing capable of redeeming lives wasted on fun and games, of giving them meaning. It is George's grasp of just how 'real' this makes the boy that finally gives him the power to turn the tables on Martha; she starts to be rattled from the moment he makes it clear that he will not differentiate between fact and fantasy: '(*a little afraid*): Truth or illusion, George. Doesn't it matter to you . . . at all?' (p. 120). This leads to the last game of all ('it's called bringing up baby'), with Martha '(*pleading*): No more games' (p. 121). Early on, Martha had dismissed George as non-existent: 'I can't even see you . . . I haven't been able to see you for years <. . .> I mean, you're a blank, a cipher <. . .> a zero' (p. 18). The decision to sacrifice their son, and the power it reflects, changes all that. Martha complains:

> You can*not*. You may not decide these things
>
> Nick: < . . . > He hasn't decided anything, lady. It's not his doing. He doesn't have the power . . .
>
> George: That's right, Martha; I'm not a God. I don't have the power over life and death, do I?
>
> (p. 136)

This is ironically disingenuous on George's part. He does not have the absolute and arbitrary powers of a god. The power he has, in a realistic sense, derives from the fact that Martha let Nick and Honey in on 'the bit' (pp. 18-19), the most secret of their games. George is able to exploit this mistake, in using Honey's drunken and confused corroboration of events to 'allow' him to kill off their son. But on another level — the level where distinctions between truth and illusion, fact and fiction really do not matter, George's power comes from his grasp of the spiritual forces engaged in their game-playing. This is the level that confirms the whole dramatic experience of the play as a tragicomedy.

Nick and Honey share vicariously in all of George and Martha's games, gradually proving themselves — and by proxy, those other unsuspecting guests, the audience — to be mirror-images of their hosts. In the middle of 'bringing up baby', the identification between hosts and guests becomes intense; Honey cries out three times 'I want a child', and when the 'death' of the boy is firmly established, she joins in the Latin Mass of the Dead which George remorselessly intones for him: 'Et lux perpetua luceat eis' (p. 138). Nick does his best to comfort Martha as a surrogate husband, and then belatedly thinks he 'understands' — with that ironic oath. This moment of shared understanding after so much confusion, bewilderment, suffering and seeming death is reminiscent of Renaissance tragicomedies, with their unexpected reversals that place everything in proper perspective, allowing characters and audience alike to share in sudden joy and wonder. It demonstrates that the bewildering experience undergone is not merely a private trauma but is something crucial to the life of the whole community, a complex moment of history and biology.

It is a moment that never comes in the tragicomedies of Beckett, Pinter and Stoppard; only its absence is carefully registered — Godot does not come, though he will surely come tomorrow. This is the only shared understanding possible in these plays, which have no equivalent characters to Nick and Honey: moments of tacit acceptance that things are as they are, rather than outbursts of joy at new prospects. In fact, Albee proves to be true to the tone and implication of other modern tragicomedies, even though his structure seems to promise something more positive. George has won this final game with Martha, but at a crippling sacrifice to himself as well as to her; it has all the hallmarks of a Pyrrhic victory about it. We are given no assurance that anything positive will emerge from their suffering and sacrifice. To the straight question, 'Are you all right?' Martha replies, 'Yes. No', an ambivalence that reflects the final emphasis of the play. Both as individuals and as tokens in the larger spiritual struggle, their future hangs in the balance.

Of all the plays considered in this book, *Who's Afraid of Virginia Woolf?* is the one whose critical stock has fallen most markedly in the twenty years since it was first produced.[10] It is undoubtedly a very effective, even harrowing piece of theatre — perhaps too much so for its own good. It has been accused of being melodramatic and pretentious, of trying to invest itself with an intellectual weight it will not carry. I do not share these reservations, though I understand them: the mixture which this play attempts of the ordinary with the extraordinary, of conventional realism with the ritual and numinous elements of tragicomedy, is inevitably a precarious one. Albee, moreover, is explicit to the point of bluntness about what he is trying to do, most notably in the titles that he gives to the individual acts. It may be that in this, and in placing Nick and Honey between the audience and the main protagonists, Albee has cheated the audience of the *real* sense of mystery and confusion which are essential ingredients of tragicomedy. These are, finally, matters of taste rather than of definition. What is indisputable is that, in its mixture of public ritual and private trauma, in its depiction of ordinary people caught up by forces they do not understand (neatly labelled for us as historical, biological and religious), the play offers us the clearest commentary possible on the more reticent and oblique forms of contemporary European tragicomedy.

5
The Homecoming,
by Harold Pinter*

At first sight, there is nothing strange or unusually challenging about *The Homecoming* as a play. There is nothing disconcerting about the staging — no equivalent, for example, of Mick on stage in the darkness at the beginning of *The Caretaker* or Anna in the half-light in *Old Times*; the presentation of events is conventionally realistic. Nor is there anything particularly mysterious about any of the characters; they are all members of the same family, whose histories and occupations are not significantly in doubt — unlike such figures as Goldberg and McCann in *The Birthday Party* or the trio in *Old Times*. In such respects, *The Homecoming* is more like *Who's Afraid of Virginia Woolf?* in being less immediately perplexing than most tragicomedies; it has a deceptively conventional surface.

It is in the relationships within the family, fraught with sexual tensions, that we first detect something unusual. This centres firstly on the figure of Max, who is sexually ambivalent or perhaps — as Lenny puts it — 'sexless' (p. 88). He is constantly associated with traditionally female roles, notably cooking; he resents this some of the time ('Who do you think I am, your mother?' p. 32) but can take a bitter pride in it when it suits him ('don't talk to me about the pain of childbirth — I suffered the pain, I've still got the pangs', p. 63). At times he can be aggressively patriarchal, wielding his stick viciously, in a manner reminiscent of his former trade — a pointedly masculine one — as a butcher; but he resents it when Lenny tries to label him as 'Dad' (p. 33) and his one real display of paternal affection, towards Teddy, is cloyingly maternal in tone: 'What about a nice cuddle and kiss, eh?' (p. 59). This

---

*First performed, London, 1965

ambivalence also manifests itself in his attitude to other members of the family, both male and female. Sometimes he evokes his dead wife, Jessie, as a paragon, 'with a will of iron, a heart of gold and a mind' (p. 62), at other times as a whore — 'a slutbitch of a wife' (p. 63). And he transposes these attitudes exactly on to Ruth, sentimentalising at one moment about the mother of three children and fulminating the next about 'a stinking pox-ridden slut' (p. 57). When he is irritated, he refers to the male members of the family indiscriminately as 'bitches' (e.g. Lenny, p. 27; Sam, p. 32; Teddy, p. 58).

The sexual peculiarities of other members of the family all seem of a piece with Max's ambivalence. His brother Sam is apparently homosexual ('Anyone could have you at the same time. You'd bend over for half a dollar on Blackfriars Bridge', p. 64), which presumably explains his pointedly a-sexual memories of Jessie — 'Used to just drive her about. It was my pleasure' (p. 32). Lennie's attitude to women seems to be fundamentally sadistic — 'I just gave her another belt in the nose and a couple of turns of the boot and sort of left it at that' (p. 47) — which makes it less of surprise when his 'profession', as he coyly refers to it for so long, turns out to be that of a pimp. Joey's masculinity is aligned with his pretensions as a boxer, and both prove suspect; as a boxer, 'you don't know how to defend yourself, and you don't know how to attack' (p. 33), while in two hours with Ruth he fails to 'go the whole hog'.

Ruth and Teddy, by contrast, seem at first a perfectly normal married couple with children. What must seem abnormal is how casually they react, in the end, to the suggestion that the family should take Ruth in and 'put her on the game' (p. 88). Teddy puts up no real resistance to the idea of losing her in this way, having apparently already 'lost' her in a previous difference about leaving early (pp. 70-4). He offers her the option — 'Or you can come home with me' (p. 92) — but leaves with no apparent regrets, making all the usual platitudinous noises with which family visits end, even taking a picture of Max for his children (pp. 95-6). Ruth is similarly dispassionate, being quite unruffled by the suggestions of prostitution and rapidly getting down to business details, as if she knows the trade of old: 'I would want at least three rooms and a bathroom' (p. 92). Her farewell to her husband — 'Eddie. (*Teddy turns. Pause.*) Don't

126

become a stranger' (p. 96) — is pointedly bland, perhaps even the sort of thing a prostitute might say without thinking. Only the unprecedented use of his name in this form, 'Eddie', points to there being something deeply unusual going on.

Initially it may seem that we need to invoke Freud and the psychoanalysts to make sense of so many sexually unstable characters, with their lurid imaginations; a family saga which in so many ways seems to hark back to the central role of the long-dead mother seems to invite comparisons with the psychological realism of Ibsen, O'Neill or D.H. Lawrence. But such parallels will not get us very far with this play. In particular, they will help us little with the reactions of Teddy and Ruth to the weird attitudes of the rest of the family. They seem prepared for what happens, to take it almost casually, in ways for which the audience have not been prepared and which have little to do with realistic psychology. For most of the play Teddy seems nervous about bringing Ruth to see his family, which is not surprising, given what he and we know about them. Not long into the second act he makes a concerted effort to get Ruth to leave earlier than they had planned, but she resists and thereafter he makes no real attempt to hold on to her, even when the family makes the most outrageous proposals. He finally leaves as if nothing untoward had happened at all. In Ruth's case, we may discern a glimmer of a 'realistic' psychological profile in her admission, 'I was . . . different . . . when I met Teddy . . . first' (p. 66). In context it is easy to read this as an admission that she had then been a prostitute. But even if this were so, we are hardly prepared for the cool and business-like way in which she picks up their proposal, effectively taking over the family in the process (as the closing tableau suggests). In each case, it is as if they were following some pre-determined course, quite independent of normal psychological prob-abilities.

What we see here, in effect, is a structured pattern of events, something deeply suggestive of myth, rather than a naturalistic family saga. This impression is reinforced if we attend to the nuances of the names in the play. It seems likely, though it is never explicitly established in the play (and it has to be set against Christian oaths and indeed discussion of Christian theology), that this is a Jewish family: the names Max, Sam,

Lenny and Joey are common enough in London Jewish families (though Teddy, the one who significantly has left home, is altogether more Anglo-Saxon). In this context, the names of Ruth and Jessie are particularly resonant. In the Old Testament, Ruth was a Moabite woman who married into a Jewish family, settling in Israel ('amid the alien corn', as Keats put it) when her first husband died; eventually she was married again, to a rich kinsman, and so became the great-grandmother of King David and hence an ancestor of Christ. Her grandson, the father of David, was Jesse, from whose 'tree' the descent of Christ is usually drawn. These associations might seem irrelevant or far-fetched, were it not for the fact that the sexual peculiarities of the family centre on the question of paternity, the establishment of the patriarchal line.

Teddy makes a revealing observation to Ruth about the house: 'Actually there was a wall, across there . . . with a door. We knocked it down . . . years ago . . . to make an open living area. The structure wasn't affected, you see. My mother was dead' (p. 37). The odd running-together of the last two statements gives the clear inference that the structure of the house and Teddy's mother were intimately connected — perhaps, in a manner of speaking, the same thing. So the present 'structure' of the house — the relationships of the characters living within it — are a legacy of when the mother was alive; they have not been changed by minor adjustments to the 'architecture' — even by anything as apparently radical as Teddy's emigration to America. The play in effect 'enacts' the structure of the house, reliving the myth-like pattern of relationships on which it is built. Jessie — the matriarch rather than the patriarch — is at the centre of everything:

Max: He was very fond of your mother, Mac was. Very fond. He always had a good word for her. (Pause.) Mind you, she wasn't such a bad woman. Even though it made me sick just to look at her rotten stinking face, she wasn't such a bad bitch.

(p. 25)

Mac is another figure from the past, who is repeatedly associated with Jessie; he inspired in Sam the same kind of aversion as Jessie did in Max, whom he tells: 'He was a lousy

stinking rotten loudmouth. A bastard uncouth sodding runt.
Mind you, he was a good friend of yours' (p. 34). Mac's name
('he was the only one they called Mac', p. 24) is pointedly
similar to Max's, perhaps suggesting that he might be some kind
of *alter ego* to the latter — but at the same time pointedly belongs
to a (Scots) outsider. These suggestive ambiguities should
perhaps prepare us for Sam's desperate final revelation:
'MacGregor had Jessie in the back of my cab as I drove them
along' (p. 94) but equally for Max's insistence that this is the
invention of a 'diseased imagination'.

Sam's 'revelation' in fact brings to a head an issue that runs
through the play, underlying its whole set of unbalanced
father/son relationships — from Lenny's prurient interest
('That night . . . you know . . . the night you got me . . . that
night with Mum, what was it like? Eh?' p. 52), to Max's
effeminate cuddle and kiss with Teddy, his complaints about
having to 'mother' Joey and his resistance to being called 'Dad'.
It is summed up in the pointed question Max asks when Ruth
reveals that she has three children: 'All yours, Ted?' (p. 59).
There is an unspoken suspicion that Max is not the father of the
family at all, that by this fundamental definition he is not a man
at all and so not essential to the 'structure' of the house. This
touches deeply primitive emotions which infect not only Max's
personality but the whole society of the family.

The tragicomic potential of the theme of jealousy or sexual
mistrust is apparent in one of the finest of Renaissance
tragicomedies, Shakespeare's *The Winter's Tale*,[11] which makes
an interesting comparison with Pinter's play. Both plays centre
on the death/disappearance of the mother-figure in a family,
and her resurrection/return, the latter occasioned by the
miraculous discovery of a daughter/daughter-in-law. Of
course, Hermione does literally return from her apparent death,
in addition to the discovery of Perdita, but Shakespeare's
staging of events runs these things together, so that the statue
scene is effectively the emotional climax of both 'resurrections'
— a concept sometimes reinforced on stage by having mother
and daughter played by the same actress.[12] Ruth in *The
Homecoming* is ambiguously both mother and daughter-in-law
(or both mother and whore) for the male members of the family,
an object alternately of reverence and lust, but always implicitly

attached to them. 'I was born quite near here', she says, echoing in Act 2 Teddy's claim in Act 1: 'I was born here': it is as much her homecoming as his. There is an ironic ambiguity, further identifying Ruth with Jessie, in Max's outburst on first seeing her: 'I've never had a whore under this roof before. Ever since your mother died' (p. 58). Early in the play, Max tells Joey to 'Go and find yourself a mother' (p. 32). By the end of the play, that is exactly what he has done: '[*Ruth*] *continues to touch Joey's head, lightly*'.

It is common, in considering the death/resurrection motifs in *The Winter's Tale*, to draw analogies with Christ or with the vegetation myths of Ceres and Proserpina from classical mythology; the text certainly draws attention to such parallels, though it is salutory to bear in mind Frank Kermode's observation that 'here, as elsewhere in Shakespeare, the divine analogues are intermittently presented'.[13] In the same way, without trying to tie the text down to a simple allegorical or mythological interpretation, we may say that *The Homecoming* has affinities with such material, cautiously alluded to in the Ruth/Jessie (Jesse) analogues. The characters are similarly caught up in forces and processes over which they have no direction. That is why psychological explanations of what is going on are ultimately limited; we are dealing with areas of experience beyond individual personality, beyond rational understanding, and beyond personal control.

So *The Homecoming*, like *The Winter's Tale*, explores areas of profound sexual disorientation which affect not only specific individuals but permeate the whole society. Leontes' jealousy is sudden, violent and unsubstantiated; it leads him to see 'gracious' Hermione as a whore, to doubt the parentage of his son, Mamillius, and to repudiate the unborn daughter, Perdita; in the second half of the play, Polixenes, the unwitting cause of this jealousy, proves equally prone to such unwarranted passion when he turns on Perdita, threatening to mar her beauty with briars — an ugly reaction, caused by his determination not to have his royal line 'sullied' but fuelled by her sexual attractiveness. These sexual disorientations give rise to confusion, suffering and several deaths, both real and supposed, before the return of Hermione and the marriage of Perdita with Florizel restore harmony in both political and sexual spheres.

Similarly in *The Homecoming* the (re-) assimilation of Ruth into the family perversely offers a resolution to the jealousy and sexual disorientation running through the play.

In the nature of things, there is rarely any doubt about who is the mother of a particular child. But paternity is a far more open question, hardly susceptible to proof. In normal circumstances we assume that the woman's husband is the father, but we do so on faith rather than evidence — faith in the wife/mother's chastity in marriage. I use the theological term, faith, deliberately to underline the analogy — which is tacitly drawn throughout *The Homecoming* — between the state of paternity ('All yours, Ted?') and the nature of religious truth. Much is made in the play of the fact that Teddy is a Doctor of Philosophy; it underlines the social and intellectual gap that he has opened up in leaving the family, but it also opens up a metaphorical way of discussing the issues of faith at the heart of the family. Lenny tries on a number of occasions to catch Teddy out, or to demonstrate that he is not overawed by his academic qualifications: 'Do you detect a certain logical incoherence in the central affirmations of Christian theism? [. . .] How can the unknown merit reverence? In other words, how can you revere that of which you're ignorant? (pp. 67-8). Teddy coolly refuses to rise to the bait on any of these, in a way that prefigures the calm with which he accedes to the family's arrangements for Ruth. His recipe for circumventing all major issues of faith and emotion is to deny that they fall within his province. In that way he endeavours to maintain what he calls an 'intellectual equilibrium' (p. 78). But these issues are, in effect, the issues at the heart of the family itself and Teddy can only ignore them by denying the family completely. The Oxford English Dictionary offers this definition of 'theism': '*esp*. Belief in one God as creator and supreme rules of the universe, without denial of revelation: in this use distinguished from *deism*'. The critical issue here, then, is the nature of religious belief and whether such belief requires supernatural evidence ('revelation') or whether it might not be a purer belief without such evidence ('deism'). It all boils down to the nature of faith itself, which makes a virtue of certain kinds of ignorance, and so invokes Lenny's second question: 'how can you revere that of which you're ignorant?' The relevance of all this to the family and the play should readily be apparent when we remember that it was also Lenny who badgered Max with 'that night with Mum, what was it like? Eh?'

Lenny's questions are always implicitly those of a cynic, an unbeliever. For the man of faith, 'logical incoherence' is no obstacle and ignorance is an irrelevance (as Ignorance proves to be in *The Pilgrim's Progress*). Faith has its own certainties on what we might call a different wavelength from those of logic and fact. It is the absence of faith, the absence of such certainties, in respect of the lost mother, Jessie, which lies at the heart of the odd behaviour within the family. Lenny comes close to admitting this, by implication, in a further philosophical interchange with Teddy:

> *Lenny*:   Well, for instance, take a table. Philosophically speaking. What is it?
> *Teddy*:   A table.
> *Lenny*:   Ah. You mean it's nothing else but a table. Well, some people would envy your certainty, wouldn't they, Joey?
>
> (p. 68)

There is no evidence, of course, that Teddy does have any 'certainty', either as a philosopher or as a member of the family, but he has cultivated an indifference which can be mistaken for it and this makes him (befitting his name) the outsider of the family, an object of resentment particularly to Lenny, the doubting Thomas of the family. This emerges critically in the incident of the cheese roll, which Teddy admits to having eaten, just before the family's proposal to Ruth: 'to pinch your younger brother's specially made cheese roll when he's out doing a spot of work, that's not equivocal, it's unequivocal' (p. 80). Teddy tries to claim that there was no ulterior motive, that he did it simply because he was hungry, but Lenny is determined to construe it as an act of spite, 'unequivocal' and certainly not outside his province. But Teddy rises neither to this provocation nor to what is then proposed to Ruth.

Ruth, by contrast, has already declared her affiliation to that which is equivocal and ambiguous in the family, in picking up the discussion about the table:

Don't be too sure though. You've forgotten something. Look at

me. I . . . move my leg. That's all there is to it. But I wear . . .
underwear . . . which moves with me . . . it . . . captures your
attention. Perhaps you misinterpret. The action is simple. It's a
leg . . . moving. My lips move. Why don't you restrict . . . your
observations to that? Perhaps the fact that they move is more
significant . . . than the words that come through them. You must
bear that . . . possibility . . . in mind.

(p. 69)

Her analysis of meaning and interpretation is sexually charged
both in the teasing deliberation with which it is conducted and
in its suggestive choice of examples (moving legs, underwear,
lips); but it is only in her next line — 'I was born quite near here'
— that we begin to see this in the context of the family, of the
possibility (meaning being so slippery) that this is *her*
homecoming rather than Teddy's. She is, in effect, a
reincarnation of the dead mother, the structure of the house,
and she speaks the family's language in a way that Teddy refuses
to do: 'You're just objects', he insists. 'You just . . . move about.
I can observe it. I can see what you do. It's the same as I do. But
you're lost in it. You won't get me being . . . I won't be lost in it'
(p. 78).

So Teddy speaks, as it were, for the rational faculties of the
audience, which view the strange and morally repugnant world
of this family essentially from the outside. But Ruth speaks for
something more basic and intuitive within us, which is more
intrigued and tantalised than offended: she voices the part of
ourselves that recognises itself in these primitive emotions.
'This thing of darkness I acknowledge mine', says Prospero of
Caliban in *The Tempest*. In true tragicomic style, *The
Homecoming* does not choose one over the other, but poses the
middle-mode, dual perspective of both options at once (though
Ruth's presence is overwhelmingly the most significant item in
the closing moments of the play). Teddy's homecoming has
been a frigid, nervous affair. Hers has been smooth,
provocatively charged, ultimately dominating. He returns to the
'normal' world and their children; she remains behind, both a
whore and a kind of goddess/mother, the centre of the closing
tableau. The ritual is complete; the spirits of jealousy and un-
faith have been exorcised in this departure and her
'resurrection'. It is a grotesque parody of the 'rebirth' of

Hermione's statue and the rediscovery of Perdita, an image of the dark things that flow beneath our sexual natures, beyond reason and comprehension.

6

Rosencrantz and Guildenstern Are Dead,
by Tom Stoppard*

Rosencrantz and Guildenstern Are Dead is strikingly similar in many respects to *Waiting for Godot*; indeed, it has widely been criticised for being too obviously derivative from the earlier play.[14] Rosencrantz and Guildenstern, for example, look suspiciously like reworkings of Estragon and Vladimir, not only in being little, ineffectual people, pawns in someone else's game, but even in their broad characterisations. Guildenstern resembles Vladimir in being a would-be intellectual, a worrier who wants to explain things rationally, as in his grapplings with the laws of probability and his outrage at the idea that mere theatricals can cope with the reality of death. Rosencrantz is more like Estragon, more interested in the physical and emotional dimensions of a problem, as for example in his one long speech (pp. 50-2), where he tries to imagine being dead and buried; he is a big slow on the uptake — note how long it takes him to pick up the sexual innuendo of the Player's offer of a performance — and always more likely to follow than to lead. As he pathetically puts it, 'I can't think of anything original. I'm only good in support' (p. 75). The action of the play also has a familiar shape to it: long periods of waiting, in which Rosencrantz and Guildenstern discuss their situation but never really come to terms with it, punctuated by interruptions from other characters, which the two principals sometimes dread and sometimes long for. The two plays are both tragicomedies in that everything within them is subsumed to the end of making sense of the strange and perplexing situation in which their principal characters find themselves.

But there are also major differences, which give *Rosencrantz*

---

*First performed, Edinburgh, 1966; in its final form, London, 1967 *and Guildenstern Are Dead* a life and tone of its own. All the most obvious ones are announced in the title, which is a quotation from *Hamlet*, a line from the rather stunned postcript to the multiple on-stage deaths which comprise the climax of Shakespeare's tragedy. In that context, it is almost an irrelevance, an afterthought to the real action, which audiences scarcely grace with their attention. In Stoppard's play, it becomes the *only* relevant fact, beside which everything else is unreal. Rosencrantz and Guildenstern are not waiting: they are dead. There is no uncertainty about the outcome of this play, except perhaps about its precise manner. Rosencrantz and Guildenstern are as dead as two people who never lived can be, since the fact of it is firmly enshrined in the most famous play in the English language. The whole play is an attempt to make sense of that fact, to give it a meaning.

In *Waiting for Godot*, Beckett invests the central dilemma of the play, the wait, with a wide range of terms of reference: Christian theology, classical mythology, even the occasional allusion to Shakespeare and other artists. These do not necessarily explain what is going on, but they help us to make a sense of it by offering us a perspective from which to view it, a useful analogy. Stoppard effectively denies himself such a range of reference, relegating mythology and religion to the level of Rosencrantz's half-hearted jokes about 'A Christian, a Moslem and a Jew' and 'a Hindu, a Buddhist and a lion-tamer' (p. 51). The only effective terms of reference are those provided by *Hamlet* itself, which becomes a kind of total mythology. We are effectively warned that this will be the case in the opening moments of the play, when Guildenstern gropes in his memory for something he once heard: 'The law of probability, it has been oddly asserted, is something to do with the proposition that if six monkeys < . . . > if six monkeys were' (p. 8). At this point he gets lost, conflating the heads and tails of monkeys with those of the coins which they are spinning, and which keep landing 'heads' with disquieting regularity. (This confusion, incidentally, is a model of what passes for rational thought in the play.) The odd proposition, in fact was that if six monkeys were left typing indefinitely, one of them would — quite randomly and by chance — eventually write *Hamlet*, word for word. The point of the proposition, which (as Guildenstern observes) is not 'a particularly rewarding speculation', relates to the difference between things done deliberately, or by genius, as opposed to occurring by sheer chance: it is hence a metaphor for the difference between a universe governed by a purposeful providence, or God, and one at the mercy of pure accident (a critical difference, of course, for Rosencrantz and Guildenstern). The further relevance of the proposition here lies in drawing attention to the, as it were, mythological status of *Hamlet* as a work of art, the dramatic equivalent of the *Mona Lisa*, which is customarily cited as the apogee of human endeavour in this sort and as a result enjoys a kind of existence independent of itself. *Hamlet* is famous for being a famous play, even to people who have never seen or read it. Stoppard continually capitalises on that fact in his efforts to give a meaningful existence to two of its least distinguished characters. Where Hamlet the Dane is an unmistakable figure from countless performances, parodies and folklore, Rosencrantz and Guildenstern are so anonymous as to be repeatedly mistaken for each other — even, at times, by themselves. The contrast could hardly be more complete.

But there is also another sense in which *Hamlet* provides the terms of reference by which we may begin to make sense of Rosencrantz and Guildenstern's dilemma. Of all Shakespeare's tragedies, it is the one which most clearly evokes the heroic pattern of separation, initiation and return.[15] Tragedy calls upon this pattern as well as tragicomedy, but with important differences: where tragicomedy tries to give a distanced, middle-mood overview, in which individual characters are seen to operate more or less blindly within a providential process, tragedy charateristically focuses on events from the perspective of the central heroic figure. His position and personality are of much more obvious significance here, and the climax of the play is invariably his private appointment with destiny — an appointment which usually (e.g. Dr. Faustus, Macbeth) but not always (e.g. Oedipus) results in death. Tragedy thus emphasises the pain and suffering of experience, concentrating heavily on the *separation* phase of the heroic cycle, but it does also characteristically *imply* the initiation and return phases. The great tragic heroes are allowed uncommon insights into the mysteries of life and providence (even though, like Faustus and

Macbeth, they may not be strong enough to use them virtuously) and the deaths or intense sufferings they undergo generally carry with them a promise that it has not all been in vain, that the future will be better for those who survive. This is why the great tragedies do not seem totally pessimistic or irredeemably gloomy in performance.

So it is with Hamlet, who is cast in the heroic mould, a courtier, soldier, scholar or complete Renaissance man, as Ophelia indicates.[16] But at the outset of the play he is already a man apart from the rest of Danish society, a misfit, as his black clothes and strange behaviour indicate. The message of the Ghost — that his father has been murdered, by the new King, Claudius — only exacerbates his isolation; Horatio is the one he can talk to, but his sceptical stoicism is not profound enough to tackle the realms of knowledge with which Hamlet is obliged to struggle: 'There are more things in heaven and earth, Horatio,/ Than are dreamt of in your philosophy' (I.v. 166-7). Perhaps mad and perhaps not, he fails to kill the King but kills Polonius instead. Being a royal prince, he is not executed for this but sent into exile in England (where, however, Claudius secretly plans to have him killed). Everything is thrown into confusion, however, by the providential intervention of the pirates, which sends Hamlet back to Denmark and destiny — and his escort of Rosencrantz and Guildernstern on to England where, with a little help from Hamlet, they meet the fate Claudius planned for him. The pirate scene is not shown in the play but is reported, firstly by letter and then in person, by Hamlet to Horatio (V.i. and V.ii.); this is tantalising, because the whole experience seems to have had a fundamental effect on Hamlet. When he first returns, there is no obvious change: the grim witticisms over Yorick's skull and his passionate affray at Ophelia's funeral might be the old Hamlet, but it soon appears (directly, in fact, after his fuller account of the events on board ship) that there has been a major change. Before, he was a man at odds with himself, moody and impetuous, unsure of himself or passionately convinced, unable to bring all the parts of his personality together; now he has a quiet conviction, an ability to see events and his own part in them with philosophical detachment: 'We defy augury. There is special providence in the fall of a sparrow. If it be now, 'tis not to come; if it be not to come, it will be now; if it be not now, yet it will come. The readiness is all' (V.ii 208-11). The experience on the boat, in short, had been what Joseph Campbell would call an *initiation*, an experience bordering on death in which Hamlet saw deeply into the mystery of things, and from which he returned with an almost mystic faith. This being tragedy rather than tragicomedy, this experience does not bring unequivocal blessings; it precipitates the final catastrophe, but out of that something positive may arise. Hamlet's new conviction allows him to take part in the duel, which leads to the death of Claudius, but also of Laertes, his mother and himself. Denmark has paid a terrible price for its redemption, but it is free of a wicked King and may look forward to an assured future under Fortinbras.

So the relationship of *Rosencrantz and Guildenstern Are Dead* to *Hamlet* is two-fold. On the one hand, Stoppard exploits the over-familiarity of Shakespeare's play, and its associated 'mythology', often to comic effect; on the other, the central dilemma of the two principal characters is always implicitly being measured against the genuine tragic heroic pattern embodied in the figure of Hamlet, in ways analogous to the use of Biblical and classical allusions in *Waiting for Godot*. The shifts in tone in the play, from a kind of flippant irreverence about *Hamlet* to a deadly seriousness, largely account for the disconcerting quality of *Rosencrantz and Guildenstern Are Dead*. We can see this, for example, in the actual picture of Hamlet — a very partial and biased one — that Stoppard chooses to give us. The early scenes in which he appears are absurdly melodramatic by twentieth-century standards, as the stage directions imply simply by sticking to the Elizabethan language of the original: '*Hamlet, with his doublet all unbraced, no hat upon his head, his stockings fouled, ungartered and downgyved to his ankle, pale as his shirt, his knees knocking each other . . . etc.*' (p. 25). Nobody today would even know what 'downgyved' meant were it not for this very use in *Hamlet*. This scene is not actually staged by Shakespeare, but is reported by Ophelia, so this introduction to the great tragic hero is a classic example of the Player's maxim about 'every exit being an entrance somewhere else' (p. 20) and takes us unawares in several senses: without the careful preparation that Shakespeare gives for Hamlet's performance as the distraught, melancholy lover, it cannot but appear ludicrously histrionic. It is the behaviour of a man from another time and different conventions. Similarly, *'Hamlet enters upstage, and pauses, weighing up the pros and cons of making his quietus'* (p. 53) — an oddly arch way of saying that he is contemplating suicide, which is only possible because of the extreme familiarity of the 'To be or not to be' soliloquy. It is a clear invitation to the actor to ham it up as much as possible, so that we almost *have* to take this dumb-show version of the famous speech as parodic: we cannot take this man and his problems seriously. It is all rather comfortably from another time and place, which we can treat rather condescendingly.

But even by the beginning of Act 2, there are hints that it may not all be quite so simple. On Claudius' orders, Rosencrantz and Guildenstern have engaged Hamlet in conversation, trying to get to the bottom of his odd behaviour. The interview proves worse than useless:

> *Rosencrantz: (simply)* He murdered us.
> *Guildenstern:* He might have had the edge.
> *Rosencrantz: (roused)* Twenty-seven — three, and you think he might have had the edge?! He *murdered* us.
>
> (p. 40)

The force of these words depends upon a very sophisticated use of dramatic irony: the reason, of course, that Rosencrantz and Guildenstern *are* dead is that, to all intents and purposes, Hamlet *did* murder them. More immediately, however, they also depend upon a tacit assumption all round that Hamlet here is not simply a joke or a hangover from another age. The whole point is that Hamlet played the two of them at their own game, as equals. The kind of witty word-play with which Hamlet banteringly engages them (in *Hamlet* II.ii.) matches the verbal games they have been playing themselves while waiting for things to happen (e.g. pp. 30-1), except that he does it so much better than they do. So, when Rosencrantz says, 'Half of what he said meant something else, and the other half didn't mean anything at all' (p. 40), he is not joining the ranks of modern critics bemused about the problem of Hamlet's real or supposed madness: he is expressing admiration for someone who speaks their own language better than they do. If the kind of verbal games that Rosencrantz and Guildenstern might be said to have inherited from Vladimir and Estragon are a sign of modernity, then Hamlet is one of the moderns — murderously so, in fact.

This is confirmed chillingly in the final act, when Stoppard stages the most crucial of all scenes that Shakespeare only reports — crucial both to Hamlet's state of mind and to the fate of Rosencrantz and Guildenstern — the events on board ship. The Hamlet we see here is suddenly very much of our time: '*Beneath the re-tilted umbrella, reclining in a deck-chair, wrapped in a rug, reading a book, possibly smoking, sits Hamlet*' (pp. 80-1). It is pointedly anachronistic; the umbrella is described as gaudy and striped, '*one of those huge six-foot diameter jobs*' (p. 72) which, like deck-chairs, were not a feature of Elizabethan sea-voyages. Given Hamlet's furtive activity with the letters a moment before this description, it is a scene we might recognise from modern spy- or detective-fiction rather than Renaissance tragedy; it underlines the fact that this is no longer a joke, that Hamlet stripped of the familiar histrionics is to be taken very seriously indeed. His last significant action in the play — spitting into the audience/wind — sums up the serio-comic role he plays throughout. At first it must seem a facetious gesture to have the great tragic hero spit at the audience; when, '*a split second later he claps his hand to his eye and wipes himself*' (p. 84) it suddenly turns into a schoolboy joke, a standard moment from farcical mimes or music-hall routines. But when we examine the moment in context, it is really none of these things. Rosencrantz and Guildenstern have just been preening themselves about their freedom of manoeuvre:

> *Guildenstern:* . . . We can relax. We can do what we like and say what we like to whomever we like, without restriction.
> *Rosencrantz:* Within limits, of course.
> *Guildenstern:* Certainly within limits.

Hamlet's spitting into the wind is a graphic demonstration of the natural limits within which man is actually enclosed, however much he may be inclined to ignore or defy them. Looked at another way, his spitting into the *audience* is a severe test of analogous limits which similarly restrict art. It would be offensive for any character in a play actually to spit into the audience — but for Hamlet the Dane to do it is unthinkable —

Stoppard would be pushing his embroidery of the Hamlet text myth too far. Hamlet just does not do that sort of thing — which is why Stoppard not only can, but *has* to turn it into a joke, albeit a pointed one. Art, like nature, is governed by limits, rules, laws: this is a fact that the parallels between *Hamlet* and *Rosencrantz and Guildenstern Are Dead* insist upon continually, taking us by metaphor to the heart of the dilemma in which Rosencrantz and Guildenstern find themselves.

The metaphor is the idea of acting: in what ways is it real, and in what ways an illusion, and how do the two relate to each other? What are the laws that determine whether it is done properly or not? These questions parallel the problem of the kind of existence, or non-existence, that Rosencrantz and Guildenstern have: they are, after all, characters in two different plays simultaneously, and so the nature of dramatic art must be central to determining the kind of identity they have. The issue always arises in its most pointed form when the Player and his tragedians appear and discuss the nature of their profession. In their first appearance (pp. 15-24), the running motif is drama as a kind of prostitution — the actors allowing themselves, for a price, to perform any role that will entertain their audience. This is signalled in a succession of broad nuances mainly for the benefit of Rosencrantz, who is slow on the uptake in such matters:

> *Player*: . . . we can do you rapiers or rape or both, by all means, faithless wives and ravished virgins — flagrante delicto at a price, but that comes under realism for which there are special terms. Getting warm, am I?
>
> *Rosencrantz*: (*doubtfully*) Well, I don't know . . .
>
> *Player*: It costs little to watch, and little more if you happen to get caught up in the action, if that's your taste and times being what they are.
>
> (pp. 16-17)

It is particularly striking that the terms normally used for discussing dramatic credibility and audience response — 'realism', 'get caught up in the action' — mark the dividing line between pornography and actual prostitution; the actors can provide forms of lewd entertainment that will do well enough, but for something really convincing, something that will really involve the audience, they have to sell themselves completely. This is clearly relevant to Rosencrantz and Guildenstern on more than one level: in terms of the story of *Hamlet* they go to their deaths because, in Hamlet's eyes, they have committed a kind of political prostitution, selling their friendship with him for Claudius' gold — and even enjoying it: 'Why, man, they did make love to this employment' (V.ii. 57). Stoppard's version does not endorse the charge in these terms. They do receive money from Claudius, though whether it is 'such thanks as fits a king's remembrance' (p. 29) is never apparent; but money never seems to interest them, except as something to play games with (e.g. pp. 9-11, 74). But perhaps in a broader sense there is some truth in the accusation. As human beings, they constantly allow themselves to be used; they are so unsure about what is going on at all that they never pause to consider the morality of their own parts in it. There is never any question of objecting on ethical grounds to the assignments which Claudius gives them. In that sense, the charge of prostitution does not entirely miss the mark. They may be covered by the old excuse of only being little men obeying orders, but how valid has that excuse ever been?

The nearness of the charge may explain Guildenstern's furious response to almost becoming involved in Alfred's one-man performance of the Rape of the Sabine Women, when he hits the Player across the face: 'It could have been — it didn't have to be *obscene* . . . It could have been — a bird out of season, dropping bright-feathered on my shoulder < . . . > But it's this, is it? No enigma, no dignity, nothing classical, portentous, only this — a comic pornographer and a rabble of prostitutes' (p. 19). It would presumably have suited his conscience or his vanity better to be caught up in something 'classical, portentous', and this prompts him to demand, as his forfeit for the lost bet, the performance of a genuine play from the tragedians, and this shifts the discussion of dramatic art into another key. The Player announces that his troupe belongs to 'the blood, love and rhetoric school', running through the permutations of style this allows but concluding:

> Blood is compulsory — they're all blood, you see.
> *Guildenstern:* Is that what people want?
> *Player:* It's what we do.
>
> (p. 23)

The tyranny of the audience, it seems, is not all-consuming. In some respects, at least, the actors are constrained by forces over which neither they nor the audience have any control. But before the implications of this can be explored, the first scenes from *Hamlet* catch up with Rosencrantz and Guildenstern, carrying them away from the tragedians. Is this perhaps a graphic underlining of the inexorable laws both of life and of art?

The next time the Player speaks, he is furious at what he sees as their betrayal: 'We're actors . . . We pledged our identities, secure in the conventions of our trade; that someone would be watching. And then, gradually, no one was' (p. 46). Whether an actor prostitutes himself or not to an audience, he needs them to give him an identity: 'We're *actors* — we're the opposite of people' (p. 45). 'People' are secure in their own personalities, but an actor only creates one in the illusion that he offers to an audience. Again, the application of this to Rosencrantz and Guildenstern is clear enough: they have no solo identities at all, but only exist in relation to the performance they put on firstly for each other and secondly for the characters who intrude on them from *Hamlet*. Rosencrantz's increasingly desperate efforts to 'please' Guildenstern in the final act are a measure of this: he cannot offer anything original or self-sustaining but is pathetically anxious to keep the performance going. The constant confusion about which of them is which is thus more than a joke: they are hollow men, only kept going by a degree of self-consciousness about that fact and by a determination (like the Player) to preserve any self-respect they can in the face of it.

It is for this reason that the nature of performance itself, and of the kinds of illusion to which it gives rise, is of particular importance to the two of them:

Guildenstern: What is the dumbshow for?
Player: Well, it's a device, really — it makes the action that follows more or less comprehensible: you understand, we are tied down to a language which makes up in obscurity what it lacks in style.

(p. 56)

The Player accepts as a matter of course that their lives and their art are indistinguishably governed by devices, conventions, rules and laws; this is what gives their existence meaning and purpose: 'We're tragedians, you see. We follow directions — there is no *choice* involved. The bad end happily, the good unluckily. That is what tragedy means' (p. 58). The fact that this is a parody of Oscar Wilde's already parodic definition of fiction in *The Importance of Being Earnest* only reinforces the Player's argument, that it is pointless, indeed even possibly in bad taste, to so much as question the rules of art — they are so pervasively accepted and acceptable. Hence his disdain for the actor who was condemned for stealing a sheep and actually hanged during one of their performances: 'he did nothing but cry all the time — right out of character — just stood there and cried' (p. 61). To be out of character in this sense is the worst loss of dignity he can imagine. This whole discussion takes place against a background of passionate scenes from *Hamlet* and a rehearsal of the dumb-show from *The Murder of Gonzago* ('The Mousetrap' in Shakespeare's play); the latter runs beyond what Shakespeare shows, to include a mime of the deaths of Rosencrantz and Guildenstern themselves, so that the relationship of art, life and performance ceases to be academic and focuses directly on the nature of *their* performances. And they struggle against the Player's conformist, determinist version of things: 'No, no, no . . . you've got it all wrong . . . you can't act death', says Guildenstern (p. 61).

The difference between them is not only a question of style; it ultimately boils down to the nature of freedom and of the dignity associated with it. The Player is happy enough that the script of his life 'is written' (p. 58), and that he has some modest leeway for interpretation: 'Between "just deserts" and "tragic irony" we are given quite a lot of scope for our particular talents.' But Rosencrantz and Guildenstern spend the greater part of the play looking for more freedom than that, for a fundamental capacity to take control of their own lives: or perhaps it would be truer to say that they spend most of the play *assuming* that this ought to exist. Art and freedom are thus inextricably mixed issues, as Guildenstern's early parable of the unicorn demonstrates (pp. 14-15). One witness sees a unicorn — something miraculous, against the laws of nature. A second witness only *thinks* he sees a unicorn and assumes he must be dreaming — a scepticism that destroys the miracle and starts the inexorable process of reducing it to a rational explanation: "'Look, look!" recites the crowd. "A horse with an arrow in its forehead! It must have been mistaken for a deer.'" The view of experience 'as thin as reality' in which unicorns are horses with arrows in their heads (for very good reasons) is essentially that of the Player who assumes that everything does and should operate according to comprehensible rules and laws — the essence of realism. What Rosencrantz and Guildenstern keep hoping for is a world in which unicorns actually exist, miracles can happen — and they can be free of the apparently inexorable laws that restrict them.

It is Rosencrantz in particular who keeps giving voice to this cheerful possibility: 'The only thing that makes it bearable is the irrational belief that somebody interesting will come on in a minute . . .' (p. 30). Nobody does, however, for quite some time. Later, when perhaps a few too many interesting people have been and gone, he changes tack: 'Keep out, then! I forbid anyone to enter! (*No one comes — Breathing heavily*) That's better . . . (*Immediately, behind him a grand procession enters . . .*)' (p. 52). At the end of Act 2, he is still undaunted: 'And besides, anything could happen yet' (p. 69). All the time he is looking for something surprising, unexpected, out of the ordinary, which would reinforce the possibility that he and Guildenstern *might* be able to act on their own initiative (which would be surprising enough in this world) — and so with the kind of dignity that independence confers. But, for all his enthusiasm, he is consistently proved wrong: nobody interesting comes when he wants them, everybody does when he does not, and nothing really could be farther from the truth than that 'anything' might happen yet. None of this categorically denies the possibility of freedom and control over one's own affairs but, like their coin-tossing, it suggests that the odds are very long indeed; as the Player later puts it, 'Life is a gamble at terrible odds' (p. 83). The more introspective Guildenstern identifies a further dimension to the problem: 'If we start being arbitrary, it'll just be a shambles; at least, let us hope so. Because if we happened, just happened to discover, or even suspect, that our spontaneity was part of their order, we'd know that we were lost' (pp. 42-43). The worry is that all the apparent freedom in the world — such as the freedom of a live performance before an audience — may only be an illusion, a playing into the hands of destiny just at the moment when it seemed possible to avoid it.

While Rosencrantz and Guildenstern continue to worry and fret about the freedom (and hence dignity) of their performances, some possibility of a miraculous intervention seems possible. But in the third act the odds swing increasingly against it: the tones of autumn and of evening point to a bleak inevitability, which is clinched by Guildenstern's reaction to the discovery that the letter they are carrying is meant to consign Hamlet to his death: 'Or to look at it another way — we are little men, we don't know the ins and outs of the matter, there are wheels within wheels, etcetera — it would be presumptuous of us to interfere with the designs of fate or even of kings. All in all, I think we'd be well advised to leave well alone' (p. 80). This is all the more striking because it was not necessary for Stoppard to include such an admission. Hamlet seems convinced that Rosencrantz and Guildenstern knew the full implications of their English mission, but Shakespeare leaves open the possibility that this is only self-justification after cold-bloodedly sending his former friends to their deaths. That is, they may only have been naive and not wicked, so that Stoppard *could* have played on our sympathy for two ingenuous pawns caught up in a very nasty game of chess. In fact, he confronts them — and us — with the moral responsibility for not acting to prevent something that they knew to be wrong. They bleat about its unfairness but in the end 'leave well alone' (a particularly unfortunate turn of phrase), pleading by way of extenuation the very argument that they have spent the whole play trying to deny — that they are little men, caught up in the wheels of fate, with no real choice in the matter . . . .. It is an ironic situation in several respects because, in the version of events that Stoppard chooses to give us, the decision not to do or say anything here is what effectively gets them killed. Had they actually warned Hamlet, he would have had no reason to switch the letters as he did, consigning them to their deaths. Of course, they would presumably still have to die as reported at the end of *Hamlet*, but not as an outcome of their own culpability; it is most poignant that they meet the fate they do as the result of specific inaction on their own part, which effectively disproves all their own fears about predestination, even as they lamely submit to them.

These ironies continue to the very end, in their reactions to the disappearance of Hamlet and to the fake death of the Player. Regarding the former, Guildenstern moans, 'Nothing will be resolved without him < . . . > We need Hamlet for our release!' (p. 87). It is as if they have belatedly come to see Hamlet as a Godot figure, a hero-redeemer who promises the happy-ever-after resolution which they cannot shape for themselves. But by this time they have lost track of the Hamlet they think they know; he is no longer the parodic figure of the early scenes, but a desperately serious actor who has in fact decided that everything so far as they are concerned *will* be resolved without him. He has already ensured their 'release'. Guildenstern's attack on the Player (when they know about the switching of the letters) is one last, hysterical attempt to find freedom, the antithesis of the Player's settled rules and conventions, in a situation where they do not appreciate that they have trapped themselves:

> If we have a destiny, then so had he — and if this is ours, then that was his — and if there are no explanations for us, then let there be none for him —
>
> (p. 89)

The fact that it proves to be a trick knife and that the Player stands up again to take the applause of his fellows makes a mockery of all Rosencrantz and Guildenstern's pretensions to freedom, to be somehow outside the rules, and they subside into very self-conscious theatrical exits, which the conventions of the play have led us to equate with their deaths:

> *Rosencrantz*: I've had enough. To tell you the truth, I'm relieved. [Perhaps echoing Francisco's famous line at the opening of *Hamlet*, 'For this relief, much thanks'].
> *Guildenstern*: Well, we'll know better next time. Now you see me, now you —
>
> (p. 91)

Guildenstern, as usual, poses the right questions with his farewell, but fails to come up with the right answers. 'We'll know better next time' is a grim piece of gallows humour from a man on the way to his death, but it is also the never-say-die optimism of an actor at the end of a dreadful performance looking forward to the following night. 'Now you see me, now you —' is a piece of facetious stage magic, a line that properly belongs to a master of illusion, not to its slave. This has all the self-conscious art and self-cancelling irony of the tradition of modern tragicomedy stemming from *Waiting for Godot*: the bewildered little men, caught up in a pattern of great events and hoping for redemption or enlightenment, retaining their dignity and the audience's sympathy by seeing things through, even achieving a kind of heroism in their sheer perseverance. In many ways, this is what we might expect of a modern fable based on *Hamlet*; the heroes of Renaissance tragedy started out so much bigger than life, and even if they were enmeshed in a web of fate, there was never any reason to doubt that they had the force of character to contribute something personal to the outcome. Hamlet may die, and half the Danish Court with him, but not before he has the satisfaction of knowing that he has killed Claudius at last. Modern men, such as Rosencrantz and Guildenstern prove to be, do not have that strength of personality: they wait, they suffer, they try to understand, they do not act. The modern world is too complex a place, too aware of the limitations on free will, too unsure of man's ultimate value, to be capable of genuine heroism.

But there is something a little too glib about this view of things, a little too convenient about the way that Rosencrantz and Guildenstern are always able to see themselves as innocent victims, realistically aware of their limitations, and Stoppard points this up too. Just before Rosencrantz's farewell line, he cries, 'We've done nothing wrong! We didn't harm anyone. Did we?' And just before Guildenstern's facetious exit, he muses: 'There must have been a moment, at the beginning, when we could have said — no. But somehow we missed it.' Both lines take us back to the discovery that they were taking Hamlet to his death and their failure to do anything about it. No, they did not harm anyone, they have not done anything wrong — except as sins of omission. There *was* a moment, albeit not at the beginning, when they *could* have said — no. And they did not miss it; they deliberately let it slip by, with fatal consequences for themselves. It is this above all that distinguishes *Rosencrantz and Guildenstern Are Dead* from *Waiting for Godot* and the classic pattern of modern tragicomedy: a moment of practical moral choice, when the characters were able to see the issues clearly and able to do *something* about them for themselves, however limited the net effect might be. But they chose not to, chose rather to believe that it was not their place to do anything. It is characteristic of Stoppard's work that for all he explores the possibility of a determinist universe, governed by a capricious or even malicious fate, he never totally endorses it. Bewildering, complex and paradoxical his tragicomic world may be, but not so complex that — even for the Rosencrantz and Guildensterns of the world — there may not be some place for moral choice, for an assertion of human decency.

7
Home
by David Storey*

David Storey is not usually associated with the so-called absurdist tradition of British drama. The theme of alienation that runs through his plays and novels clearly has associations with the varieties of distorted communication and emotional antagonism that we find, say, in the plays of Pinter. But Storey's depiction of alienated characters usually blends with an analysis of the social conditions which helped to make them the way they are — the British class system, for example, is often a prominent issue. And this is not characteristic of the works of Beckett or Pinter. Nevertheless, in *Home*, Storey struck a balance which puts the play firmly in a line with the works of those dramatists. The play indicates the appeal of modern tragicomic form at this time, even for a writer for whom it was not an habitual mode.

By the standards of the more enigmatic works of Beckett and Pinter, *Home* is not an unduly perplexing play. We can make adequate sense of it scene by scene. Yet the characters and the situation in which they are fixed retain certain mysteries to the end. The opening scene is typical in this respect, and sets the mode. The conversation between Jack and Harry is a standard piece of modern, naturalistic dialogue, brief interchanges, with frequent hesitations, deviations and one character often anticipating the other. The only hint of artifice lies in the fluency with which it is kept up:

Harry:	*My* wife was coming up this morning.
Jack:	Really?
Harry:	Slight headache. Thought might be better . . .
Jack:	Indoors. Well. Best make sure.

---

*First performed, London, 1970

151

Harry:	When I was in the army . . .
Jack:	Really? What regiment?
Harry:	Fusiliers.
Jack:	Really? How extraordinary.
Harry:	You?
Jack:	No. No. A cousin.
Harry:	Well . . .
Jack:	Different time, of course.
Harry:	Ah.
Jack:	Used to bring his rifle . . . No. That was Arthur. Got them muddled. (*Laughs*)
Harry:	Still.
Jack:	Never leaves you.
Harry:	No. No.
Jack:	In good stead.
Harry:	Oh, yes.
Jack:	All your life.
Harry:	Oh, yes.
Jack:	I was — for a very short while — in the Royal Air Force.
Harry:	Really?
Jack:	Nothing to boast about.
Harry:	Oh, now. Flying?
Jack:	On the ground.
Harry:	Chrysanthemums is my wife's hobby.

(pp. 14-15)

It is only when we look at such a sustained passage as a whole that we may begin to suspect that all is not as it seems to be, that the words do not say what they seem to. On the surface, everything is polite deference and mutual concern between the speakers. Yet the constant stab of 'Really?' to so many of the statements they both make gives us cause to doubt both the spirit of what is said and its truthfulness. 'Really?' is ostensibly an expression of polite interest, an invitation to continue, but repeated too often it can take on a sarcastic edge of incredulity. It is never quite clear on which side of the line it falls in the conversation of Jack and Harry — perhaps ambiguously on the line itself. There is some evidence, however, that each regards the 'Really?' of the other as something of a challenge and reacts by toning down or steering away from the implications of his original statement. So Harry's claim that *his* wife was coming up (a response to an earlier discussion of Jack's wife) has to be shuffled off with a lame excuse about a headache. The fact is that she had *not* come and Jack will not overlook it: her very existence remains unproven and Harry will not gain some obscure credit simply by mentioning her. The apparently casual introduction of the claim that he had been in the army thus might be construed as an attempt to gain/save face in another sphere, which is challenged in turn by 'What regiment?'. Fusiliers might be the truth or it might be a bluff — a name picked out of the blue for effect — so that Jack's 'How extraordinary' carries the challenge a stage further, but only by implying a claim of his own, which might equally be a bluff and which Harry calls with his 'You?' (effectively a variant of 'Really?'). At this point, if indeed they have been bluffing, Jack backs down, invoking one of the many well-connected (but unverifiable) relations, who pepper his conversation. He even covers his tracks further by throwing in 'Different time, of course' — obviating any serious discussion of names and places — even though he does not actually know when Harry might have been in the army. The 'used to bring his rifle' remark and its attendant confusions thus sounds like an attempt to salvage *something* — an association with the army, though nothing too precise. This may be an unnecessarily jaundiced reading of the passage, but it is striking that the same formula recurs, though with the shoe on the other foot, when Jack claims to have been in the R.A.F. Any possible advantage that might derive from this claim is rapidly scotched — indeed grounded — by his partner's response. The word 'ground' itself gives the cue for the most marked deviation of all — from the R.A.F. to chrysanthemums. The charitable explanation of this — as of so much else in their conversation — would be that it is a random association made by an old man (though Harry is described as 'a middle-aged man in his forties'. p. 11); less charitably, we might construe it as a firm stamping on Jack's attempt to make capital out of the R.A.F. and in turn to regain some of the *kudos* he lost in the earlier effort to introduce his wife into the conversation.

In short, the passages rides a very fine line between polite but aimless conversation and a tacit game of verbal chess, with every feint matched by an appropriate challenge, though neither player feels confident enough to launch a forthright attack. The further the scene goes, the more evidence we accumulate in favour of the latter reading. Towards the end, for example, Jack says:

> I don't think I've met your wife.
>
> *Harry*: No. No . . . As a matter of fact. We've been separated for a little while.
>
> (p. 36)

This could be a gambit like any other — we have no corroboration — but it is very difficult to square with the earlier claim that his wife 'was coming up this morning'. The contradiction only confirms suspicions that he is lying, or at best embroidering the truth, at least some of the time. The same may be said of Marjorie's implication that Harry is an arsonist: 'Burn the whole bleedin' building, he will. Given up smoking because they won't let him have any matches' (p. 50). This casts a ghoulish hindsight on Harry's claim to be a 'heating engineer' (p. 35) and may even cause us to wonder as to the circumstances in which he 'separated' from his wife. But then Marjorie is not a particularly reliable witness and, if we assume that Harry is consistently making things up, we have also to take into account the fact that Jack matches him throughout, virtually claim for claim. There are 'explanations' for Jack too. Kathleen asks: 'Your friend come in for following little girls?' to which Harry hesitantly replies: 'I believe there were . . . er . . . certain proclivities, shall we say' (p. 58). Marjorie is much blunter:

> | | Girl? |
> |---|---|
> | *Jack*: | Girl? |
> | *Marjorie*: | Girls. |
> | *Jack*: | Girls? |
> | *Marjorie*: | In the street. |
> | *Jack*: | Really? |
>
> (pp. 66-7)

Harry's credibility is already suspect, and he hedges on this question with his 'I believe'. The disingenuousness of Jack's reactions, moreover, suggest that Marjorie could be mistaken, which would be quite in keeping with her fondness for indiscriminate tittle-tattle. On all such critical issues there is no reliable witness to whom we can turn. We are left in each case with innuendoes, suggestions, tacit refutations, and we can do no more than weigh up the balance of possibilities.

This is true not only of specific details about the characters but of the play as a whole. Beneath its naturalistic surface, *Home* is a tissue of innuendo and suggestion, centring on ambiguities in its title that are never fully resolved. For all we are told in the first scene, the characters might well be in a rest home (Jack explains that he has 'Been laid up for a few days', p. 12) or even a seaside hotel — something large enough to explain the number of people Jack and Harry see (though we do not) and the slightly institutional metalwork furniture which constitutes the set. If the title has any resonance at all, it perhaps focuses attention on the 'homes' that Jack and Harry have left for no very apparent reason; much of their conversation focuses on wives, families and the surrogate families provided by the armed forces. The second scene, however, forces us to think again. Kathleen's claim that 'they' have taken her laced shoes — 'Thought I'd hang myself, didn't they?' (p. 39) — and her references to having been in 'this other place' suggest very strongly that they are in some form of mental institution and that they may not be there of their own free will: 'Were you the feller they caught climbing out of a window here last week?' (p. 48). These suggestions are intensified in Act 2, with frequent references to doctors, 'Remedials' and 'the padded whatsit' (p. 67). They seem to be clinched in the figure of Alfred, of whom Marjorie says: 'Thinks he's at home, he does < . . . > Took a bit of his brain, haven't they?' (p. 69). The running together of 'home' and lobotomy comes as close as anything to fixing this play in a mental asylum. But nothing in the action or scenery of the play ever renders the issue unequivocal. We see no doctors, nurses or details of the institution. No one does or says anything which is unambiguously insane.

Storey himself has described *Home* as 'a play which, halfway through the writing, I discovered was taking place in a lunatic asylum'.[17] But I take this to be an example of the disingenuousness which seems to afflict all writers in the tragicomic mode when discussing their works.[18] A structure which introduces us successively to two characters who — mainly with the benefit of hindsight — we may say are 'possibly' insane, two more who are 'probably insane' and one who is 'certainly' insane inevitably calls into question the whole definition of insanity. Yet it does so in the obliquest and least tendentious way. The fact that we know so little for certain about the characters and their past histories makes it impossible for use to pass judgement on them as individual cases. And although there are references to a 'they' who control things, the emphasis never falls on the ethics or politics of psychiatric treatment as it does, say, in Ken Kesey's *One Flew Over the Cuckoo's Nest*, or even Pinter's uncharacterisically explicit early play, *The Hothouse*. Even the dubious practice of lobotomy comes in for no particular comment; the play never takes an overtly critical stance. As with all the other features of the 'home' they inhabit — the food, the furniture, the fact that people hardly speak to one another — the characters simply accept it as a fact of life.

Since the characters' dialogue offers us neither clear-cut factual evidence nor a critical perspective on their lives, we are left to infer what we can about their 'abnormality' from the ways in which they speak. The style of what they say is at least as revealing as the substance. As we noticed earlier, the conversation of Jack and Harry is both spare and ambiguous, a polite game of deferences in which the primary object seems to be to gain as much advantage as possible over the opponent without leaving oneself vulnerable. It is couched impeccably in what used to be known as the Queen's English, though the grammar is often clipped to the bone ('Indoors. Well. Best make sure') because the characters pay each other the mutual compliment — for all their unspoken rivalry — of assuming that they are speaking on the same wavelength, so to speak, sharing the same general attitudes and approaches to life: the attitudes of nostalgic, slightly Blimpish, middle-class Britons. In most respects, the language of Kathleen and Marjorie could hardly be more different; Kathleen repeats 'Cor blimey!' eight times in the first two pages of their dialogue (pp. 38-9), emphatically announcing that they are working-class Cockneys. Their conversation has a gusto which Jack and Harry's never does; this is largely because, rather than looking back over past achievements and family status, they are primarily concerned with the physical realities of the present moment — whether it be the weather, the food, aching feet, Alfred's brain or the sexual potential of the situation (the latter giving rise to a good deal of unsubtle double-entendre and rib-tickling). The contrast between the two couples — broadly the life of the mind and that of the body — thus resembles the pairings of Vladimir and Estragon, Rosencrantz and Guildenstern in the neatness of the symmetry.

The one respect in which the women's dialogue significantly resembles that of the men lies in the mutual assurance of their idiom: they pick up each other's phrases instinctively, turning them to their own advantage in what, at times, is a much more openly antagonistic game of words than that which the men play:

> *Margorie*: Mind she doesn't stroll you to the bushes.
> *Kathleen*: Mind she doesn't splash.
> *Marjorie*: See the doctor about you, my girl!
> *Kathleen*: See him all the time: your trouble. Not right in the head.
> (p. 65)

Both pairs of characters are symbiotically bonded by the kind of language they use, or rather by the social and cultural assumptions that lie behind their linguistic styles. At the same time, however, that bonding is shot through with mutual antagonism, a competitive instinct not to let the other person gain a perceptible advantage. The mixing of the two pairs is inevitably fraught and much of the tension of the play hinges on the question of how the tensions within each relationship will resolve themselves under the new pressures. In the face of the women's ebullience, Jack and Harry retreat ever further into their middle-class correctness, with frequent recourse to the impersonal 'one' construction ('one sees it', 'one says hello', 'one doesn't wish') and statements repeatedly prefaced with a defensive 'oh' ('Oh, yes', 'Oh, now', 'Oh, no' etc.). But the frankness of the women about why people are in the 'home' (which perhaps ought not to be confused with truthfulness) leads Harry in particular to admit things about himself and about Jack ('certain proclivities') which would never figure in their own conversations. On the other hand, it is the presence of the men which brings to the surface the latent competition between the women, as Kathleen's sexual appetite ('Can't keep away from men', p. 66) ceases to be a matter of banter and begins to focus on Harry, to the exclusion of Marjorie. This leaves Jack and Marjorie to a frosty duet which is only saved from collapse by the entrance of Alfred, who deflects any fleeting and embarrassing suggestion of intimacy ('Very rare. Well . . . find someone to communicate', p. 67).

Both attempts at pairings across the sexes and across the classes collapse in embarrassed failure:

Kathleen:	(*to Harry*) Wanna hold my hand?
Marjorie:	Not seen so many tears. Haven't.
Kathleen:	Not since Christmas.
Marjorie:	Not since Christmas, girl.
Kathleen:	Ooooh!
Marjorie	(*to Jack*): You all right?

    (*Jack doesn't answer. Stands stiffly turned away, looking off.*)
        Think you and I better be on our way, girl.

(p. 76)

The men retreat into a characteristic mutual silence, the women into their ebullient double-act. The forces holding together the symbiotic bonds are stronger than those, like sex or mutual antagonism or the need for genuine sympathy, that might break them apart. The sterile implications of this are summed up in the lobotomised figure of Alfred; the only representative of a younger generation, he is virtually monosyllabic, with no active personality, apparently finding some meaning in life through the lifting and moving of the furniture. The stage directions describe how he '*lifts the table up and down ceremoniously*' and '*lowers the table slowly, almost like a ritual*' (p. 55). He parodically underlines the lack of true ceremony or fertile ritual in the lives of the other characters.

When the women have withdrawn, Jack and Harry resume the dialogue with which the play began, though now intermittently under Alfred's gaze. They return to themes they had rehearsed before:

Jack:	That is the nature of this little island.
Harry:	Extraordinary when you think.
Jack:	When you think what came from it.
Harry:	Oh, yes.

Jack:	Radar.
Harry:	Oh, yes.
Jack:	Jet propulsion.
Harry:	My word.
Jack:	Television.
Harry:	Oh . . .
Jack:	Steam-engine.
Harry:	Goodness.
Jack:	Empire the like of which no one has ever seen.
Harry:	No. My word.
Jack:	Light of the world.
Harry:	Oh, yes.
Jack:	Penicillin.
Harry:	Penicillin.
Jack:	Darwin.
Harry:	Darwin.
Jack:	Newton.
Harry:	Newton.
Jack:	Milton.
Harry:	My word.
Jack:	Sir Walter Raleigh.
Harry:	Goodness. Sir . . .
Jack:	Lost his head.
Harry:	Oh, yes. (*Rises: comes downstage.*)
Jack:	This little island.
Harry:	Shan't see its like.
Jack:	Oh, no.
Harry:	The sun has set.
Jack:	Couple of hours . . .

(p. 79. Compare the dialogue on pp. 19 and 22)

There is no sense of competition here, they are falling back on the shared little-Englander attitudes and assumptions that lie behind their symbiosis, taking comfort from them after the disruptions caused by the women. Harry dutifully endorses everything that Jack says, until the telling moment when he comes downstage and interrupts the flow with the observation that 'the sun has set', which Jack takes to be a reference to the fact that night has fallen. Perhaps it has, but it also echoes or mocks the boast of the Empire they have just been eulogising: that the sun never set on it. The confusion is significant because it brings to the surface what had previously been only a latent implication: that the 'home' is not some specific institution but

Britain itself, what is left of the glorious Empire in which Jack and Harry take so much pride. It is a possibility that the non-specific nature of the characterisation and the staging always leaves open.[19]

In that context, we may see the play as an open-ended social allegory, noting in particular how — when so much else about the characters was in doubt — their class backgrounds were unmistakable, in a way that would simply not have been possible in most other modern cultures, even ones like the United States which purport to use the same language. This is not to make the British class system or nostalgia for the Empire 'keys' to the play, explaining every aspect of its strangeness and turning it primarily into a work of social/political criticism, though it does help to place *Home* more firmly in the mainstream of David Storey's own works. It is rather to suggest that, like Albee in *Who's Afraid of Virginia Woolf?* and Stoppard in *Jumpers*, Storey has here recaptured one of the essential features of Renaissance tragicomedy as it was practised by Shakespeare and Fletcher. Renaissance tragicomedy invariably had, in the broadest sense, political dimensions. The resolution of the perplexities of the major characters was not only a matter of personal import, but carried with it implications for the nation as a whole — indeed (as in *The Winter's Tale* and *The Tempest*) sometimes for more than one nation, as two states may be joined together in a glorious Empire by the marriage of the younger generation. This is not only a matter of dynastic politics but symbolises the tangible blessings of providence upon countries and cultures that have undergone great distress. The microcosmic lovers, in finding resolutions to their emotional and intellectual perplexities, reflect the macrocosmic pattern.

In the manner of modern tragicomedy, it is the absence of such a blessing in *Home* which affects us most profoundly: the bleak and wintry lives of these characters are mocked by memories of British greatness and by the possibility of sexual fulfilment. These are the principal symptoms of the various 'insanities' with which they appear to be afflicted. If the two couples had been able to 'communicate' with each other, to break free of their repressed and alienated selves, some form of redemption might have been possible — an 'imperial marriage' that would overturn the sterility, fear and antagonism of their lives. The absence of such a providential resolution, and the continued presence of Alfred — his actions 'almost like a ritual' — are an eloquent testimony to Storey's analysis of what is wrong with modern Britain.

8

Old Times
by Harold Pinter*

Kate:	If you only have one of something you can't say it's the best of anything.
Deeley:	Because you have nothing to compare it with?
Kate:	Mnn.
	(*Pause*)
Deeley:	(*Smiling*) She was incomparable.
Kate:	Oh, I'm sure she wasn't.

(p. 5)

This early interchange between Kate and Deeley points us towards several of the recurrent features of this elegantly spare but intensely suggestive play. Firstly, the principle of comparison — character against character, statement against statement, fact against fact, always vying with each other for precedence but not achieving absolute status ('the best') until perhaps the very end of the play. Secondly, the slippery nature of language: Deeley's use of 'incomparable' here is (to judge from the *smiling*) wilfully wrong in context, since he is pretending that it means 'happened not to have been compared' when he knows full well that it actually means 'could never be compared, matchless'. Thirdly (a function of the other two) the battle of wills between the characters: Deeley is pressing in the conversation here to establish or confirm a superiority over Kate, which she seems not to respond to or be aware of, answering with the half-hearted 'Mnn' and not rising to the bait of 'incomparable'.

These features define the 'strangeness' of this tragicomedy, which is signalled to the audience at the very beginning by the unexplained presence on stage of Anna, whose '*figure remains*

---

*First performed, London, 1971

still in dim light at the window' (p. 3), while Kate and Deeley in full lighting discuss her as if she were not there. Then she suddenly '*turns from the window, speaking, and moves down to them*' (p. 13), without making any form of conventional entrance. This cinematic device is quite disconcerting, falling as it does within the trio of features I have outlined. Anna's presence, even while she is being described/imagined fuels the audience's instinct to compare what is being said with the reality (an instinct characteristically frustrated by the fact that she remains in semi-darkness — no facts are ever really *clear* in this play). That presence is, moreover, as ambiguous or mischievous as Deeley's 'incomparable'. We may feel that we can construe it metaphorically — Anna, present in their thoughts and memories, is by a form of theatrical shorthand suddenly present on the visit they were anticipating. Nevertheless, there must remain a question about her 'reality'; she is a provisional and mysterious figure who, moreover, calls into question our 'realistic' acceptance even of the other two characters. It is this provisionality which makes her an important element in the battle of wills between Deeley and Kate; she is a plastic figure at this stage, able to be shaped to the apparent advantage of the stronger protagonist. This is a quality which will pass to each of the other characters in turn, as the play unfolds and the battle of wills shifts ground.

All of this is quietly underlined by the setting of the play. The two acts, although set in different rooms, physically mirror each other: '*The divans and armchair are disposed in precisely the same relation to each other as the furniture in the first act, but in reversed positions*' (p. 43). Deeley draws attention to the point in his usual over-emphatic and literal-minded way: 'The great thing about these beds is that they are susceptible to any amount of permutation. They can be separated as they are now. Or placed at right angles, or one can bisect the other, or you can sleep feet to feet, or head to head, or side by side. It's the castors that make all this possible' (p. 44). The invitation to compare and contrast, to examine the situation from a variety of possible angles, is unmistakable. This is all the more fitting in what we are told is 'a converted farmhouse', old on the outside but modishly and anonymously modern within: it is an architectural ambiguity, which can be used (as in Kate's appropriation for a time of the bathroom) in the evolving battle of wills.

This trio of features I have been outlining is thus present throughout the play, but it is most clearly apparent in the reminiscences of the characters, and particularly those surrounding the film, *Odd Man Out*. The first account we have of this comes from Deeley, who recalls how 'I marched in on this excruciatingly hot summer afternoon in the middle of nowhere and watched Odd Man Out and thought Robert Newton was fantastic' (pp. 25-6). He insists that 'there was only one other person in the cinema, one other person in the whole of the whole cinema, and there she is. And there she was, very dim, very still' — presumably, though it is never established explicitly, this is/was Kate, who later 'told me she thought Robert Newton was remarkable. So it was Robert Newton who brought us together and it is only Robert Newton who can tear us apart'. Anna coolly replies to this emotional account: 'F.J.McCormick was good too', which establishes that she too had seen the film, though when Deeley tries to ascertain when, she vaguely replies, 'Oh . . . long ago'. Kate, in her only comment on this topic — like Anna earlier, she has all but faded into the background — simply admits that she remembers the film: 'Oh yes. Very well'.

Shortly thereafter Anna gives a very different account of how she and Kate saw the film: 'I remember one Sunday she said to me, looking up from the paper, come quick, quick, come with me quickly, and we seized our handbags and went, on a bus, to some totally obscure, some totally unfamiliar district and, almost alone, saw a wonderful film called Odd Man Out' (p. 34). It is by no means necessary to conclude that the two viewings of the film are one and the same, but is is in keeping with this feature of the play that we are virtually compelled to compare them, to explore this possibility: it is, after all, already something of a coincidence that two characters should independently recall seeing the same film, perhaps twenty years before. (*Odd Man Out* was first released in 1946). Deeley is quite categorical that there was only 'one other person in the cinema', whom we infer to be Kate; Anna merely comments that she and Kate were 'almost alone' — which would not preclude the possibility that Deeley had in fact first picked up Kate on this occasion, though we should have to explain how, in his version of things, he completely overlooks Anna.

It is striking in this regard that Deeley's description of Kate ('very dim, very still') invites comparison itself with our first view of Anna in the play (*'remains still in dim light'*). It is only one of a number of details in the play — the accounts of Anna stealing/borrowing Kate's underwear are another — which invite us to consider the possibility that Kate and Anna are, in some metaphorical sense, the same person, perhaps different facets of the same person. But it is a possibility for which (like 'incomparable') the evidence is tantalisingly incomplete and ambiguous.

In the absence of more conclusive evidence we are driven back to consider that the recollections of the film are not random and disembodied but very much *in character* for the speakers: the emphasis, attitude and chosen detail in each case may lead us to question the objectivity of the memories. For Deeley, the whole experience is charged with thoughts of his childhood and of repressed sexuality; the cinema was in the neighbourhood where his father had bought him his 'first' and 'only' tricycle, while one of the usherettes 'was stroking her breasts and the other one was saying "dirty bitch" $<$ . . . $>$ I left when the film was over, noticing $<$ . . . $>$ that the first usherette appeared to be utterly exhausted' (p. 25). It is in this context that the film led to his 'trueblue pickup' of Kate, with later sexual consequences. For Anna, seeing the film was part and parcel of the life she and Kate had had together as young women in London: it comes at the end of a burst of reminiscences about art galleries, old churches, old buildings, theatres, chamber concerts, reading the review pages of the Sunday newspapers. In this light, the two accounts of seeing the film belong to the battle of wills — here between Deeley and Anna over 'possession' of Kate. Deeley's account pointedly leaves out Anna in wanting to emphasise, in rather boorishly masculine fashion, how he acquired Kate; Anna's account pointedly leaves out Deeley in wanting to emphasise the gregarious urban sophistication of her relationship with Kate (something very much lacking in this converted farmhouse by the sea). The objective 'truth' of what happened in the past is totally subsumed by the battle of wills in the present.

Anna alludes to this possibility without admitting to the competitive element in it: 'There are some things one remembers even though they may never have happened. There are things I remember which may never have happened but as I recall them so they take place' (pp. 27-8). This is typical of her pose throughout the play — arty, sophisticated, imaginative, stylish, and gregarious. It is a pose which seems alternately to intrigue and affront Deeley. At times he tries none too successfully, to match it with bluster about his own cosmopolitan life-style ('My name is Orson Welles', p. 38); but more frequently he responds with a blunt, not to say boorish, literal-mindedness, as if he finds Anna's 'sophistication' offensive. His response to this speech, for example, is an incredulous '*What?*' When she then tells a mysterious story of a man in her and Kate's room, Deeley presses for factual details; she concludes with the fanciful observation, 'It was as if he had never been there', to which Deeley responds with all the force of fact: 'Of course he'd been. He went twice and came once' (p. 29). He will not allow her to tamper with the past in this imaginative way. This is of a piece with his aggrieved outburst in the closing phase of the play, after Anna has been talking in very intimate terms about her relations with Kate: 'Of course it's my bloody province. I'm her husband. *Pause.* I mean I'd like to ask a question. Am I alone in beginning to find all this distateful?' (p. 62). 'I'm her husband' is an appeal to a brand of common sense and conventional decency, in the face of Anna's much more stylish and metaphorical construction of past reality, which increasingly carries with it connotations of illicit and promiscuous sexuality. Moments like this bring home the irony of the fact that, when Anna and Deeley rehearse their old songs, he is the one who clings to the refrain: 'No [Or 'Oh'], no, they can't take that away from me' (pp. 23, 54), singing it three times in all to her once. Anna is effectively trying to take that (meaning Kate and all that she represents to him) away from him in her reconstruction of the past. His assertiveness, like his insistence on facts, is ultimately a measure of how much he feels threatened rather than of self-confidence.

It will be apparent from this analysis that the choice of *Odd Man Out* as the film which focuses so much of all this emotional energy is far from accidental. Its title gives voice to the 'game' which is constantly being played beneath the surface of the dialogue in *Old Times*: at any one time, one of the characters is 'odd man out' as the other two personalities measure up to each other. Anna is theatrically 'odd man out' as the play opens, but relegates that role to Kate for the mid-part of Act 1, when the latter is virtually ignored — to the extent that she finally protests: 'You talk of me as if I were dead' (p. 30). From there, however, she reasserts herself, and by the end of the act the collusion of the two women virtually excludes Deeley, who reacts by becoming increasingly strident and outrageous: 'I wrote the film and directed it. My name is Orson Welles < . . . > I've been there. There's nothing more to see, there's nothing more to investigate, nothing. There's nothing more in Sicily to investigate' (pp. 38-9) — before lapsing into silence. Kate, however, then moves into self-imposed isolation in the bath, literally leaving the stage to Deeley and Anna. By now, however, it is clear that the title of 'odd man out' does not relate to which character is silent or off-stage, but to which of Anna and Deeley will fail to hang on to Kate — either in their memories or in the present. When she returns from the bath, both of them turn to her:

Anna: (to Deeley) Doesn't she look beautiful?
Deeley: Doesn't she?

                                                                    (p. 55)

Kate is only odd man out in the sense that she proves to have a strength of self-sufficiency which the other two lack; this is symbolised in the solitary bath, concerning which she spurns both Anna's offer to run it for her (p. 42) and Deeley's tentative offer to help her dry herself (p. 56). This is the strength that enables her to silence the other two in the final moments of the play.

The prominence accorded to *Odd Man Out* is contrary to Pinter's usual practice in several respects, and raises some interesting questions about an audience's response to the play as a whole. Firstly, Pinter normally keeps specific references to real people, events or works of art to a minimum; the worlds he depicts are plausibly like our own but also remarkably self-contained, not defined by reference to external co-ordinates. For many members of his audience, this may well be the case with *Odd Man Out*, which has never achieved the kind of cultural currency, say, of Carol Reed's later film, *The Third Man*. Most people will have no idea of what it is about, where it is set, what sort of style it is in; and Pinter tells us nothing of this, merely that it starred James Mason (who died in it), Robert Newton (who Deeley thought was 'fantastic') and F.J. McCormick (who Anna thought 'was good too'; she thought the film as a whole was 'wonderful'). So, for many people, the resonant title is all that the film will convey, but anyone who has seen it will know that it is about 'an IRA gunman wounded and on the run in Belfast, [who] is helped and hindered by a variety of people'.[20] The Irish connection would immediately focus the odd-man-out implication on Deeley, whose name is unmistakably Irish, even though — interestingly — it is never voiced in the course of the play.[21] Even if we did not know his name, however, his words occasionally take on an unmistakable Irish phrasing: 'Myself I was a student then, juggling with my future, wondering should I bejasus saddle myself with a slip of a girl . . .' (p. 31).[22] And there is even a hint of violence about him when, in his enthusiasm for Robert Newton, he claims 'And I would commit murder for him, even now' (p. 25).[23] But, like so much about him, this is surely a piece of bravado. Nor is it altogether clear just how authentic his Irishness is. His brogue (at least on paper) is far from consistent, and he seems to have long-standing connections with London: he associates the neighbourhood of the cinema (assuming it *is* in London) with his childhood and expresses affection for his old friends in the 'Edgware Road gang' and the 'Maida Vale group'. In short, Deeley remains an ambiguity — an Irish Londoner or an Irishman living in London and this (rather than any fanciful association with the I.R.A.) is surely the significance of his close association with that film. It underlines yet another of the ways that Deeley is an odd man out — the outsider intellectually, sexually, even racially, in the sophisticated, cosmopolitan world that Anna evokes around herself and Kate.

One further dimension to the emphasis placed on *Odd Man Out* suggests itself, which relates to our response to cinema: what Deeley and Anna remember most about the film is not the story, the setting, the style or even really the characters of the film. What they remember is the actors who were in it. 'James Mason was dead'; 'Robert Newton was fantastic'; 'F.J.

McCormick was good too', as if the acting of the roles was somehow separate from and more important than the roles themselves. This reflects tellingly on the speakers: the battle of wills between Deeley and Anna is essentially a matter of the roles with which they try to invest themselves. The relationship between those roles and 'reality' is unknowable because of the ambiguities in which they are couched and the contradictions with which they are hedged: so what we are left with is the conviction with which they carry off these roles and with which they respond to the attempts of the other person to upstage or undermine them. The flaws in Deeley's 'performance' are perhaps the more obvious: there is always an edge of desperation in his literal-minded responses to Anna's 'sophistication' and even more in what look like his attempts to cap it with a sophistication of his own: 'I mean let's put it on the table, I have my eye on a number of pulses, pulses all round the globe, deprivations and insults, why should I waste valuable space listening to two —'.[24] It is at this moment, as the self-importance degenerates into bluster, that Kate effectively deflates him:

(*Swiftly*.): If you don't like it go. (p. 63)

By contrast, Anna's 'performance' seems so much more assured. And yet she is almost too enthusiastic in her memories of the past and too solicitous — too anxious to be of service — in the present. When she insists that 'Katey had always been interested in the arts', Kate coolly replies: 'I was interested once in the arts, but I can't remember now which ones they were' (p. 33). And, though it is never too pointed, Kate contrives to turn down a whole succession of her offers: to run her bath, read to her, make fresh coffee, do the hem of her black dress, phone old friends. To this extent we may feel that it is not just a case of Deeley being crass when he challenges some of her over-subtle reflections on memory and creativity; she is too eager both to ingratiate herself and make an impression. Her early slip:

Anna:	You have a wonderful casserole.
Deeley:	What?
Anna:	I mean wife. So sorry. A wonderful wife.

(p. 16)

is an indication of her over-intense performance. Similarly, although she seems coolly self-possessed about memories/ inventions of men in her room or Deeley staring up her skirt at a party, she reacts almost with hysteria to the idea of walking across the park: 'The park is dirty at night, all sorts of horrible people, men hiding behind trees and women with terrible voices' (p. 79). In her way, she is as vulnerable as Deeley, her 'performance' as flawed and in the end liable to an even more terrible, silencing judgement from Kate: 'I remember you lying dead' (p. 67).

Kate's final soliloquy and the actions that follow from it (pp. 67-71) may thus be seen as an appropriate resolution, if not explanation, of the tensions that underlie the play's 'strangeness'. The recurrent invitation in the play to compare and contrast persons and events has, until then, been partly frustrated by the absence of Kate's point of view: she has not offered any perspective on events that might endorse or corroborate those of Deeley or Anna, perhaps favouring one over the other. Kate does not actually comment on details — *Odd Man Out*, The Wayfarers Tavern, old parties — but she 'places' both Anna and Deeley in particular ways that reduce the one to a recumbent figure in the shadows, the other to tears. In so doing, she establishes her own will as stronger than either of theirs — the passive figure with whom Deeley sported at the beginning has returned from her purifying bath with decisive powers. But none of this reduces the play's pervasive ambiguity. In Deeley's last major speech (p. 65), he voices one of the symbolic readings which might help us to reduce the play to a single, manageable 'meaning': '[Anna] thought she was you, said little, so little. Maybe she was you. Maybe it was you < . . . >'. The possibility that Anna and Kate are different facets of the same personality, or that Anna is Kate's past, or that they were lovers, or that all three characters, including Deeley, are all facets of the same personality — all of these are suggested by the play's remorseless comparative mode. None is confirmed by the closing moments, but none is excluded either. In Kate's final dominance the truth is established, but not explained: it is a concluding moment of ritual rather than of factual revelation.

'Last rites I did not feel necessary. Or any celebration,' says

Kate (p. 68) about the 'dead' Anna (though it was a death from which she 'woke'). This picks up Anna's earlier claim: 'I came here not to disrupt but to celebrate. *Pause*. To celebrate a very old and treasured friendship' (p. 64). The play as a whole has been a rite, in a perverse sort of way a celebration, of the insubstantiality of memory, experience and personality. Just as 'James Mason was dead', Anna was 'dead' — symbolically both sullied and buried with earth. Deeley 'resisted with force. He would not let me dirty his face, or smudge it, he wouldn't let me. He suggested a wedding instead, and a change of environment. *Slight pause*. Neither mattered' (p. 69). So Deeley resisted the rite of death — so central to the mysteries of tragicomedy, both Renaissance and modern — substituting for it the rite of marriage and the ritual change of environment, in the hope that they would bring him the miraculous fulfilment he sought. But, as Kate chillingly adds: Neither mattered. That, surely, is the force of this tragicomedy: so much energy, so much will, such a faith in what people could make of themselves, all finally seen as meaningless. The miraculous rites have not worked in the past and they will not do so now. The acting of roles on the stage or on the screen has become a perfect metaphor for the lives of these characters: an intriguingly ambiguous performance that makes nothing happen and means only itself.

9
Jumpers,
by Tom Stoppard*

I mean no backhanded compliment to a play as original and inventive as *Jumpers* if I start by observing how significantly it echoes two plays we have previously considered. In the first place, the lecture which George is preparing throughout the play, around the question 'Is God?' presumably has much in common with the lecture which Goldberg in Pinter's *The Birthday Party* claims once to have given in the Ethical Hall, Bayswater, under the title 'The Necessary and the Possible'.[25] Although we never hear the substance of Goldberg's lecture, the title suggests that it would have been concerned with a philosophical analysis of the chain of cause and effect in the history of men's lives, with the predication or otherwise of God as the ultimate cause in the universe and so of providence in its continuing operations; the issue of free will or its absence would also probably be involved. These certainly form the substance of George's lecture as we fragmentarily hear it, though his argument has a specifically ethical slant to it (concerning the derivation and nature of 'the good') which we have no reason to suppose would have interested Goldberg, for all that he was talking in The *Ethical* Hall.

Secondly, in the dying moments of the play, Archie — the play's cynical, pragmatist factotum — starts quoting St. Augustine on the lesson to be learned from the two thieves who died on the Cross with Christ: 'Do not despair — many are happy much of the time; more eat than starve, more are healthy than sick, more curable than dying; not so many dying as dead; and one of the thieves was saved' (p. 87). As we have already seen, the issue of·the thieves on the Cross is a critical one in *Waiting for Godot* and Beckett has more than once quoted

---

*First performed, London, 1972

St. Augustine's perfectly balanced dictum on the subject when asked about that play's meaning.[26] Archie's glibly partial quotation and specious argument are surely, in part, a wry genuflexion to Beckett's seminal work, with a significance I shall consider later. For the moment, I cite these two echoes of earlier works primarily to establish the tragicomic provenance of *Jumpers* and to emphasise how this play — for all its elements of farce and black comedy — returns repeatedly to the key tragicomic themes: the intrusion of strange, mysterious forces into everyday lives, the bewilderment that surrounds the intrusion, and the possibility of a redeeming grace arising from it.

We may see the opening section of the play as an oblique spelling out of these themes, teasing the audience in a variety of ways about how much they are able to see or understand. The concatenation of events from the beginning of the play (p. 7) until George's first stab at the lecture (p. 23) is simply bewildering — far more so for an audience in the theatre than Stoppard's stage directions imply, since they incorporate a good deal of hindsight and (re. Dotty) character analysis not available to an audience. It all seems simply impossible in any normal, rational scheme of things. In the course of the play, however, we are to learn that it all has a rational explanation.

It must seem at the outset that we are in a music hall, with Dotty being announced as a 'much-loved star of the musical stage' by a disembodied voice; the term 'hostess' would suit a variety show well enough. What this has to do with a 'momentous victory at the polls' is far from clear, though nobody harps on this point. Dotty's 'drying' in the middle of 'Shine on Harvest Moon' has all the credibility of a professional entertainer's nightmare, and the sudden appearance of the girl on the swing (she is not a 'secretary' to the audience's knowledge), like the subsequent entrance of the Jumpers, maintains the music-hall illusion. Crouch's entrance and his obscuring of the girl's striptease raises several layers of confusion: is he really part of the girl's 'act', in which case the whole thing is a deliberate joke, a tease upon a tease? (It certainly is for the audience of Stoppard's play, but what about the 'unseen watchers' within the play?) If not — and the 'unseen watchers' certainly do not see it in that light — what is this drinks waiter doing here? Are we in a variety club, where drinks are served, rather than a true music hall? The reappearance of Dotty, seemingly not 'performing' for any unseen audience, only compounds the confusion: is this an extension of the embarrassment of her 'drying', perhaps confirming her to be drunk if not actually deranged? Or could it be an elaborate on-stage joke: she keeps complaining that the Jumpers are not 'incredible', as the introductory voice claimed they would be, but that could be a rhetorical trick, preparing us for some genuinely stunning acrobatics later in their display. George's entrance in the midst of this makes comprehension no easier; his complaint about it being after 2 a.m. makes no sense in any of the contexts to which we are attuned unless (like Crouch) he can be seen as a stooge, a deliberate part of a theatrical routine.

Dolly's furious rejoinder, 'It's my bloody party, George!' (p. 19) is perhaps the turning point, where we *have* to reassess our premises: the tone is now too earnest for some theatrical in-joke, and we have to grapple with the possibility that this actually is a party — not an easy thing to do, since few people have houses in which acrobats can form human pyramids or someone can perform on a swing slung from a chandelier. (It does, however, make immediate sense of Crouch and George.) Only much later is it explained that George and Dotty's apartment incorporates what was once a ballroom. Alternatively, we may respond to the increasingly apparent fact that Dolly is at the centre of things, obsessively trying to get her moon songs right, and decide that everything we see is a figment of her deranged imagination. That scenario is perfectly in tune with the introduction of the T.V. screen which Dotty manipulates — perhaps projecting her fantasies. It is perfectly credible, in 1972, that there should be T.V. pictures of a moon landing, even — with a little poetic licence — a British moon landing, but that its crew should be called Scott and Oates and involved in events that amount to a disrespectful parody of the tragic 1912 polar expedition, is surely fantasy. A military-style celebration in the streets of London must equally smack more of imagination than of reality: the British are well used to royal pageants and sober ceremonies of Thanksgiving or Remembrance, but this is clearly what we associate with Latin American dictatorships and not with British democracy. The random advertisement we also see may be a hint that this is all-too-real, but is not conclusive enough as evidence.

We are thus caught between three possible explanations of what we are seeing — a pretty disastrous musical variety show, a lavish but unhappy party, and Dotty's paranoid hallucinations — when the pivotal event of the play, the shooting of the Jumper, takes place. We may therefore interpret it initially as part of the act, either on stage or in the party : a jokey way of ending an acrobatic routine — or we may see it as another piece of fantasy. It is presumably the blood which stains Dotty's dress that tells us that something 'real' has happened, within such realistic confines as this play will eventually admit to. From this point on, the terms of the play's mystery begin to alter. The confusion about what is going on gives way to an analysis of what has actually happened — not merely an investigation into who shot the Jumper and why, though that is a central concern, but also an examination of why Dotty cannot sing her moon tunes, why the Jumpers jump, even (obliquely) why the secretary might have been doing the striptease, why George is annoyed and why those unlikely images have been appearing on television screens.

Certain 'facts' appear: Dotty *is* a professional musical variety entertainer but retired, and what we have seen was not a real show, but a succession of party turns, made possible by the unusual nature of her house; she *is* mentally disturbed, and so cannot sing, but she is not hallucinating — the Jumper really was shot and the events on the T.V. are real too. Crouch confirms not only the fact of the moonflight but also the unlikely coincidence of names when he refers to 'the first Captain Oates, out there in the Antarctic wastes' (p. 80), and the reality of the military-style celebrations (for the Radical Liberals' election victory — or *coup d'état* as Archie calls it) is attested when the jets scream over the house rather than on the screen (p. 34). Neither the Jumpers nor the stripper were professional entertainers; the former combine gymnastics with their academic studies (less implausible, perhaps, in the wake of the Sixties than in the Eighties, but metaphorically apt at any time) while the latter is eventually revealed to have had a love-affair with the dead Jumper — suggesting that she is altogether more passionate than her staid secretarial demeanour implies and not so unlikely a stripper as first appears. George's annoyance is not really to do with the lateness of the hour — it is linked in a complex way to his sexual frustrations with Dotty, his dislike of her theatrical connections and the frustrations of his own career (all of which relate also to the multi-faceted figure of Archie, the focus of all his jealousies). In this way, all the mystery of the opening phase of the play is dispelled, reduced to a set of mundane and comprehensible facts.

Indeed, the play seems resolute in its determination to reduce the mysterious to the commonplace, as in the mini-mystery of the disappearance of Thumper, finally explained as the consequence of George's premature firing of the arrow. But what is not explained — what in effect becomes more mysterious the further the play progresses — is the *connection* between all these commonplace facts, between the faltering marriage of George and Dotty and the landings on the moon, between the death of a Professor of Logic and a military-style takeover of Britain, between a lecture on 'Is God?', a dead rabbit and several presumptions of adultery. Connections are frequently implied but never fully established. What is missing, essentially, is the significance of these facts, the broader context which will give them an interlinked meaning. The secretary's striptease may thus be seen as a metaphor of the play as a whole: more and more is revealed, but just as the revelations are becoming interesting they are obscured from view, and the naked truth is never apparent, though it is forceful enough to knock Crouch 'arse over tip'.

The starting point for any attempt to connect these apparently disparate 'facts', and so reveal the naked truth, must be the one fact which is never fully elucidated — who killed the Jumper, and why? There is no shortage of candidates. The stage directions, for example, emphasise that Dotty *could* have done it, though her only motive would seem to be her disappointment that the Jumpers were not 'incredible'. George could have done it, jealous of the fact that the Jumper, McPhee, held a superior Chair to his own. Archie could have done it; the fact that he had no apparent motive ought not to rule him out — he is such a cynical manipulator that he could have found his own reasons. These might (for instance) not be unconnected with Crouch's late revelation that McPhee had been having serious misgivings about his life's work 'giving philosophical respectability to a new pragmatism in public life, of which there have been many disturbing examples both here and on the moon' (pp. 79-80): a reference to Archie as Vice-Chancellor, or is it broader disapproval of the extremely pragmatic Radical Liberals who have just secured an election victory? Could McPhee have been shot for political reasons? Just as Archie begins to look a shade uncomfortable about how much Crouch knows — 'You must have been a close friend of his' — the evidence swings in an entirely different direction, bringing revelations of McPhee's 'secret betrothal' to the secretary and his belated decision to retire to a monastery. All this seems very pointed as the *'grim, tense, unsmiling'* secretary *'snaps her handbag shut with a sharp sound'* and prepares to go home. But then, McPhee's wife knew about the affair and had just as great a motive. Crouch confesses: 'It makes no sense to me at all' and it is left to Archie to draw the platitudinous moral: 'The truth to us philosophers, Mr. Crouch, is always an interim judgement. We will never even know for certain who did shoot McPhee. Unlike mystery novels, life does not guarantee a denouement; and if it came, how would one know whether to believe it?' (p. 81). This bland dismissal of the possibility of objective, verifiable truth is something we might well have expected in a modern tragicomedy. In the endless suspense of whether Godot will come or the endless ambiguities of a Pinter text, objective truth seems a redundant concept; and it is tempting, after the bewildering twists and turns of Stoppard's play, simply to take Archie's words at face value. But this is a luxury the text does not allow us. In the first place, the words belong to Archie and not to Stoppard, and Archie is not the most reliable of men — certainly with women, possibly with guns: it should not escape our attention that it may well be in his own interest to pull the philosophical wool over everyone's eyes. Secondly, the events which follow this speech and bring the second act to a close directly contradict what he has said: blood on the secretary's coat leads to an investigation on top of the cupboard, to the discovery of a dead Thumper, impaled on what is unmistakably George's arrow. The chain of cause and effect could not be clearer or less subject to doubt, but Stoppard makes the point doubly clear by then directing George to step *'backwards, down'* and so tread on the tortoise,

Pat, with fatal consequences. If two deaths can be explained so unequivocally, why not a third?

McPhee's death never is explained in such terms, but that is not to say that it *could not* be. Life may not guarantee us a denouement, 'unlike mystery novels', but that does not deny the existence of the objective facts which would provide such a denouement if we knew how to set about looking for them properly (which no one in this play appears to do). And even if we are frustrated of such an explanation, it does not follow that the fact of McPhee's death is without significance — as the drift of Archie's argument suggests. Dotty's response to it in particular should give us pause: 'O horror, horror, horror! Confusion now hath made its masterpiece . . . most sacrilegious murder! — (*Different voice.*) Woe, alas! What, in our house?' (p. 24) The effect of this in the theatre is so multi-faceted as almost to defy description. In the first place, it is two quotations from *Macbeth* — Macduff's discovery of the murdered King Duncan followed by Lady Macbeth's hypocritically pious shock that it should have happened in the Macbeths' castle. The possibility that the quotation is apt enough to amount to Dotty's confession that her ambitious husband killed McPhee, with her own collusion, cannot be overlooked. But the very fact that these are quotations from *Macbeth*, rather than any other play, raises other possibilities. Everyone knows that 'the Scottish play' has attracted more superstition for bad luck than anything else in the theatre; many theatrical people will not quote from it at all, so we may take it that the old trouper, Dotty, has been profoundly shocked to break this taboo. (And so is innocent?) It is her desperate attempt to communicate with George, who has other things on his mind, so he reacts neither to the quotation nor to the breaking of the taboo.

The fact that Stoppard has allowed himself to use the quotation in his play is firstly an in-joke — 'Look at me breaking the rules' — on a par with Dotty's later plea for attention, '*Fire!*' (p. 28), which breaks the old safety rule about not shouting 'fire' in a theatre for fear of causing panic. (That this incident causes George to 'fire' the arrow which kills Thumper only proves how sensible the old rule is . . . .) But there is an additional dimension to such in-jokes, which is most apparent in such moments as that when George perpetrates one of the most execrable puns of modern theatre — 'Now might I do it, Pat', bringing his pet tortoise into Hamlet's line on discovering Claudius at prayer (p. 43) — or when Archie implicitly admits his own Machiavellianism when he starts quoting (with amendments) from *Richard III* (III.iv.31-3); 'My Lord Archbishop, when I was last in Lambeth I saw good strawberries in your garden —' (p. 85). Such self-conscious moments amount to a tacit admission of the playwright's own shaping hand in his creation: the joke does not work unless we appreciate the artist playing fast and loose with the 'rules'. And such a playing fast and loose reminds us that the artist is a kind of god, determining the processes of cause and effect, the apportionment of significance and insignificance, innocence and guilt, which will emerge in the course of his play. This is so important for Stoppard that he keeps reminding us of it in other contexts, such as what Archie dubs the Cognomen Syndrome (p. 61), the fact that characters in and around the play have distressingly appropriate names. Inspector Bones' brother was an osteopath, Bones the Bones, who changed his name to Foot but became a chiropodist. George Moore has the name of the author of *Principia Ethica*. Dotty Moore really is dotty. And Archie's name is Jumper. At the bottom of the list — and easiest to overlook, since Stoppard carefully refrains from underlining it — is Professor McPhee. Dotty's outburst from 'the Scottish play' is all the more apt when we know that the murdered Jumper is actually a Scot called Duncan — something that does not emerge until half-way through the play (p. 49, to be precise).

But the Cognomen Syndrome and the clever quotations are like so much of the play, facts without inherent significance, unless we recognise that they are not gratuitous exercises in wit, but carry with them moral and ethical implications. To cite a few obvious examples: 'Now might I do it pat' leads Hamlet to the conclusion that he will not do it now (that is, kill Claudius in revenge for his father) because Claudius is at prayer and so likely to go to heaven if he dies at this moment, for all his past sins. It is a complex weighing of practical opportunities and moral absolutes. Richard III's ingratiating request for strawberries is actually, in context, a device for getting the Bishop of Ely out of the way so that he can plot more devilish business with

Buckingham: it is the proverbial line of the amoral manipulator. The death of Duncan in *Macbeth* is no ordinary murder; in killing his King, his friend and his guest Macbeth has indeed committed 'sacrilegious murder', invoking a weight of moral responsibility that is remorselessly visited upon him before the play is through. The names in the play similarly carry connotations beyond the obvious witty or factual ones: Inspector Bones, for example, introduces himself to George with the explanation, 'As in rags-and' and 'Bones' the name, as in dem bones, dem bones . . . (*Pause.*) . . . dem dry bones' (p. 44). Both of these prove apter than he intends. The old spiritual from which he quotes is all about the connection of one bone to another to build the human skeleton and so create man — 'Now hear the word of the Lord!' As a policeman, it is Bones' job to connect one thing with another and so come up with the 'mystery novel' explanation of events which Archie is so keen to eliminate. At this he proves singularly inept, largely because, as he repeatedly says: 'Show business is my main interest, closely followed by crime detection' (p. 46). That being the case, he is always more interested in appearances than in facts — 'This is a British murder enquiry and some degree of justice must be seen to be more or less done' (pp. 65-6) — and in Dorothy Moore than the murder investigation. He is more than susceptible to the bribes which Archie is offering him when Dotty's cries drag him away, and his behaviour in her bedroom proves to be less than judicial. In short, and ethically speaking, Bones really is a pile of rag and bones who has never heard the word of the Lord. Similarly, the fact that Archie is called Jumper underlines his Machiavellian morality, the fact that Dotty is dotty is scandalously ignored by George, Archie and Bones (who all ignore or try to take advantage of her) and the fact that George Moore is *not* the author of *Principia Ethica*, though widely thought to be so, points to the radical flaws in his philosophising. As he admits himself: 'The fact that I cut a ludicrous figure in the academic world is largely due to my aptitude for traducing a complex and logical thesis to a mysticism of staggering banality' (p. 72). Dotty puts it more succinctly in describing him as 'the last of the metaphysical egocentrics' (p. 74) — so wrapped up in misplaced thoughts of his own importance that he has considerable difficulty acknowledging either his wife's madness or the fact that one of his colleagues has been killed in his own house.

Thus, Stoppard's in-jokes, allusions and farcical games carry with them a weight of moral and ethical inference that the characters, for the most part, ignore. Wherever we look in the play, modern thought — and its foundations in modern philosophy — are cut off from the business of making moral and ethical judgements in the everyday world. Archie is a prime culprit here. Dotty, for example, quotes his assertion: 'But good and bad, better and worse, these are not real properties of things, they are just expressions of our feeling about them' (p. 41), a fitting argument for someone able to maintain 'that belief in God and the conviction that God doesn't exist amount to much the same thing' (p. 68). This is a cynical relativism, one of whose consequences is policemen like Inspector Bones. It ought, of course, to find its rebuttal in the thinking of a man called George Moore, particularly if he holds a Chair of Moral Philosophy. But *moral* philosophy is always the last thing on George's mind; he is far more interested in the Chair of Logic and its senior status, and the lecture we hear being put together is far more concerned with abstruse metaphysical speculations (constantly in danger of collapsing into 'a mysticism of staggering banality') than with moral applications. It is entirely appropriate that, in attempting to refute Zeno's Paradox, he should overlook the practical effect of wayward arrows, and that he should deride Bertrand Russell's attempts to telephone Mao Tse-Tung: 'I was simply trying to bring his mind back to matters of universal import, and away from the day-to-day parochialism of international politics' (p. 31). George has little time for 'day-to-day' realities, except perhaps when they impinge on his own dignity; this accounts for his appallingly unsympathetic treatment of Dotty — 'I'm sorry if it's one of your bad days, but things will get better' (p. 41) — and the length of time it takes him to realise that McPhee is dead.

This then is the central concern of the play, the abandonment of ethics in modern thinking. The play is full of echoes of a time gone by when moral do's-and-don'ts had a comprehensible place in people's thinking, when Chairs of Divinity were held in esteem, when Archbishops of Canterbury were devout clergymen and not agnostic politicians, when Captain Oates sacrificed himself gallantly for his friends. All of these are correlated with the time when Dotty was still a star of musical variety and could sing her moon songs to the applause of such as Inspector Bones — notably the one that Stoppard wrote especially for the play, 'Forget Yesterday' (words printed, p. 89). Her malaise, then, reflects the malaise which has overcome modern Britain, and she identifies its onset with the first landing on the moon: 'When they first landed, it was as though I'd seen a unicorn on the television news . . .. It was very interesting, of course. But it certainly spoiled unicorns' (p. 38).[27] Technological advance has taken a very specific slice out of the mystery and wonder of life, and since then she has not been able to sing the songs that celebrate that wonder. The moons of all those trite and corny songs have lost their meaning, as have those of the poets Keats, Milton and Shelley: *Oh yes, things were in place then!* (p. 41). Nobody, of course, understands what she is saying, least of all George, on whose uncomprehending heart she weeps — they have all suffered the same fall, but none of them understands it. That is the reason for their false and devious philosophies, their lack of moral concern, Astronaut Scott's disgraceful behaviour and the military takeover of Britain. The breakdown of true mystery (as opposed to relativistic obfuscation) has led to a breakdown of moral responsibility, on which concepts like altruism, democracy and even love depend:

> *Dotty*: Well, it's all over now. Not only are we no longer the still centre of God's universe, we're not even uniquely graced by his footprint in man's image . . .. Man is on the Moon, his feet on solid ground, and he has seen us whole, all in one go, *little-local* . . . and all our absolutes, the thou-shalts and the thou-shalt-nots that seemed to be the very condition of our existence, how did *they* look to two moonmen with a single neck to save between them? < . . . > There is going to be such . . . breakage, such gnashing of unclean meats, such coveting of neighbours' oxen and knowing of neighbours' wives . . .
>
> (p. 75)

Dotty's wry little joke about the start of her relationship with

George — 'And so our tutorials descended, from the metaphysical to the merely physical' (p. 35) — sums it all up: the desire for self-gratification, wrapped up as it may be in philosophical cant, has obliterated any real concern for wider issues and other people. It is never spelled out in so many words, but we may infer that it was the realisation that his own philosophy had led everyone down this slippery slope that directly caused McPhee's death. His decision to retire to a monastery, in effect recanting the trendy views by which he sanctioned both political deviousness and his own affair with his secretary, made him a marked man, a logical target for someone who felt betrayed — which, in effect, means any of the possible suspects. That is what makes McPhee a true martyr, a real Duncan in this play, and not just any random murder victim. Note the demand of the people for just such a sense of redemptive martyrdom in the wake of Radical Liberals' atheist/agnostic takeover: 'Give us the blood of the lamb. Give us the bread of the body of Christ' (p. 84).

As with *Rosencrantz and Guildenstern Are Dead*, then, Stoppard has devised a play which follows the formula of modern tragicomedy, tracing the relationship between the strange, the mysterious or the metaphysical and the ordinary, commonplace or 'merely physical', and wrapping it with bewildering farce around a scapegoat death, about which we know few facts, though its significance grows and grows throughout the play. But Stoppard has carefully dissociated himself from some of the implications of the Beckett/Pinter tradition from which he obviously borrows so much: however bewildering and untrustworthy the world seems in *Jumpers* it does not absolve the characters of moral responsibility towards other people, in marriage, in politics, or even in murder. The emphasis in both Beckett and Pinter, in their different ways, is on characters driven by forces over which they have no control, caught up in situations where individuality is a meaningless concept as also, by inference, is individual choice. Stoppard refuses to allow that this is the case, which is surely the significance of Archie's allusions to Beckett and St. Augustine in the closing moments of the play. His Panglossian assertion that all is for the best is as specious as his previous assertion that truth is always 'an interim judgement', both Machiavellian attempts to make people forget that moral choice exists and can have a bearing on events. It is when people forget such things that democracies fall, McPhees are shot and their killers not found, Oateses are left on the moon, and marriages reach the distressing state of that of George and Dotty:

> *Dotty*:   George . . .
> (*But George won't or can't . . .*)
>
> (p. 75)

Whether it is 'won't or 'can't', it is ultimately a moral failure on George's part, an egocentric solipsism, rather than an unshakable fact of existence. In that distinction lies the difference between Stoppard and his predecessors in tragicomedy.

10
Travesties
by Tom Stoppard*

Travesties is not, in my view, a tragicomedy, not even a revisionist tragicomedy in the manner of *Rosencrantz and Guildenstern Are Dead* and *Jumpers*, as I have described them. This may seem a surprising claim, since it is unmistakably by the same author: it has the same capacity to tease and tantalise an audience with its wit, to turn a corny joke into a profound thought (and vice versa). It shows the same playful capacity for plagiarising the classic dramatic tradition, using *The Importance of Being Earnest* where *Rosencrantz and Guildenstern Are Dead* used *Hamlet* and *Jumpers* capitalised on the mystery thriller genre, embellished with a range of Shakespearean allusions. It even shares the concern of both of these plays with (to use Goldberg's terms from Pinter's *The Birthday Party*) the Necessary and the Possible, being preoccupied with the themes of fate and accident, and the role of the individual in both art and history. What *Travesties* lacks compared with its predecessors, is a mysterious core, the genuine bewilderment of both characters and audience caught up in processes they do not understand and over which they have no apparent control. The play also lacks any obvious candidate for the role of scapegoat victim, just as it lacks any dimension that might be construed as sacrificial ritual; a case might be made for seeing the deaths of the First World War or the Russian Revolution in this light — something of this is clearly implied in the play — but we would be straining definitions very hard. These omissions do not make *Travesties* a bad play — on the contrary, it is a fine play — but they do prevent its being a tragicomedy.

I include a brief consideration of the play here because it

---

*First performed, London, 1974

marks a significant development in Stoppard's career and so in the history of modern tragicomedy. When Stoppard first emerged in the mid-Sixties, he was immediately identified with the tradition of Beckett and Pinter. He had a distinctively witty and playful style, but his concentration on lost and confused characters struggling with the meaning of their lives (and indeed with the meaning of meaning) seemed much more of a piece with the work of Beckett and Pinter than with the more overtly social and political concerns of dramatists like Osborne, Wesker, Arden or Bond. Nevertheless, as I have tried to demonstrate in the two earlier chapters, there has always been a side of Stoppard concerned with what we may call the moral practicalities of life. His plays always reflect the complexities of modern thought, often with the brilliance that only parody at its best can achieve; they demonstrate the confusions, ambiguities and paradoxes to which even the most honest modern thinking must be prone, but also the evasions and double-think which it allows an unscrupulous agent to engage in all too easily (c.f. Archie in *Jumpers*). But Stoppard never lets these complexities stand as an excuse for fundamentally inhumane behaviour: Rosencrantz and Guildenstern's failure, for example, to do anything when they discover that the letter they are carrying is Hamlet's death-warrant, and George's failure to respond to Dotty's cries for help in *Jumpers*, both emerge as pieces of callousness that cannot be excused by the fact that these characters are genuinely confused about the nature of the universe they inhabit. Basic human decencies cut across any amount of philosophical perplexity, and the failure to attend to such basics is what leads to a denial of human rights and decencies on a much larger scale (instanced by the triumph of the military-style Radical Liberal party in *Jumpers*).

In Stoppard's later works — notably the T.V. plays, *Professional Foul* and *Squaring the Circle*, the play-with-music, *Every Good Boy Deserves Favour* and the stage works, *Night and Day* and *The Real Thing* — this emphasis on the loss of human rights, on repressive or totalitarian societies and the culpable inattentions to basic decencies which allow them to exist, has loomed larger and larger. These works, in short, have an overt social/political dimension which is not compatible with tragicomedy. Tragicomedy is *not* inherently an apolitical form

of drama, as it has sometimes been accused of being;
Shakespeare's late plays, for example, or *Jumpers* itself, *Who's
Afraid of Virginia Woolf?* and *Home* all demonstrate ways in
which tragicomedy can incorporate significant social and
political issues. Even the 'purest', most self-referential
tragicomedies, like *Waiting for Godot, The Caretaker* and *Old
Times*, analyse the soul or psyche of a society in ways that have
tacit political implications. These authors do not live in a
separate world and we may sense some of their 'beliefs',
however obliquely, in their writing; it came as no surprise, for
example, that Pinter's early but long-unperformed play, *The
Hothouse* turned out to be quite clearly opposed to such
psychiatric practices as enforced electrotherapy. But tragicomedy chooses to concentrate on the most mysterious areas of
human activity, on those aspects of relationships and behaviour
least susceptible to rational analysis, where people are driven by
forces — either from outside or from deep within themselves —
which they do not understand and over which they have no
control. These are parts of a wider human reality which political
analysis very often ignores (though perhaps recent events in
such places as Iran and India ought to prompt a rethink on this
— human beings are not just socio-economic statistics).
Nevertheless, tragicomedy is not concerned with what we might
call partisan politics or with any overt attempt to change
people's thinking. And, while Stoppard has never adopted the
overt political stance of Seventies playwrights like Howard
Brenton, David Edgar, Howard Barker or David Hare, his later
plays have provocatively confronted overt political issues. The
main reason that Stoppard seems unlikely ever to be identified
with this slightly younger generation of dramatists is that they
are all explicitly on the left of the political spectrum, whereas
Stoppard — in as much as he allows his personal sympathies to
obtrude — seems at heart to be something of an old-fashioned
liberal, always chary of -isms and orthodoxies but concerned for
individual liberties, particularly on behalf of those least able to
defend themselves.

Travesties, then, seems to me an important transitional work,
still in touch with the tragicomic mode of Stoppard's first two
full-length plays but clearly anticipating later developments. As
such, it is a revealing document not only in Stoppard's own

career but also in the general abandonment of tragicomedy that took place in the early Seventies. The play is a fantastic embroidery on the facts of history: the Russian revolutionary Lenin, the Irish novelist James Joyce and the Rumanian Dadaist Tristan Tzara are all known to have lived in Zurich during the First World War. But their paths are not known to have crossed, and Joyce is the only one of them to have been involved with a consular official named Henry Carr in a production of Oscar Wilde's *The Importance of Being Earnest*. In Stoppard's play, the three famous characters meet each other (and Carr), and Tzara seems to take part in the production. It is an arrangement fraught with possibilities for all the strange confusion and bewilderment characteristic of tragicomedy, and these possibilities promise to be realised in the opening scene of the play, where the three famous men are all at work in their individual styles in a Zurich library. Tzara is cutting up pieces of writing and allowing them to rearrange themselves randomly, according to the dictates of his Dadaist faith — we hear some of the unintelligible results; Joyce is dictating a portion of his Modernist novel, *Ulysses*, going for inspiration to scraps of paper in his pockets — the results are just as unintelligible as anything of Tzara's, being a complex collection of Latin, German, Italian and English phrases, puns, arcane allusions, portmanteau words and syllables arranged as much for assonance as for sense; Lenin proves to be at work on a book of political economy, but his first contributions to the dialogue are a conversation with his wife, in Russian — it is not until the second half of the play (p. 70), when their conversation is repeated with a stilted accompanying translation, that the average English theatre-goer learns that they have been discussing the first news of revolution in Russia.

But just as this chaos of Dadaist, Modernist and Russian unintelligibility threatens to engulf the play, Stoppard draws back from the brink and introduces the aged figure of Henry Carr, self-consciously rehearsing his memoirs. From that point on, there will be no *real* confusion in the play: although it will take all kinds of liberties with narrative form, will have characters talking in doggerel or limericks, will merge on and off with dialogue and situations from *The Importance of Being Earnest*, and will repeat itself from time to time, like a record stuck in a groove, the audience recognises everything, including the historical improprieties, as the vagaries of an old man's mind. As Carr disarmingly puts it: 'But I digress. No apologies required, constant digression being the saving grace of senile reminiscence' (p. 22). And Stoppard adds an important note: '*the scene (and most of the play) is under the erratic control of Old Carr's memory, which is not notably reliable, and also of his various prejudices and delusions. One result is that the story (like a toy train perhaps) occasionally jumps the rails and has to be restarted at the point where it goes wild* < . . . > *At any rate the effect of these time-slips is not meant to be bewildering, and it should be made clear what is happening*' (p. 27).

In place of the genuine mysteries of *Rosencrantz and Guildenstern Are Dead* and *Jumpers*, we are faced with confusions that are perfectly comprehensible, given what we know of the vagaries of both memory and prejudice. Both of the earlier plays at least *consider* the possibility that some inscrutable providence is responsible for the perplexities of human life, and reflect this in the perplexities which they pose for the audience, but *Travesties* avoids these metaphysical speculations — or at least keeps them firmly at arm's length. There are no strange gods to be appeased in the play (except perhaps those being appeased off-stage by the ritual slaughter of the First World War); we are dealing rather with human vanities. What Carr's unreliable memory brings about and acts out before us is a rich confrontation of philosophies not so much opposed to as serenely oblivious of each other — until the quirks of that memory and the blatantly theatrical device of exchanged identical folders (like the handbags in *The Importance of Being Earnest*) bring them face to face. Dadaism ('*Dada!* — down with reason, logic, causality, coherence, tradition, proportion, sense and consequence', p. 25) confronts Joyce's view of the perfectionist artist ('An artist is the magician put among men to gratify — capriciously — their urge for immortality', p. 62) and both of them have to contend with the Leninist dictum that: 'The sole duty and justification for art is social criticism' (p. 74).

The fact that three such distinct and articulate opinions are represented, rather than two in simple opposition, ensures that the play never endorses one position over the others. It rather subjects each in turn to parodic distortions, stripping them of their self-imposed dignities, but never to the extent of dismissing any one of them. It is helped in this process by the frequent allusions to, and lapses into, *The Importance of Being Earnest*, a play of self-consuming brilliance, the perfect embodiment of art for art's sake — an attitude at odds with all of the three protagonists. Its perfectly-shaped but vacuous plot and its epigrammatic but hollow wit defy both Joyce's sense of the purpose of art and Tzara's sense of its purposelessness, not to mention Lenin's insistence on art's social function. What is particularly at issue in these parodic confrontations is the question of individual freedoms — both metaphysical and social. According to Tzara: 'The clever people try to impose a design on the world and when it goes calamitously wrong they call it fate. In point of fact, everything is Chance, including design' (p. 37). Joyce, of course, is one of those 'clever people', whose *Ulysses* is precisely an attempt to impose design — a lasting artistic order — on a day in Dublin in 1904. Lenin, equally obviously, has a basically Marxist view of the inexorable progress of history, in which the role of the artist may have to be regulated for the greater good of all: 'Today, literature must become party literature. Down with non-partisan literature! Down with literary supermen! < . . . > we shall establish a free press, free not simply from the police, but also from capital, from careerism, and what is more, *free from bourgeois anarchist individualism*' (p. 85). This definition of freedom would, of course, be anathema equally to Tzara and to Joyce, though for totally different reasons. Nor would it have suited the 'Irish Gomorrahist', Wilde, whose play (at least, as refracted in Carr's memory) seems to endorse or eschew in equal measure randomness, artistic purpose and historical determinism.

As this three- (or four-) sided confrontation goes on, an unexpected additional dimension emerges — that provided by Henry Carr. Carr is neither famous nor an original thinker. For the most part, his attitudes are those of an averagely intelligent member of the Edwardian upper classes. He is happy enough, for example, to offer the bland opinion that: 'It is the duty of the artist to beautify existence' (p. 37). He is resolute, in the face of Tzara's mockery, in his determination that the First World War *means* something. He is sceptical about Joyce's neutralist position respecting the war. And he tries — belatedly — to have

Lenin prevented from returning to Russia, on the grounds that the provisional government there has the makings of a liberal democracy on Western lines. He is, in fact, a middle-of-the-road nonentity, someone passed over by the supposedly great movements of art and history; the very survival of his name into the Seventies, so that he can figure in Stoppard's play, is the result of a most insignificant difference of opinion with Joyce over payments for the production of *The Importance of Being Earnest*. It would be very easy to dismiss Stoppard's Carr as a vain, rather blimpish Englishman of the old school, not really up to the intellectual challenges of the twentieth century. The play certainly gets plenty of comic mileage out of old Carr's self-important memoirs and young Carr's sartorial affectations — everything revolves around what he might be wearing, so that even Joyce's resumé of *The Importance of Being Earnest* (p. 52) is nothing more than a recitation of Carr's costume changes. Similarly, his gallant attempts to protect Gwendolen from the realities of Wilde's sexual reputation is made to look doubly foolish by her 'advanced' reaction: 'Gomorrahist . . . Silly bugger' (p. 53).

It would be a mistake, however, to write Carr off simply as the butt of the jokes of history and of people cleverer than himself. For all his vaguenesses and vanities, a stream of common sense runs through his conversations with the great men of history, as when he observes to Tzara that 'to be an artist *in Zurich, in 1917*, implies a degree of self-absorption that would have glazed over the eyes of Narcissus' (p. 38). Later, when Tzara shows some enthusiasm for the Bolshevik revolution, Carr tells what is surely the truth: 'if the revolution came you wouldn't know what hit you. You're nothing. You're an artist. And multi-coloured micturition is no trick to those boys, they'll have you pissing blood' (p. 83). His decision to try to have Lenin prevented from returning to Russia comes too late but it is by no means inherently foolish. Only someone with perfect hindsight could argue that the Russian Revolution was bound to run its course exactly as it did. Stoppard's account (pp. 79-84) of the hare-brained schemes and labyrinthine negotiations that finally resulted in the famous journey to the Finland Station underlines just how fortuitous it was that Lenin ever got back to Russia in time to play the role that he did. Carr could have been right.

Similarly, it is far from clear who was in the wrong in the altercation between Joyce and Carr over the payments in respect of the production of the play: it is not obviously the case that the greater artist was the better man. What does emerge in Stoppard's account is that Carr was more incensed by Joyce's manners than by the sums of money concerned: 'Came round to the dressing room and handed me ten francs like a *tip* — bloody nerve — Sponger — < . . . > *You are a swindler and a cad!*' (p. 96). Joyce, of course, took his revenge both in the courts and by portraying Carr in a most uncomplimentary light in *Ulysses*, and to that extent he 'won', the permanence of his art affording him a moral victory to which Carr cannot answer back. But in Stoppard's play Carr does answer back, no more overawed by Joyce's genius than he is by Lenin's historical greatness. He is just an ordinary person, who happens to find Joyce's manner devious and off-putting, which it may well have been.

The point, surely, is that Henry Carr — a Rosencrantz or Guildenstern of history rather than of art — was a real human being, whose thoughts and feelings were every bit as real and as valid as those of the more famous contemporaries whose lives brushed briefly against is own. His views are old-fashioned and not particularly intellectual; he can be snobbish and patronising, especially to foreigners (this appears in his dealings both with the Rumanian Tzara and the Irish Joyce) and to women. But who is to say that this personality and the opinions it generates are worth any more or less than those of men who fortuitously become better known? The whole mode of the play, located in Carr's erratic memory, emphasises both the waywardness of human faculties and their propensity for construing reality as individuals would like it to be, rather than necessarily as it is. The closing scene, in which the old Cecily corrects the old Carr on his facts, particularly underlines this point. But it is a truth that extends to great men as well as to little ones; their theories of art or history are just as much the products of limited faculties as are Carr's memories, construing reality as they would like it to be and trying to foist it on other people.

This is the inference to be drawn from the play's nominal comic climax, where the confusion of the identical folders' is finally explained. Tzara returns to Joyce what he conceives to be the latter's typescript, observing that it 'has much in common with your dress. As an arrangement of words it is graceless without being random; as a narrative it lacks charm or even vulgarity; as an experience it is like sharing a cell with a fanatic in search of a mania' (p. 96). The audience absorbs this, like Joyce, as Tzara's characteristic assessment of *Ulysses*, until Joyce reveals that the text is actually 'an ill-tempered thesis purporting to prove, amongst other things, that Ramsay MacDonald is a bourgeois lickspittle gentleman's gentleman' — in other words, a piece of Lenin's political propaganda. Of course, Tzara's views on art being what they are, his comments on the chapter of *Ulysses* might have been exactly the same. Carr proves, in fact, to have the missing extract from *Ulysses*, which he describes as 'a chapter, inordinate in length and erratic in style, remotely connected with midwifery'. To which Joyce frostily replies that: 'It is a chapter which by a miracle of compression, uses the gamut of English literature from Chaucer to Carlyle to describe events taking place in a lying-in hospital in Dublin' (p. 97). Each of the three is correct according to his own lights, even — by his beloved Chance — Tzara. There is no way of saying that any one of them is any more correct than the others.

Lenin's reactions to literature and music (described at length, pp. 86-9) underline further the relativity of human judgements and the propensity of human faculties to reconstruct reality in an arbitrary manner. Lenin's general view of art is a consequence of his view of history and politics and keeps finding itself at odds with his reactions to particular works. He admires Tolstoy's *War and Peace*, but finds it necessary to criticise Tolstoy as a man and a thinker. He can find nothing to admire in Mayakovsky, though he is a revolutionary writer, and prefers Pushkin, though he is a bourgeois one. He claims to admire Gorki but is irritated by an actual performance of *The Lower Depths*. He claims to be deeply moved by Beethoven's Appassionata Sonata but cannot listen to music much because it 'makes me want to say nice stupid things'. That is, there is a continual discrepancy between what Lenin admits he actually feels and politically finds it necessary to believe. It is a waywardness of human faculties at least as disconcerting as Carr's erratic memory, and with far more disturbing consequences.

So it is that Carr emerges as the true hero of *Travesties*, not because there is anything special about him but precisely because he is so ordinary — a man with weaknesses and foibles which we see, warts and all, not dressed up with the doctrines of art or of history. The confusions and complexities of the play stem directly from that ordinariness, from a memory and a vanity trying to impose a design upon reality which it never really had. A Joyce, a Lenin, or even in his own way a Tzara, could doubtless have imposed such a design more impressively — that is why they are remembered. But Carr's very human failure in this respect is perhaps (paradoxically) truer to reality than their successes would have been.

It is precisely the centrality of Carr to *Travesties* which prevents the play from becoming a tragicomedy. The confusions and complexities of the play, although they have much in common with what we have encountered in other tragicomedies, prove to be firmly grounded in human nature; they are not mysteries but products of human vanity. The more Stoppard insists upon this point, the more a tacit moral emerges. If no one is to say that Carr's view of reality is inherently any less perfect than anyone else's, it follows that no one has any right to *impose* his own views upon anyone else. Neither Tzara nor Joyce would wish to do that, though as artists each might hope to convince other people of the force of his personal vision. They are in fact intensely self-absorbed, resolutely pursuing their obsessions in a way that ignores the appalling realities of wars and revolutions. Tzara is so concerned 'to jeer and howl and belch' (p. 37) at the existing world that he naively believes the new Communist one will welcome artists like himself. Joyce calmly announces that: 'As an artist, naturally I attach no importance to the swings and roundabouts of political history' (p. 50). Both of these in effect leave the way open for Lenin, the one man in the play who *is* determined to impose his views on other people. For all the blatant flaws in his ideology, Lenin is prepared to use all the force at his disposal to impose it, as he does on the 'bourgeois intellectuals of the near-Cadet type' about whom he writes so callously to Gorki (p. 88). Tzara, Joyce and Carr would all have fared very badly in Lenin's Russia; the play implicitly condemns such absolutism — and also regards with scepticism any art so self-absorbed as to ignore it. This final emphasis on personal freedom and on the moral responsibility of art is what ultimately separates *Travesties* from the tradition of modern tragicomedy and aligns it, however obliquely, with the era's plays of political commitment.

11
No Man's Land,
by Harold Pinter*

There is good reason to suppose that *No Man's Land* represents the swan-song of the form of modern tragicomedy with which this book has been concerned. Pinter's only subsequent full-length plays to date, *Betrayal* (1978) and *One for the Road* (1984), are significantly different in style and emphasis from his earlier works and are not, by my definitions, tragicomedies. None of the other authors I have considered has written in the tragicomic mode since then, nor has it attracted new practitioners. As is the way with literary genres and sub-genres, its day seems — at least for the present — to have passed.

It is notable in this context that *No Man's Land* echoes many of Pinter's own earlier works, almost as if recapitulating his recurrent themes and motifs in a final, crystalline form. As Martin Esslin points out: 'Like Davies, at the end of *The Caretaker*, Spooner's hopes of gaining a foothold in a new home are defeated; as in *Old Times* a dual of wits is conducted in terms of one spurious reminiscence topping another; Briggs and Foster are a pair of brutal thugs in the line of Ben and Gus of *The Dumb Waiter*, Goldberg and McCann of *The Birthday Party*, or, indeed, Lenny and Joey in *The Homecoming*'.[28] Bernard F. Dukore also draws attention to this feature of the play: 'With resonances of *The Caretaker* (a seedy visitor who fails to establish himself as a mainstay in the house of a benefactor), *Old Times* (the unreliability of memory), *The Collector* (hints of homosexuality), *The Homecoming* (malicious taunting beneath a veneer of affability), *Tea Party* (self-appraisal that proves inaccurate) and no doubt other works as well . . . *No Man's Land* is an echo chamber of the Pinter canon'.[29] As both of these

---

*First performed, London, 1975

authors go on to point out, however, the echoes and resonances do not constitute a laziness on Pinter's part; he has subsumed them into an entirely original and effective work, a fitting finale to modern tragicomedy, which invokes not only his own earlier works but also those of other authors in the genre:

> *Spooner*: < . . . > I have gone too far, you think?
> *Hirst*:   I'm expecting you to go very much further.
> *Spooner*: Really? That doesn't mean I interest you, I hope?
> *Hirst*:   Not in the least.
> *Spooner*: Thank goodness for that. For a moment my heart sank.
>
> (p. 82)

This is reminiscent of Hamm and Clov in *Endgame*:

> *Hamm*: We're not beginning to . . . to . . . mean something?
> *Clov*: Mean something! You and I, mean something (*Brief laugh.*) Ah that's a good one.
>
> (p. 27)

The concept that characters might 'interest' each other, or the audience, or that they might 'mean something' to each other or the audience, are closely analogous in the context of a dramatic performance, in which the processes of entertainment (interest) and signification (generating meaning) run so closely together. In *Waiting for Godot* and *Endgame*, Beckett constantly draws on music-hall routine and silent-comedy films as forms of innocent (i.e. meaningless) entertainment, self-consciously teasing the audience both about what they find interesting and about the sense they are making of it:

> *Clov*: (*picks up the telescope, turns it on the auditorium*) I see . . . a multitude . . . in transports . . . of joy. (*Pause.*) That's what I call a magnifier.
>
> (p. 25)

Stoppard, in *Rosencrantz and Guildenstern Are Dead*, carries this a stage further by implying an element of titillation, not to say prostitution, about the relationship between a performance and its audience:

> *Guildenstern*: You said something — about getting caught up in the action —

Player: *(gaily freeing himself)* I did! — I did! — You're quicker
            than your friend . . . *(Confidingly.)* Now for a handful
            of guilders I happen to have a private and uncut
            performance of the Rape of the Sabine Women — or
            rather woman, or rather Alfred — *(Over his shoulder.)*
            Get your skirt on, Alfred — *(The Boy starts struggling
            into a female robe.)* . . . and for eight you can
            participate. *(Guil. backs. Player follows.)* . . . or both for
            ten.

(pp. 18-19)

Spooner's line in *No Man's Land* — 'That doesn't mean I
interest you, I hope?' — clearly also carries a strain of
(homosexual) flirtation in it. Homosexuality is implicitly a
theme throughout the play, from the possible nuances of 'Do
you often hang about Hampstead Heath?' (p. 79) to Foster's
marked sexual ambiguity: 'I was in Bali when they sent for me. I
didn't have to leave, I didn't have to come here < . . . > I was
only a boy. But I was nondescript and anonymous. A famous
writer wanted me' (p. 144). But in Spooner's line it goes beyond
being an issue between the characters and becomes, as in
Stoppard, though much more discreetly, an issue between the
performance and the audience.

There is a parallel example in Spooner's comment when he
finally elicits a personal statement of sorts from the
unforthcoming Hirst: 'A metaphor. Things are looking up'
(p. 94). Just as Hamm and Clov repeatedly allude to theatrical
conventions such as asides and soliloquies, and Rosencrantz and
Guildenstern make much of the formal rules of philosophical
debate (rhetoric, statements, *non-sequiturs* etc.), this focuses
attention very self-consciously on the whole question of
communication. If the characters are only relating to each other
via the slippery medium of metaphor, what is the relationship
between the performance of which they form a part and the
audience? What form of communication is taking place? How
effective is it? The issue is reiterated on a number of occasions,
invariably by Spooner:

I decided to paint a picture — of the canal, the waiter, the child, the
fisherman, the lovers, the fish, and in background, in shadow, the
man at the other table, and to call it The Whistler. The Whistler. If

198

you had seen the picture, and the title, would the title have baffled you? (p. 101)

Translating verse is an extremely difficult task. Only the Rumanians remain respectable exponents of the craft. (p. 122)

terza rima, a form which, if you will forgive my saying so, you have never been able to master. (p. 135)

You could read your own work to an interested and informed audience, to an audience brimming over with potential for the greatest possible enthusiasm < . . . > Let us content ourselves with the idea of an intimate reading, in a pleasing and conducive environment, let us consider an evening to be remembered, by all who take part in her. (pp. 148-9)

Significantly, after a silence, it is this latter proposition — an evocation of a perfectly controlled communication of Hirst's works to a receptive audience — that shifts the play into its final, lyrically-chilling coda, defining the terms of No Man's Land. It is perhaps to be expected that, in a play where both the central characters claim to be authors of sorts, the issue of communication should arise. But it does so here persistently, and at critical moments, with a self-consciousness that is unusual in Pinter — though not, as we have seen, in Beckett or Stoppard. It is as if, in this play, Pinter has turned to confront the 'strangeness' of his plays, the ways in which they tantalise or infuriate his audiences, though in so doing he can hardly be said to have alleviated the problem. As with Shakespeare in *The Tempest*, (the parallels between the plays are quite marked), Pinter foregrounds the processes of creativity and communication in *No Man's Land*. But he does so in a way that dispels none of their essential mystery. The more he seems to put his cards on the table, the more we suspect he has up his sleeve.

There is a perfect illustration of this in the play's use of cricket imagery. At one point Spooner discusses Hirst's hypothetical wife in the jargon of the true cricket enthusiast:

Tell me with what speed she swung in the air, with what velocity she came off the wicket, whether she was responsive to finger spin, whether you could bowl a shooter with her, or an offbreak with a legbreak action. In other words, did she google?

(p. 92)

Later, when Hirst addresses Spooner as Charles Wetherby, he recall their 'last encounter': 'Pavilion at Lord's in '39, against the West Indies, Hutton and Compton batting superbly, Constantine bowling, war looming. Surely I'm right?' (p. 127). It is by now something of an open secret[30] that cricket is a particular passion of Pinter's — a fact which has been construed as throwing light of a sort on his plays: the game is ridiculously arcane in its rules, unintelligible to the uninitiated, a strange mixture of polite behaviour, style and sudden violence — all qualities that have been attributed to Pinter's drama. So the fact that he invokes cricket explicitly here, in the mysterious contexts both of Spooner and Hirst's past and of their sexuality, might been seen as an in-joke, a pointedly self-conscious reference to the game-playing which lies at the heart of the play's process of communication. It is not at all clear, however, that this explanation will help us with another apparent cricketing allusion in the play, which is the fact that the names of all four characters (including the somewhat unusual Spooner) happen to be those of English test cricketers from around the turn of the century.[31] This may, of course, be entirely coincidental. Even if it is not coincidental, there may be no particular point to it — *Wisden* might simply have been closer to hand than the telephone directory when Pinter was looking for names. Certainly, if this is a deliberate allusion on Pinter's part, it is a very obscure one; these are not names to conjure with (as Hutton, Compton and Constantine are) except for a very few enthusiasts — who might just make something of the fact that Hirst, Briggs and Foster were primarily slow left-arm bowlers, while Spooner was an elegant batsman. To the mass of the audience these would be nothing more than dry extracts from the record-books, even if the allusion were recognised. So this is hardly an in-joke — more, perhaps, an inscrutable private gesture. The mystery of creativity and communication remains intact, for all that Pinter flaunts it so provocatively.

It is in this context that we may begin to appreciate the measured irony of the play's opening lines:

Hirst: As it is?

Spooner: As it is, yes please, absolutely as it is.

(p. 77)

The literal reference is to the drink that Hirst is pouring for Spooner. This is an apt starting point, since Hirst and Spooner are rarely without a drink in the course of the play and Spooner's identity in particular seems to revolve around his association with drink — notably his sharing a drink with a Hungarian émigré in Jack Straw's Castle, where apparently he also met Hirst (pp. 85-7); his claim to be a 'champagne drinker' (p. 121); and his association with The Bull's Head pub in Chalk Farm, where Briggs knows him as someone who collects the glasses but he projects himself as a friend of the landlord, who allows him to use an upper room for select literary gatherings (pp. 99, 123-4, 148-9). Drink is thus associated with social cachet and literary sophistication, but also with various forms of degradation — most graphically when Hirst crawls off-stage, after a fierce bout of whisky and vodka, and Spooner laconically rhymes: 'I have known this before. The exit through the door, by way of belly and floor' (p. 96). So the bluff certainties of the opening lines ('absolutely as it is') disintegrate as the various capacities of drink manifest themselves in the course of the play. And this parallels the 'strangeness' of the play itself, which promises at times — as in the cricket and literary metaphors — to be so much more open-handed and self-revealing than Pinter's earlier plays, but in the end never is. The 'as it is' may tempt us to look for something literal and uncomplicated, but we shall not find it.

The more self-conscious Pinter becomes about the tragicomic themes and conventions of *No Man's Land*, the more oblique and mysterious the play actually becomes. The paradox is pointed up by Spooner who, while preferring not to be too categorical about himself, is anxious to pierce the mysteries surrounding Hirst. Some of these he ascribes to a form of Hirst's own 'impotence' (sexual? philosophical? literary?):

I would say < . . . > that you lack the essential quality of manliness, which is to put your money where your mouth is, to pick up a pintpot and know it to be a pintpot, and knowing it to be a pintpot, to declare it as a pintpot, and to stay faithful to that pintpot as though you have given birth to it out of your own arse.

(pp. 94-5)

The image of the pintpot, of course, tells us at least as much about Spooner (alcoholically speaking) as it does about Hirst: the asumption, moreover, that a pintpot is always a pintpot and invariably knowable as such is far from self-evident, and we might well conclude that this tells us as much about Spooner's inadequacies as it does about Hirst's lack of 'manliness'. The same tendency to reveal his own limitations, rather than penetrate to the truth of things, is apparent in the story of Foster's little mystery of the disappearing coin. Spooner announces confidently that the old tramp 'was a con artist':

> *Foster*: Do you think so?
> *Spooner*: You would be wise to grant the event no integrity whatsoever.
> *Foster*: You don't subscribe to the mystery of the Orient?
> *Spooner*: A typical Eastern con trick.
> *Foster*: Double Dutch, you mean?
> *Spooner*: Certainly. Your good health. (*Drinks.*)
>
> (pp. 104-5)

Spooner wishes to seem the perfect rationalist, impervious to all mysteries, which he dismisses as trickery. As such, he is antipathetic to the very spirit of tragicomedy, which resists all the literal, realistic implications of 'as it is'. Foster's rejoinder, 'Double Dutch' is particularly ironic, evoking as it does Spooner's own recent tale of wishing to paint a scene which he would enigmatically call The Whistler (p. 101). That scene was itself in Amsterdam, and so a rather literal example of the Double Dutch which Spooner here disdains. The fact that Spooner misses the irony and has another self-satisfied drink underlines his lack of authority throughout. He seeks to take over Hirst, to pierce the sexual, personal and literary mysteries that surround him, but he is thwarted as much by his own limitations as by any real resistance put up by Hirst, Foster and Briggs. He is to that extent an image of the confused or unimaginative rationalist in Pinter's audience, who wants his drama 'as it is', without con tricks or Double Dutch, not appreciating how impossible or untruthful that would actually be — or how much such a desire represents *his own* limitations.

In thus flaunting his usual tragicomic conventions — the strangeness, the lack of realistic definition of his plots and characters — Pinter confronts and challenges his audience with an unusual directness, as in the closing of the first act:

> *Foster*: You know what it's like when you're in a room with the light on and then suddenly the light goes out? I'll show you. It's like this.
>
> (p. 115)

Foster's plunging of Spooner into darkness simultaneously plunges the audience into darkness, and we are made forcefully aware of the artificiality of all theatrical conventions. The actor playing Foster after all only *pretends* to put out the light. Technicians elsewhere turn off the stage lights which *pretend* to be the room lights, thereby also putting the audience into darkness.

Here, as in all the other examples I have traced, Pinter is drawing attention to the make-believe element central to all drama (indeed, to all literature) but paramount to tragicomedy, where the imaginative possibilities of other worlds, other modes of understanding, even metamorphosis into other modes of being, are explored. This is perfectly, if paradoxically, exemplified in Briggs' long and detailed account of meeting Foster (pp. 120-1). His tale of directing Foster to Bolsover Street is positively baroque in its accumulation of verifiable detail — one-way systems, hardware stores, lefts and rights, the Post Office Tower. It is realism gone mad, as perhaps we begin to suspect by the time this near-thug starts talking about writing to *The Times*. But where in earlier plays Pinter might have left us to infer the unreliability of such garrulousness (in the cases, say, of Mick's cosmopolitan airs in *The Caretaker* or Deeley's memories in *Old Times*), he here tops and tails the whole speech with the same *caveat*: 'I should tell you he'll deny this account. His story will be different.' He admits that this is, at best, a personal version of events, at worst pure fantasy; whether as a result of the vagaries of memory, or of perception, or of wilful distortion, the story has no absolute validity. It is, in short, a piece of invention, of imagination — as much on Briggs' part as on Pinter's. And it calls attention to the fact that the play itself is a fabrication, something that obeys the mysterious rules of imagination, and in no way answerable to the grey consensus we call reality.

This kind of self-consciousness, with its apparent insistence on a form of art for art's sake, answerable only to itself, is something for which tragicomedy has repeatedly been castigated. Lytton Strachey, for example, dismissed Shakespeare's late tragicomedies as the works of a man 'bored with people, bored with real life, bored with drama, bored with everything, in fact, except poetry and poetical dreams'.[32] And the self-consciousness in Fletcher's works is repeatedly equated with decadence. But such criticism is fundamentally misconceived. It ignores the fact that, at heart, tragicomedy is always concerned with the act of imagination, the capacity both to conjure up and communicate 'far other worlds and other seas', as Marvell put it.[33] The self-consciousness, or the drawing of attention to its own artificiality, is thus always a way of drawing attention to its own central metaphors, the creation of something out of nothing, of new life out of death, of the act of faith between drama and audience out of a bare stage. In Renaissance tragicomedy the miracle invariably worked, at least within given limits: providence repaid the act of faith (c.f. Prospero's 'prayer' for release at the end of *The Tempest*). In modern tragicomedy, however hard we try, the miracle does not work: perhaps the faith is lacking. And that, surely, is the central theme, as well as the central fact, of *No Man's Land*.

Hirst and Spooner are both poets or men of letters; at least, both have pretentions to be so. Yet both display radical inadequacies — Hirst in his chronic drinking and faintly sordid dependence on Foster and Briggs, Spooner in his over-anxiety to impress and to establish a foothold. These inadequacies extend to most areas of their personalities — sexual, social and economic: the possibility of impotence is alluded to more than once, as are a number of infertile sexual practices; it is never clear if either actually had the wives or families that are repeatedly implied. Spooner may actually be reduced to collecting glasses in a pub and, while Hirst shows every sign of being affluent, he also appears to be under the control of those who purport to be his servants. At the heart of these inadequacies, however, lies the question of their being artists, men of imagination — a faculty which, whatever vitality it may have had in the past, they have both apparently lost by the time of this play. This issue lies behind the photograph album which

Hirst thinks of showing to Spooner, which may revive the ghosts of their pasts: 'Allow the love of the good ghost. They possess all that emotion . . . trapped. Bow to it < . . . > You think it cruel . . . to quicken them, when they are fixed, imprisoned? No. . . no. Deeply, deeply, they wish to respond to your touch, to your look, and when you smile, their joy . . . is unbounded' (p. 137). In the terms of this play memory is like art, an act of imagination, which can be a vital, positive force.

Briggs, of course, cannot allow this possibility: 'They're blank, mate, blank. The blank dead.' But the tantalising element of this play — the half-promise of the miracle — is that, with Spooner present, Hirst shows signs of rediscovering his creative imagination. Early on, he says: 'Tonight . . . my friend . . . you find me in the last lap of a race . . . I had long forgotten to run' (p. 94). Now he shows signs of trying to run again, resisting Briggs' pessimism ('Nonsense') and talking of getting on with a critical essay he is supposed to be writing.

Whether or not Hirst and Spooner really knew each other at Oxford before the war, and had strings of acquaintances with Noel-Cowardish names, whether or not one had an affair with the other's wife, they acknowledge an affinity with each other, while remaining guarded and even antagonistic. They both belong to the tradition of English gentlemen, with its Arcadian ideals of life and literature. However muted and parodied it may be, this theme adds a nationalistic strain to the tragicomedy:

Spooner: All we have left is the English language. Can it be salvaged? That is my question.

Hirst: You mean in what rests its salvation?

Spooner: More or less.

Hirst: Its salvation must rest in you.

Spooner: It's uncommonly kind of you to say so. In you too, perhaps, although I haven't sufficient evidence to go on, as yet.

(pp. 80-1)

Spooner: What happened to our cottages? What happened to our lawns? *(Pause.)* Be frank. Tell me. You've revealed something. You've made an unequivocal reference to your past. Don't go back on it. We share something. A memory of the bucolic life. We're both English.

(p. 91)[34]

This may all be fantasy, but it is a fantasy with the power almost to galvanise the drink-sodden Hirst into new life; he painfully relives the dream of the drowning man (whom Spooner claims to be, p. 109) which seems to symbolise the passing into his present state of limbo — a surrogate death which Spooner's presence now offers hope of reversing. It is significant that the major speech in which Spooner offers Hirst the prospect of an intimately communicative poetry reading uses terms that all but imply a resurrection:

> I beg you to consider seriously the social implications of such an adventure. You would be there in body. It would bring you to the young, the young to you. The elderly, also, those who have almost lost hope, would on this occasion leave their homes and present themselves.
>
> (p. 148)

At the last moment, however, Hirst falters, falling back on Foster and Briggs rather than rising to the opportunity/ challenge that Spooner represents. It is a falling back on moribund literalism at the expense of the imaginative vitality, of the living tradition, which Spooner nearly revived:

> *Hirst*: Let us change the subject. *(Pause.)* For the last time. *(Pause.)* What have I said?[35]
> *Foster*: You said you're changing the subject for the last time.
> *Hirst*: But what does that mean?
> *Foster*: It means you'll never change the subject again.
>
> (p. 149)

As with his turning out of the light at the end of the first act, Foster's words have a literal force that is intensified by the artificial conventions of the drama itself. There is no time for Hirst to change the subject again. The play is coming to an end, the limitations of time and performance circumscribing the possibilities of further creativity. Appropriately, the play self-consciously enacts its own final meaning, its closing words reiterating earlier words with new force and finality. Spooner fleshes out Hirst's earlier (p. 96) 'explanation' of the play's title:

> No. You are in no man's land. Which never moves, which never

changes, which never grows older, but which remains forever, icy and silent.

Silence.

If the title was enigmatic earlier, like Spooner's 'The Whistler', it is hardly so now, as the silence in the theatre underscores the silent life-in-death which Spooner here pronounces, final confirmation of the modern tragicomic truth that no miracle is possible. Hirst caps it in the only possible way: 'I'll drink to that.' It is a fitting epitaph for modern tragicomedy.

In Conclusion

Many questions, of course, remain. Why should modern tragicomedy have flourished when it did, and only then? Why should it, for all the obvious differences, have had so much in common with Renaissance tragicomedy? It is always tempting to try to answer such questions in terms of the prevailing culture — the social, political and philosophical pressures of the day. Modern tragicomedy as I have described it is a post-war phenomenon, a contemporary of the hydrogen bomb, television, the decline of the British Empire — and all of these 'influences' can be traced in it. But they can also be traced in other plays of the period — those of John Osborne, Edward Bond, Stephen Poliakoff, for example — and only offer a partial explanation for the flourishing of this unique form at this particular time.

I would point to one central characteristic of all the works we have considered here as further partial explanation. That is the emphasis on the diminished status of the individual. I do not only mean social status, though it is certainly symptomatic that so many of these plays should concentrate on tramps, drop-outs and people pushed to the side of life's mainstream. I refer also to the recurrent suggestion that individuals can have no say in their own futures and little or no control over their own actions: they are at the mercy of larger forces, however we define them — economics, biology, history, providence. So often locked in sterile symbiotic relationships, they have lost the power to regenerate, to create new generations. Indeed, individuals are so ineffectual that they are constantly in danger of losing their identities altogether, interchangeable Rosencrantzes and Guildensterns, Vladimirs and Estragons. Frequently we feel that the characters on stage — like Hamm and Clov in *Endgame* or Anna and Kate in *Old Times* — are so nebulous as to seem only parts of a personality, not the entire substance.

The genre as a whole represents a sustained doubting of the concept of the free, rational, purposive individual which is central to liberal democratic societies and was for so long (though perhaps is no longer) the mainstay of the novel as a literary form. Identity, the self itself, is repeatedly exposed as vulnerable and, what is perhaps more worrying, insignificant. Two of the most forceful images in this connection are those of Hamm autocratically but pathetically insisting on his own centrality and Aston in *The Caretaker* falteringly remembering (or inventing) the electrotherapy that changed his life.

This may help us to explain some of the parallels with Renaissance tragicomedy. We no longer think of the Renaissance quite as confidently as we once did as an age of aggressive 'individualism'; what is undoubtedly the case, however, is that the status and integrity of the free moral individual was one of the key issues for all writers and thinkers from, say, Machiavelli to Descartes. The tragicomedy of Guarini, and successors like Fletcher and Shakespeare, may be seen as a reaction to this; it embodies a mystic, essentially irrational sense of bewildered and ineffectual individuals achieving significance not by their own efforts but by playing their parts in a wider pattern of experience, whose existence is a matter of faith rather than of material demonstration. Echoes of this pattern of experience — suggestions of rebirth, initiations into new mysteries — recur throughout modern tragicomedy, but it is the bewilderment that predominates. What is lacking is the faith: no one really expects Godot to come, the Buddha is smashed, Guildenstern and Dotty can only be wistful about the lack of unicorns. If the 'miracle' endings of Renaissance tragicomedies constituted a challenge to their audiences to redefine the 'real', how much more does the absence of such miracles today throw down the gauntlet: what is at stake is our definition of our*selves* and the qualities of integrity that depend upon that definition.

Notes

Preface

1. See *At the Royal Court. Twenty-five Years of the English Stage Company* ed. Richard Findlater (Ambergate, Derbyshire, 1981) for a history/celebration of the English Stage Company, with pictures from early products of several of the plays discussed here.
2. Published by Methuen, London, 1984, 1985. The second edition includes 'A Play and Its Politics, a Conversation between Harold Pinter and Nicholas Hern'.

Part I

1. J.L. Styan, *The Dark Comedy: the Development of Modern Comic Tragedy*, (Cambridge U.P., Cambridge, 2nd edn. 1968), p.vi.
2. P. 244.
3. Eric Bentley, *The Life of the Drama* (Atheneum, New York, 1964); Karl S. Guthke, *Modern Tragicomedy* (Random House, New York, 1966); Ruby Cohn, *Currents in Contemporary Drama* (Indiana U.P., Bloomington, 1969); Bernard F. Dukore, *Where Laughter Stops: Pinter's Tragicomedy* (University of Missouri Press, Columbia and London, 1976); David L. Hirst, *Tragicomedy* (Methuen, London and New York, 1984).
4. See Pinter's interview with Lawrence M. Bensky in *The Paris Review*, No. 39 (1966), reprinted in *Writers at Work, The Paris Review Interviews*, Third Series (Viking Press, New York, 1967; Secker and Warburg, London, 1968) and elsewhere. This gives the most detailed personal account of Pinter's early life, reading and influences.
5. See Martin Esslin, *The Theatre of the Absurd*, 1968.
6. Quoted in Herrick (1955), p. 3. Aristotle discusses categories of drama in the *Poetics*. Horace, in the *Art of Poetry* (89-93) does admit that exceptions are possible. But he seems rather to think that the boundaries of tragedy and comedy are somewhat elastic than that elements of the two modes may legitimately be mixed.
7. Quoted in Herrick (1955), p. 1.

211

8. Sir Philip Sidney, 'An Apology for Poetry', in *English Critical Texts: 16th to 20th Century*, ed. D.J. Enright and E. de Chickera (Oxford U.P., London, 1962), p. 42.

9. Written in 1543, but revised before its publication in 1554.

10. *Discorso*. Quoted in A.H. Gilbert, *Literary Criticism: Plato to Dryden*, (Wayne State U.P., Detroit, 1962; first published New York, 1940), p. 255.

11. Aristotle, 'On the Art of Poetry' (i.e. the *Poetics*), in *Classical Literary Criticism*, trans. T.S. Dorsch (Penguin Books, Harmondsworth, 1965), p. 48.

12. *Altile* (published 1583), p. 9. Quoted in Herrick (1955), p. 67.

13. Taken from *A Critical Edition of Sir Richard Fanshawe's 1647 Translation of . . . 'Il Pastor Fido'*, by W.F. Staton Jr. and W.E. Simeone (Clarendon Press, Oxford. 1964), Appendix I, pp. 177-8.

14. Staton and Simeone (1964) Introduction, p. xiii.

15. Translated in Gilbert (1962), pp. 511-12.

16. M.C. Bradbrook, 1962 Introduction to *Beaumont and Fletcher: Selected Plays* (Dent, London, 1911), p. x.

17. *The Faithful Shepherdess* was actually by Fletcher alone. This is not the place to rehearse the vexed question of their respective authorship in the large canon of work which goes under their joint names, but which certainly contains contributions from Massinger, Rowley and others. I wish here to identify a style of drama which they first made popular in England in the years 1608-13, when they were certainly collaborating closely.

18. Everyman edn., (1911), p. 242.

19. E.M. Waith, *The Pattern of Tragicomedy in Beaumont and Fletcher*, (Yale U.P., New Haven, Conn., 1952; Archon Books, New York, 1969), pp. 36-42.

20. References to *Philaster* are to Andrew Gurr's Revels edition (Methuen, London, 1969).

21. T.S. Eliot, 'Ben Jonson' in *Selected Essays* (3rd edn., Faber and Faber, London, 1951) 147-60, p. 156.

22. See J.F. Danby, *Elizabethan and Jacobean Poets* (Faber and Faber, London, 1965). Chapter 5, 'Beaumont and Fletcher: Jacobean Absolutists' has a very detailed and unsympathetic reading of *Philaster* in this connection.

23. See *Philaster*, ed. Gurr, 1969, Introduction, pp. xxv-lxi.

24. Edward Bond, *Plays Two*, The Master Playwrights (Methuen, London, 1978), Introduction, p. x.

25. 'Shakespeare's Final Period', first published in the *Independent Review*, August 1904, pp. 405-18, but often reprinted.

26. See *Philaster*, ed. Gurr, pp. xlv-l, and *Cymbeline*, ed. J.M. Nosworthy (Methuen, London, 1955), pp. xxxvii-xl.

27. Ashley Thorndike, *The Influence of Beaumont and Fletcher on Shakespeare* (New York, 1966; first published, 1901), p. 150.

28. U. Ellis-Fermor, *The Jacobean Drama* (Methuen, London, 1936), p. 268. See also E.M. Tillyard, *Shakespeare's Last Plays* (Chatto and Windus, London, 1938), pp. 5-10.

29. J. Hartwig, *Shakespeare's Tragicomic Vision* (Baton Rouge, Louisiana, 1972).

30. Herrick (1955) pp. 258-60.

31. George Bernard Shaw among them. See *Shaw on Shakespeare*, ed. E. Wilson (Penguin Books, Harmondsworth, 1969), p. 171.

32. Preface to Johnson's edition of *The Plays of William Shakespeare*, taken from *Samuel Johnson on Shakespeare*, ed. W.K. Wimsatt Jr. (Macgibbon and Kee, London, 1960), pp. 28-9.

33. *Ibid.* Notes to the Plays, p. 108.

34. See 'Oberon' in *Jacobean and Caroline Masques*, Vol. I, ed. R. Dutton (Nottingham Drama Texts, 1981) p. 127, note to 1.221.

35. See, for example, I.ii.67-82; III.i.22; IV.i.24; V.ii.105-6; V.iii.121-3.

36. The main plot is counterpointed here with the story of the gaoler's daughter, who falls distractedly in love with Palamon. I omit details here, since they are not relevant to the business on hand.

37. The collaboration between Shakespeare and Fletcher was not perfect, and this probably accounts for some inconsistencies of characterisation and tone, which are however very different from the dramatically significant transformations in, say, *The Winter's Tale*. See N.W. Bawcutt's edition of the play (Penguin Books, Harmondsworth, 1977), Introduction, pp. 28-31.

38. *Ibid.* p. 26.

39. See G. Wilson Knight, *The Crown of Life* (rev. edn., Methuen, London, 1958).

40. For example, Tillyard (1938) and R.A. Foakes (*Shakespeare: The Dark Comedies to the last Plays: From Satire to Celebration* (Routledge, London, 1971) do not mention the play at all.

41. See R. Dutton, *Ben Jonson: to the First Folio* (Cambridge U.P., Cambridge, 1983), Chapter 7: *'Bartholomew Fair'*.

42. See Note 19.

43. Waith (1952) pp. 41-2, 85, 98.

44. See 'The Sunne Rising'; 'A Valediction: forbidding mourning'; 'Good Friday, 1613, Riding Westward'.

45. See David L. Hirst's *Tragicomedy* for a full history of the genre as a whole.

46. John Fletcher and John Spurling, *Beckett the playwright* (3rd edn., Methuen, London, 1985), p. 16.

47. Raymond Williams, *Modern Tragedy* (Chatto and Windus, London, 1966), p. 43.

Part II

1. Campbell, *The Hero With a Thousand Faces* (1968). I recommend the book without in any way condoning its arch and purple prose.

2. The play was written firstly in French, with the title *En Attendant Godot*, which can be translated either as 'waiting for Godot' or as 'while attending on Godot'.

3. See Genesis, 4.
4. See the title essay in Edmund Wilson's *The Wound and the Bow* (Methuen, London, 1961).
5. See Part I, pp. 14-15; 25; 26-27.
6. Part of James Boswell's entry for August 6th 1763 in his *The Life of Samuel Johnson*. See the Oxford Standard Authors edition by R.W. Chapman, revised by J.D. Fleeman (Oxford, 1976), p. 333.
7. See Part I, pp. 51-2.
8. As quoted in Martin Esclin, *The Theatre of the Absurd* (1968), p. 52. Note that Esslin himself is quoting from two sources here.
9. See Part I, pp. 49-52.

Part III

1. In fact, Conan Doyle depicted Holmes smoking *straight* pipes. The popular association of him with curved pipes like the meerschaum derives from stage and film versions. See *The Annotated Sherlock Holmes*, ed. W.S. Baring-Gould (2nd edn., New York, 1971), Vol. I, p. 107, Note 3.
2. See Part I, p. 12.
3. Some of the reviews — including the honourable exception of Harold Hobson's piece for the *Sunday Times* which hailed 'the most original, disturbing and arresting talent in the theatrical London' — are reprinted in Esslin's *Pinter the Playwright* (1982), pp. 20-3.
4. See Part I, p. 53, on the use of the term 'ritual'.
5. See Part II, pp. 57-8.
6. See Part I, p. 24.
7. See, for example, pp. 22, 23, 32, 68.
8. See the *Paris Review* interview, cited in Part I, Note 4.
9. P. 82. Mick's accusation of Davies is, of course, an extremely revealing comment about the play as a whole, and indeed about all of Pinter's plays. The sense of words is usually delimited by the context in which they are used, but the *context* itself is always such an ambiguous quantity in Pinter's plays that the words of his characters are indeed often 'open to any number of different interpretations'.
10. Along with the reputation of the author generally and of the Mike Nichols' film of the play, starring Richard Burton and Elizabeth Taylor. The decline in Albee's reputation is well reflected in *A Collection of Critical Essays*, ed. C.W.E. Bigsby: Twentieth Century Views (Prentice Hall, Englewood Cliffs, N.J., 1975).
11. See Part I, pp. 31-40.
12. Judi Dench, for example, did this with the Royal Shakespeare Company in the early Seventies.
13. 'The Final Plays' in *Renaissance Essays* (Collins, London, 1973), 219-59, p. 246.
14. See, for example, Axel Kruse, 'Tragicomedy and Tragic Burlesque: *Waiting for Godot* and *Rosencrantz and Guildenstern Are Dead*', *Sydney Studies in English*, I, (1975-6) 76-96.

15. See Part II, pp. 57-8.
16. *Hamlet*, III.i.151.
1. See Findlater (1981), p. 113.
18. See any speech or interview given by Pinter or Beckett. A particularly good example is the speech Pinter reprints as the Introduction to his *Plays: Four* (Methuen, London, 1981), pp. ix-xiii. Stoppard is superficially more forthcoming, though in fact he characteristically ducks behind aphorisms and witticisms whenever he is pressed closely on his work, as distinct from general questions on his life and beliefs. See, for example, Mel Gussow's 'The Real Tom Stoppard' in *The New York Times Sunday Magazine*, 1 January 1984.
19. Compare this with two other 'hospital' works, Peter Nichols' play and film, *The National Health* and Lindsay Anderson's film, *Britannia Hospital*.
20. *Halliwell's Film Guide* (3rd edn. London, 1981), p. 724. Halliwell's comment on the film is by no means definitive, but it is interesting: 'Superbly crafted but rather empty dramatic charade, visually and emotionally memorable but with nothing whatever to say'. This is precisely the sort of thing that unsympathetic critics say about Pinter's own plays and about tragicomedy in general. It compares strikingly with Anna's 'wonderful'.
21. Anna's name is only voiced once, just before the end. Kate is named several times, often in Anna's pet form, Katey. The literal anonymity of the other two underlines her real strength.
22. The original casting of the Irish actor, Colin Blakely, in the part removed any real ambiguity about this. That original production was stunningly memorable.
23. Pinter returns several times to the theme of Celtic violence, notably with McCann in *The Birthday Party*, who all but claims to be a member of the I.R.A, and 'that Scotch git' by whom Davies in *The Caretaker* claims to have been attacked.
24. Deeley comes very close at times to voicing the 'common man's' rational, literal-minded response to tragicomedy as a whole, with its sophisticated mysteries. This is an example of the densely textured self-referential nature of tragicomedy at its best.
25. See above, p. 99.
26. See Part II, p. 77.
27. Compare this with Guildenstern on the subject of unicorns (*Rosencrantz and Guildenstern Are Dead*, pp. 14-15).
28. Martin Esslin, *Pinter the Playwright* (1982), p. 202.
29. B.F. Dukore, *Where Laughter Stops: Pinter's Tragicomedy*, (1976), pp. 62-3.
30. See the Preface.
31. See a letter to *The Times*, 7 June 1971, by D.A. Cairns, an extract from which is quoted in Dukore, (1976), p. 70.
32. See above, Part I, Note 24.
33. 'The Garden', l. 46.
34. These passages and the 'Charles Wetherby' sequence (pp. 126-36) show

Pinter at his closest to David Storey in *Home*. It is not accidental that the parts of Jack and Harry, Hirst and Spooner, have so much in common, since both were written specifically for the pair of theatrical knights, John Gielgud and Ralph Richardson. Both Pinter and Storey exploited the public personae of these two great actors as an additional dimension of their tragicomic self-consciousness. But both plays are strong enough to survive without these particular incarnations. Both plays also have a 'national' identity to them, with a streak of nostalgia for an older England that is not quite dead and might conceivably be revived — though it is far from clear that either dramatist actually *advocates* such a revival.

35.   Echoing, whether consciously or not, Vladimir's pivotal question near the end of *Waiting for Godot* (p. 91), another example of the play taking a retrospective view of the genre as a whole.

Select Bibliography

There is already a considerable literature relating to most of the plays and authors discussed in this book. What follows is necessarily, therefore, a very selective list, incorporating all the main works on which I have drawn in my own writing and some which are likely starting places for further reading.

(i) Tragicomedy

E. Bentley, *The Life of Drama*, (Atheneum, New York, 1964).

J.R. Brown and B. Harris, eds., *Jacobean Theatre*, Stratford Upon Avon Studies 1 (Edward Arnold, London, 1960).

— *Later Shakespeare*, Stratford Upon Avon Studies 8 (Edward Arnold, London, 1966).

J. Campbell, *The Hero with a Thousand Faces*, Bollingen Series 17 (2nd edn. Princeton U.P., Princeton, N.J., 1968).

H. Felperin, *Shakespearean Romance*, (Princeton U.P., Princeton, N.J., 1973).

N. Frye, *A Natural Perspective: the Development of Shakespearean Comedy and Romance* (Columbia U.P., New York, 1965).

A.H. Gilbert, *Literary Criticism: Plato to Dryden* (Wayne State U.P., Detroit, 1940).

K.S. Guthke, *Modern Tragicomedy* (Random House, New York, 1966).

J.L. Hartwig, *Shakespeare's Tragicomic Vision* (Louisiana U.P., Baton Rouge, 1972).

M.T. Herrick, *Tragicomedy: its Origin and Development in Italy, France and England* (Illinois U.P., Urbana, 1962).

D.L. Hirst, *Tragicomedy*, The Critical Idiom Series (Methuen, London and New York, 1984).

C. Hoy, *The Hyacinth Room: An Investigation into the Nature of Comedy, Tragedy and Tragicomedy* (Chatto and Windus, London, 1967).

W. Kerr, *Tragedy and Comedy* (Bodley Head, London, 1968).
C. Leech, *The John Fletcher Plays* (Chatto and Windus, London, 1962).
D.L. Peterson, *Time, Tide and Tempest: a study of Shakespeare's Romances* (Huntington Library, San Marino, California, 1973).
J.L. Styan, *The Dark Comedy: the Development of Modern Comic Tragedy* (Cambridge U.P., Cambridge, 1962; 2nd edn. 1968).
E.M. Waith, *The Pattern of Tragicomedy in Beaumont and Fletcher* (Yale U.P., New Haven, 1952; New York, 1969).

(ii) Modern Drama

M. Bradbury and D.J. Palmer, eds., with C.W.E. Bigsby, *Contemporary English Drama*, Stratford Upon Avon Studies 19 (Edward Arnold, London, 1981).
R. Cohn, *Currents in Contemporary Drama* (Indiana U.P., Bloomington, 1969).
M. Esslin, *The Theatre of the Absurd* (first published 1961; revised and enlarged edition, Penguin, Harmondsworth, 1968).
R. Findlater, ed., *At the Royal Court: Twenty-five Years of the English Stage Company* (Amber Lane Press, Ambergate, Derbyshire, 1981).
O. Kerensky, *The New British Drama: Fourteen Playwrights since Osborne and Pinter* (Hamish Hamilton, London, 1977).
E.H. Mikhail, *Contemporary British Drama 1950-1971: an Annotated Critical Bibliography* (Macmillan, London, 1976).
J.R. Taylor, *Anger and After, A Guide to the New British Drama* (rev. edn. Methuen, London, 1969).
—*The Second Wave. British Drama in the Seventies* (Methuen, London, 1981).
R. Williams, *Modern Tragedy* (Chatto and Windus, London, 1966).

(iii) Edward Albee

R. Amacher, *Edward Albee* (Twayne, New York, 1969).
C.W.E. Bigsby, *Albee* (Oliver and Boyd, Edinburgh, 1969).
— ed., *A Collection of Critical Essays*, Twentieth Century Views (Prentice Hall, Englewood Cliffs, N.J., 1975).
R. Cohn, *Edward Albee* (Minnesota U.P., Minneapolis, 1969).
L. Kerjan, *Albee* (Seghers, Paris, 1971).
G. McCarthy, *Edward Albee*, Macmillan Modern Dramatists (Macmillan, London, 1983).

A. Paolucci, *From Tension to Tonic: The Plays of Edward Albee* (Southern Illinois U.P., Carbondale, 1972).
M.E. Rutenberg, *Edward Albee: Playwright in Protest* (Avon, New York, 1969).

(iv) Samuel Beckett

G.B. Chevigny, ed., *Twentieth Century Interpretations of 'Endgame'* (Prentice Hall, Englewood Cliffs, N.J., 1969).
R.N. Coe, *Beckett* (rev. edn. Oliver and Boyd, Edinburgh, 1968).
R. Cohn, *Samuel Beckett: the Comic Gamut* (Rutgers U.P., New Brunswick, N.J., 1962).
___ ed., *A Casebook on 'Waiting for Godot'* (Grove Press, New York, 1967).
_____ *Back to Beckett* (Princeton U.P., Princeton, N.J., 1973).
_____ *Just Play: Beckett's Theatre* (Princeton U.P., Princeton, N.J., 1980).
J.E. Dearlove, *Accommodating the Chaos: Samuel Beckett's non-relational art* (Duke U.P., Durham, N.C., 1982).
M. Esslin, ed., *Samuel Beckett: a Collection of Critical Essays*, Twentieth Century Views (Prentice Hall, Englewood Cliffs, N.J., 1965).
B.S. Fletcher, *et al.*, *A Student's Guide to the Plays of Samuel Beckett* (Faber and Faber, London, 1978).
J. Fletcher and J. Spurling, *Beckett the playwright* (3rd edn., Methuen, London, 1985).
M.J. Friedman, ed., *Samuel Beckett now: critical approaches to his novels, poetry, and plays* (2nd edn., Chicago U.P., Chicago, 1975)
L. Graver and R. Federman, *Samuel Beckett: The Critical Heritage* (Routledge, London, 1979).
R. Hayman, *Samuel Beckett* (3rd edn., Heinemann, London, 1980).
H. Kenner, *A Reader's Guide to Beckett* (Thames and Hudson, London, 1973).
C.R. Lyons, *Samuel Beckett*, Macmillan Modern Dramatists (Macmillan, London, 1983).
V. Mercier, *Beckett/Beckett* (Oxford U.P., New York, 1974).
M. Robinson, *The Long Sonata of the Dead: a study of Samuel Beckett* (Hart-Davis, London, 1969; Grove Press, New York, 1970).
B.O. States, *The Shape of Paradox: an essay on 'Waiting for Godot'* (California U.P., Berkeley, 1978).
E. Webb, *The Plays of Samuel Beckett* (Peter Owen, London 1972).

(v) Harold Pinter

G. Almansi and S. Henderson, *Harold Pinter* (Methuen, London, 1983).

W. Baker and S.E. Tabachnik, *Harold Pinter* (Oliver and Boyd, Edinburgh, 1973).

B.F. Dukore, *Where Laughter Stops: Pinter's Tragicomedy* (Missouri U.P., Columbia, Missouri, 1976).

— *Harold Pinter*, Macmillan Modern Dramatists (Macmillan, London, 1982).

M. Esslin, *Pinter: the Playwright* (4th edn., Methuen, London, 1982; revised version of *The Peopled Wound: the Plays of Harold Pinter*, 1973).

L.P. Gabbard, *The Dream Structure of Pinter's Plays: A Psychoanalytic Approach* (Fairleigh Dickinson U.P., Rutherford, N.J., 1976).

S.H. Gale, *Butter's Going Up: A Critical Analysis of Harold Pinter's Work* (Duke U.P., Durham, N.C., 1977).

— *Harold Pinter: An Annotated Bibliography* (G.K. Hall, Boston, Mass., 1978).

A. Ganz, ed., *Pinter: A Collection of Critical Essays*, Twentieth Century Views (Prentice Hall, Englewood Cliffs, N.J., 1972).

L.G. Gordon, *Stratagems to Uncover Nakedness: the Dramas of Harold Pinter* (Missouri U.P., Columbia, Missouri, 1968).

R. Hayman, *Harold Pinter* (4th edn. Heinemann, London, 1980).

A.P. Hinchcliffe, *Harold Pinter* (Twayne, New York, 1967).

J.R. Hollis, *Harold Pinter: the Poetics of Silence* (Southern Illinois U.P., Carbondale, Illinois, 1970).

R. Imhof, *Pinter: a Bibliography* (TQ Publications, London, 1975).

W. Kerr, *Harold Pinter* (Columbia U.P., London and New York, 1967).

J. and A. Lahr, eds., *A Casebook on Harold Pinter's 'The Homecoming'* (Grove Press, New York, 1971).

A.E. Quigley, *The Pinter Problem* (Princeton U.P., Princeton, N.J., 1975).

J.R. Taylor, *Harold Pinter* (Longmans Green, London, 1969).

D.T. Thompson, *Pinter: the player's playwright* (Macmillan, Basingstoke & London, 1985).

S. Trussler, *The Plays of Harold Pinter, an assessment* (Gollancz, London, 1973).

(vi) Tom Stoppard

C.W.E. Bigsby, *Tom Stoppard* (rev. ed. Longman Group for the British Council, London, 1979).

T. Braswell, *Tom Stoppard: an assessment* (Macmillan, London & Basingstoke, 1985).

V.L. Cahn, *Beyond Absurdity: the Plays of Tom Stoppard* (Fairleigh Dickinson U.P., Rutherford,, N.J., 1979).

C.A. Carpenter, 'Bond, Shaffer, Stoppard, Storey: An International Checklist of Commentary', *Modern Drama*, 24 (1981) 546-56.

R. Corballis, *Stoppard: the Mystery and the Clockwork* (Amber Lane Press, Oxford; Methuen, New York, 1984).

J.F. Dean, *Tom Stoppard: Comedy as a Moral Matrix* (Missouri U.P., Columbia, Missouri, 1981).

R. Hayman, *Tom Stoppard* (3rd edn., Heinemann, London, 1979).

J. Hunter, *Tom Stoppard's Plays* (Grove Press, New York, 1982).

F.H. Londré, *Tom Stoppard* (Frederick Ungar, New York, 1981).

T.R. Whittaker, *Tom Stoppard*, Macmillan Modern Dramatists (Macmillan, London, 1983).

(vii) David Storey

It is remarkable, considering his eminence both as a novelist and a dramatist, how little has been written on David Storey. There is no full-length book (Taylor's work is only a British Council pamphlet). The following chapters and articles are those most relevant to the present study. See Carpenter's bibliography for a full list of what is available.

C.A. Carpenter, 'Bond, Shaffer, Stoppard, Storey: An International Checklist of Commentary', *Modern Drama* 24 (1981), 546-56.

O. Kerensky, *The New British Drama* (Hamish Hamilton, London, 1977), pp. 3-17.

A.E. Quigley, 'The emblematic structure and setting of David Storey's plays', *Modern Drama* 22 (1979), 259-76.

J. Reinelt, 'The central event in David Storey's plays', *Theatre Journal* 31 (1979), 210-20.

C. Rosen, 'Symbolic naturalism in David Storey's *Home*', *Modern Drama* 22 (1979), 277-89.

J.R. Taylor, *David Storey* (Longman Group for the British Council, London, 1974).

__ *The Second Wave: British Drama for the Seventies* (Methuen, London, 1971), pp. 141-54.

Acknowledgements

Acknowledgement is made to the following: *Waiting for Godot* and *The Endgame* by Samuel Beckett (Faber and Faber Limited, London and Grove Press, Inc., New York); *The Birthday Party, The Caretaker, The Homecoming, Old Times* and *No Man's Land* by Harold Pinter (Methuen London Ltd and Grove Press, Inc., New York); *Who's Afraid of Virginia Woolf?* by Edward Albee (Jonathan Cape Ltd, London and Atheneum, New York); *Jumpers, Rosencrantz and Guildenstern Are Dead* and *Travesties* by Tom Stoppard (Faber and Faber Limited, London and Grove Press, Inc., New York) and *Home* by David Storey (Jonathan Cape Ltd, London).

In the United States the following copyrights are applicable: *Jumpers*, copyright 1972 by Tom Stoppard; *Rosencrantz and Guildenstern Are Dead*, copyright 1967 by Tom Stoppard; *Travesties*, copyright 1975 by Tom Stoppard; *Endgame*, copyright 1959 by Grove Press, Inc; *Waiting for Godot*, copyright 1954 by Grove Press, Inc., copyright 1982 by Samuel Beckett; *The Birthday Party*, copyright 1959 by Harold Pinter; *The Caretaker*, copyright 1960 by Theatre Promotions Limited; *The Homecoming*, copyright 1965 and 1966 by H. Pinter Ltd.; *No Man's Land*, copyright 1975 by H. Pinter Ltd. and *Old Times*, copyright 1971 by Harold Pinter Ltd.

Index

Note: Bold type-face indicates main entries

Index

Wilde, Oscar: 1, 27
  *The Importance of Being
  Earnest:* 145, 185, 188, 190,
  191

Williams, Raymond: 53
Williams, Tennessee: 113